In Search
of Elena Ferrante

In Search of Elena Ferrante

The Novels and the Question of Authorship

KAREN BOJAR

McFarland & Company, Inc., Publishers
Jefferson, North Carolina

LIBRARY OF CONGRESS CATALOGUING-IN-PUBLICATION DATA

Names: Bojar, Karen, author.
Title: In search of Elena Ferrante : the novels and the question of authorship / Karen Bojar.
Description: Jefferson, North Carolina : McFarland & Company, Inc., Publishers, 2018. | Includes bibliographical references and index.
Identifiers: LCCN 2018025658 | ISBN 9781476674681 (softcover : acid free paper) ∞
Subjects: LCSH: Ferrante, Elena—Criticism and interpretation.
Classification: LCC PQ4866.E6345 Z58 2018 | DDC 853/.92—dc23
LC record available at https://lccn.loc.gov/2018025658

BRITISH LIBRARY CATALOGUING DATA ARE AVAILABLE

ISBN (print) 978-1-4766-7468-1
ISBN (ebook) 978-1-4766-3362-6

© 2018 Karen Bojar. All rights reserved

No part of this book may be reproduced or transmitted in any form or by any means, electronic or mechanical, including photocopying or recording, or by any information storage and retrieval system, without permission in writing from the publisher.

Front cover image of Bay of Naples © 2018 Angelafoto/iStock

Manufactured in the United States of America

McFarland & Company, Inc., Publishers
 Box 611, Jefferson, North Carolina 28640
  www.mcfarlandpub.com

Table of Contents

Preface and Acknowledgments   1

Introduction   5

1. Ferrante Fever   13
2. Who Is Elena Ferrante? Does It Matter?   23
3. Ann Goldstein and the Challenges of Translation   37
4. The Novellas   49
5. The Neapolitan Novels: Women's Friendship   66
6. The Neapolitan Novels: Mothers and Daughters   83
7. The Neapolitan Novels: Love, Sex, Betrayal   94
8. The Neapolitan Novels: Violence and Masculinity   108
9. The Neapolitan Novels: The Climb Up the Class Ladder   121
10. Italy in the Years of Lead: Ferrante as Political Analyst   135
11. Ferrante as Feminist Theorist   150
12. Naples and the Camorra   168

Conclusion   184

Chapter Notes   191

Bibliography   205

Index   213

Preface and Acknowledgments

I count myself among those in the grip of "Ferrante Fever" and this book is my attempt to understand why Elena Ferrante's work has meant so much to me and to millions of readers around the globe. When I searched for material about Ferrante, I found countless reviews, essays, and blog posts but only two full-length studies: *Naples' Little Women: The Fiction of Elena Ferrante* by Lisa Mullenneaux and *The Works of Elena Ferrante: Reconfiguring the Margins* edited by Grace Bullaro and Stephanie Love. I searched without success for a comprehensive study of Ferrante that would explore the complicated interweaving of thematic strands, including analysis of the political dimension, an aspect of Ferrante's work not addressed by either of the above-cited texts and largely ignored by reviewers. Finally, I decided to try to write the book I wanted to read.

In Search of Elena Ferrante explores the international reaction to Ferrante, dubbed "Ferrante Fever," the controversy surrounding Ferrante's decision to write under a pseudonym, and the special challenges posed by a work in translation. In her many in-person interviews, Ann Goldstein has provided insights into the process of translating Ferrante's work, along with her sense of the themes and preoccupations of the elusive author. Furthermore, Ferrante, in numerous interviews conducted solely through letters and email, has provided a running commentary on her work. I cannot recall another instance when readers have had the benefit of both the author's and translator's insights into the creative process.

One of the great pleasures of reading Ferrante's work is observing her weave some of the same material into different situations, a theme and variations approach to narrative structure. Although Ferrante's three novellas (*Troubling Love, The Days of Abandonment* and *The Lost Daughter*) stand alone as powerful literary texts, they also prefigure much that is contained in the Neapolitan novels. Although not as immediately engaging as the Neapolitan Quartet, the novellas deserve to be read in their own right rather than as preparatory studies for the Neapolitan novels. If Ferrante had continued to write in the style of the novellas—brief, emotionally-charged novels about moments of extreme tension in a woman's life—she would have had her devoted readers, but it's unlikely that she would have attracted a global readership.

The major themes of the novellas reappear in the Neapolitan Novels: the burdens and joys of motherhood; the increasing fragility of relationships between men and women; male violence against women; the difficulty of ever erasing the imprint of one's background interwoven with an exploration of the social and economic divisions in Italy. However, the friendship theme that looms so large in the Neapolitan Quartet is not present in the novellas; also in the Quartet Ferrante locates her complex tapestry of themes within a densely populated social world, far different from the novellas' intense concentration on the inner life of the principal character.

The complicated narrative structure of the Neapolitan novels encompasses many interwoven thematic strands impossible to fully grasp on a first reading. The personal conflicts among friends, lovers, and family members play out against a background of tremendous social inequality and the struggle against that inequality—the political battles of the 1960s and 1970s. Most of Ferrante's readers and reviewers have focused on the exploration of personal relationships, particularly the theme of female friendship, and have largely ignored the political dimension. However, the Neapolitan Quartet is deeply political in that the characters' personal histories are interwoven with the larger social drama although there is no easily extractable political philosophy. Ferrante has intertwined the political and personal strands so effectively that the political debate never feels intrusive, with the characters' political beliefs emerging organically from their circumstances and personalities.

Ferrante portrays both her male and female characters as prisoners of gender, their lives constrained by the expectations of a deeply sexist society. Although many readers have seen the Neapolitan Quartet as a searing portrait of man's inhumanity towards women, I argue that Ferrante's portrayal of gender roles is far more nuanced, with some of her male characters taking tentative steps towards gender equality. Ferrante's sympathies extend to the young men who are trapped in the sexist script written for them from time immemorial. Ferrante portrays a world in a world in which gender roles are changing, with at least some of her male characters a part of that change.

I owe a great deal to the members of my feminist book club: Kathy Black, Gloria Gilman, Caryn Hunt and Beth Lewis. They went along with my suggestion to read Ferrante's novels, although Ferrante was just beginning to be known in the United States, and at the time none had heard of her. The opportunity to discuss Ferrante's novels with them certainly helped me to clarify my thinking and deepen my appreciation for Ferrante's work. I owe a special debt to my good friend Kathy Black who read and critiqued an earlier draft of this book.

Most of all I owe a debt to my husband, Richard Bojar, for his invaluable assistance in critiquing and proofreading the manuscript. I have drawn heavily upon his unpublished work, *Translation: Treason or Trust*, and am especially indebted to him for his insights into the special challenges of analyzing a work in translation as well as insights into the process of translation itself. In a sense, this book has become a collaborative effort.

Citations from Ferrante's novels are noted in the text with the following abbreviations:

(TL) *Troubling Love*, trans. Ann Goldstein (New York: Europa Editions, 2006).

(DA) *The Days of Abandonment*, trans. Ann Goldstein (New York: Europa Editions, 2005).

(LD) *The Lost Daughter*, trans. Ann Goldstein (New York: Europa Editions, 2008).

(BF) *My Brilliant Friend*, trans. Ann Goldstein (New York: Europa Editions, 2012).

(SNN) *The Story of a New Name*, trans. Ann Goldstein (New York: Europa Editions, 2013).

(TWL) *Those Who Leave and Those Who Stay*, trans. Ann Goldstein (New York: Europa Editions, 2014).

(SLC) *Story of the Lost Child*, trans. Ann Goldstein (New York: Europa Editions, 2015).

Citations from *Frantumaglia: A Writer's Journey*, an edited collection of Ferrante's letters and interviews, many of which were previously published, are included in the chapter notes in order to indicate where interviews were first published, the interviewer(s), and date of interview(s).

Introduction

I wrote this book to help me unlock the secrets of Elena Ferrante's power, to better understand why these books have had such a hold on my imagination and that of millions of readers worldwide. I was introduced to Ferrante by James Woods' January 2013 article in the *New Yorker*.[1] Rarely does a review send me straight to an online bookstore to purchase a book and pay extra for expedited shipping, but Woods made a compelling case for Ferrante. I was not disappointed. Since then I've read all her books at least three times. The English translations of the Neapolitan Quartet were released over a three-year period and while waiting impatiently for the next volume I read Ferrante's earlier books—three powerful novellas which, although they lacked the fully-realized social world of the Neapolitan novels, deepened my interest in Ferrante, drawing me more and more into her world.

Although there have been numerous reviews of Ferrante's work in periodicals, as of this writing only two book-length studies have been published: Lisa Mullenneaux' *Naples' Little Women: The Fiction of Elena Ferrante*[2] and *The Works of Elena Ferrante: Reconfiguring the Margins* edited by Grace Bullaro and Stephanie Love.[3] *Naples' Little Women*, an e-book, apparently intended for the general reader, discusses Ferrante's work in the context of contemporary Italian literature and feminist theory, but does not explore the political themes of the Neapolitan novels. Apparently written before Claudio Gatti's revelations about Ferrante's identity, Mullenneaux does not deal with questions of authorship. *The Works of Elena Ferrante: Reconfiguring the Margins* is a collection of essays focused on specific topics, intended for an academic audience. The collection does not include an analysis of Ferrante's depiction of the political struggles of the 1960s and 1970s, nor does it address "the vexed question of Ferrante's anonymity" which the editors consider more "a distraction from the work itself than as a way of deepening our understanding of it."[4] I searched for a comprehensive study of Ferrante that would include close readings of her works; information about the historical background; analysis of how she has integrated that material into the Neapolitan novels; commentary on the complicated interweaving of thematic strands, including the largely ignored political themes; and finally a discussion of questions of authorship sparked by Ferrante's choice to write under a pseudonym. When I could not locate that comprehensive study I decided to try to write the book I wanted to read. I have approached Ferrante's work as part of world literature, rather than Italian literature. The Italianists can do a better job than I in that regard.

Certainly part of the reason the Neapolitan novels resonated with me was that the historical period they cover follows the trajectory of my life. Like Elena and Lila, I was born in 1944, and although there were of course differences between my life and theirs, there were also some striking similarities, among them the dramatic changes in the status of women and the heady excitement of the 1960s and 1970s, when all established institutions were challenged. The belief that a new world was in the making was soon followed by disillusion when the left turned increasingly to sectarianism and violence. In the early 1980s, the realization grew that the political pendulum had shifted and a generation that spent its youth in a time of social possibility would spend its middle and later years in a time of reaction.

Ferrante's characters and their world were so vividly realized that initially I had difficulty accepting that I would know nothing certain about the author of the books I loved so much. I obsessively followed the speculation about Ferrante's identity and like many of her women readers thought it was impossible that the books could have been written by a man. (See Chapter 2.) There were just too many intimate details of life in a female body. After reading Ferrante's reasons for choosing to write under a pseudonym, I eventually accepted her explanation and no longer engaged in speculation about her identity. It was a closed matter. Then came journalist Claudio Gatti's well-documented claim that Ferrante was Anita Raja who, unlike Ferrante, did not grow up in an impoverished Neapolitan neighborhood but rather left Naples at the age of three and lived in middle class comfort in Rome.[5] Presumably, Raja had ready access to the educational opportunities that Ferrante's characters struggled to obtain.

Most of Ferrante's readers appeared not to be disturbed by this deception and tended to view the falsely claimed Neapolitan background of Ferrante as a literary device. Ferrante herself was a "fictional character" and Gatti just did not understand how literature worked. However, I was troubled by Raja's dishonesty and not convinced by her defenders, who saw nothing problematic in Raja's attempt to create the impression that her background was similar to that of her characters. Ferrante's devoted readers have become something of a tribe and I count myself as a member. It was disorienting to be out of synch with the tribe.

Many Ferrante fans expressed relief that at least Gatti identified a woman as the author; however, Gatti also left open the possibility of Raja's collaboration with her husband, Domenico Starnone. Interestingly, most of Ferrante's readers have ignored this possibility. However, Gatti's revelations do provide further support for the oft-made claim that Starnone was involved in writing the Neapolitan novels. The powerfully rendered portrait of growing up in deep poverty in 1950s Naples feels like it was written from firsthand experience. Raja did not have this direct experience but Starnone, like the fictional Ferrante, was the son of a seamstress and did grow up in Naples, thus lending further support to the claim that Starnone was Raja's co-author. Also, four groups of analysts using different text analysis programs independently came to the same conclusion that Starnone was in all likelihood the principal author of the books attributed to Elena Ferrante. When I first read about the identification of Starnone as the probable author (or co-author), I dismissed it out of hand. I had made up my mind that it was impossible that a man could have written any part of this deeply felt account of female experience. I am no longer convinced this is the case and can no longer discount the mounting evidence pointing to Starnone's authorship.

Certainly many of Ferrante's fans would be deeply disappointed to learn that the books were not solely the work of a woman, but there are surely others intrigued by the collaboration of a man and woman on books that so powerfully explore issues of gender. The whole experience has challenged some of my assumptions about literature—principally that there is such a thing as an authentic female voice that can be recognized as such. As Ferrante herself has said in her collection of interviews and letters, *Frantumaglia: A Writer's Journey*, "A good writer, male or female can imitate the two sexes with equal effectiveness."[6] So does all this matter? The books have not changed. But will we read them differently knowing that the author is not a woman whose perspective has been shaped by her own experience of growing up in poverty, subjected to class and gender discrimination? Will we read the books differently if we learn that Starnone is Raja's collaborator or if he turns out to be the principal author?

Any translated work is of course in some sense a collaboration and Ann Goldstein is widely praised for her excellent translations of Ferrante's novels. Functioning as a stand-in for Ferrante who has refused all in-person interviews, Goldstein has provided many insights into the process of translating Ferrante's work along with her sense of the themes and preoccupations of the elusive author. In addition to Goldstein's observations, Ferrante in numerous interviews conducted solely through letters and email and collected in *Frantumaglia* has provided a running commentary on her work. Of course this is complicated by the fact that Ferrante is a fictional character and the reader is faced with the task of disentangling what may be the author's perspective from what may be that of the fictional character Elena Ferrante. Despite this complication, many of Ferrante's readers have found *Frantumaglia* a source of valuable information about Ferrante's work. I cannot recall another instance when readers have had the benefit of both the author and translator of a major work of literature providing so many insights into the creative process.

Curious as to how much of the power of the works was attributable to Ferrante and how much to Goldstein, I struggled to read Ferrante in Italian. (The results of my efforts are described in Chapter 3.) Very few of the critical responses to Ferrante's work in the Anglophone world have analyzed her style on the sentence level—no doubt a consequence of the writers' lack of knowledge of Italian. My limited knowledge of Italian precludes close textual analysis of Ferrante's prose in the novellas (Chapter 4) and the Neapolitan Quartet (Chapter 5–9). Instead, I draw primarily on analysis of narrative structure and recurrent themes and images, contextualizing the novels by exploring Ferrante's world: the political and cultural history of Italy during the years covered in the Neapolitan novels (Chapter 10); the feminist movement which profoundly influenced Elena Greco, the narrator of the Neapolitan novels; and the feminist writers Ferrante cites as influences (Chapter 11).

Reviewers have generally ignored the political dimension of the Neapolitan novels and have focused primarily on Ferrante's exploration of personal relationships, in particular female friendship. However, the Neapolitan Quartet is very much a political text. In these novels, Ferrante incorporates the political currents of the 1960s and 1970s and does so with a sophistication that may not be apparent to readers unfamiliar with this history. It is familiar territory for me, as a participant and as a student of the social movements of those years, but my knowledge is largely the North American context. Before undertaking this study I knew relatively little about the history of 1960s–1970s Italian left-wing politics beyond what was covered in the international press, such as the kidnapping and murder of former prime minister Aldo Moro.[7]

Ferrante explores a current that ran throughout leftist movements in the developed world, the repudiation of an older generation of communists and socialists by a younger, more visionary left. In the United States, the Communist Party and Socialist Workers Party (the largest left wing organizations) were never major social forces and by the 1960s had been consigned to the margins of political life. In Italy, the Communist and Socialist parties historically had been a major social force and still wielded considerable power in the 1960s and 1970s; thus the conflict between Old and New Left played out very differently in Italy. In addition, Italy's parliamentary system presented challenges and opportunities not present in the United States.

Ferrante has claimed not to be interested in the specifics of political conflicts; in the Neapolitan novels, however, she has presented a sophisticated political analysis deeply interwoven with the personal histories of her characters. For the most part, Lila Cerullo articulates a New Left point of view; Nino Sarratore, a reformer and a technocrat, accommodates to the Socialist Party and then like many of his generation moves to the right; Pasquale Peluso repudiates the Communist Party in which he grew up and embraces the violent strand of the New Left. The narrator, Elena Greco, was broadly sympathetic to the left but primarily concerned with learning the viewpoints then current among the educated upper middle class, knowledge which would assist her in her upward rise. Class conflict and class mobility are major themes of the Neapolitan novels, intertwined with gender as Ferrante contrasts the opportunities and constraints experienced by Nino Sarratore and Elena Greco, both of whom managed to emerge from "the neighborhood" to enter Italy's upper middle class. (See Chapter 9.)

Ferrante integrates both the story of the Italian New Left and that of the feminist movement that arose in part as a reaction to left-wing machismo and in part to the deeply rooted sexism of Italian society. Ferrante has acknowledged her debt to feminist theory, characterizing herself as "a passionate reader of feminist thought."[8] The constraints of gender and its intersection with class/ethnicity emerges as the major theme of the Neapolitan novels. (See Chapter 11.) My initial reaction to the Neapolitan novels was very similar to my response to Simone de Beauvoir's *The Second Sex*, which I read for the first time in its entirety in 1999 when I attended a conference at the Sorbonne on Beauvoir's legacy.[9] So many of the issues central to the second wave feminist movement were explored by Beauvoir. Just about every concept addressed within the academic discipline of Women's Studies is contained in *The Second Sex*; Beauvoir mapped the terrain.

Like Beauvoir's *Second Sex*, Ferrante's Neapolitan novels contain the wide range of issues subsumed under the rubric of feminist thought—among them the tension-filled relationships between mothers and daughters; ambivalence towards children and the difficulty of balancing professional aspirations with care for children; the ongoing struggle to get men to assume domestic responsibilities; the complexity of female friendship; the omnipresence of gender-based violence. Ferrante, whose first novel was published almost half a century later than *The Second Sex*, went beyond Beauvoir to explore the ways in which gender is experienced differently by women of different regions, classes—in short what we now call an intersectional analysis.

Drawing on my lifetime of reading in and teaching about feminist thought, I have tried to place Ferrante in the tradition of feminist theory and feminist literature; I have read and re-read works which have influenced Ferrante as well as historical background material about her world. Unfortunately, many key works of Italian feminist theory have not been translated into English, and my attempt to contextualize Ferrante within the tradition of Italian feminist thought is limited by my lack of an adequate reading knowledge of Italian. Although Ferrante has clearly read widely in feminist thought and has claimed to have been influenced by feminist theorists, I suspect the conception of her characters and their world would not have been very different if she had not read the authors she has cited as influences in *Frantumaglia: A Writer's Journey* and in her many interviews. Ferrante's work certainly reads like it has been drawn from lived experience.

Finally, to deepen my understanding of Ferrante's world, I travelled to Naples in November 2016. (See Chapter 12.) My husband and I had been in Naples in March of 1999 as part of a sabbatical year trip to Italy. We

Introduction

foolishly believed all the guidebook warnings about avoiding Naples and stayed for a week in Sorrento, a beautiful but not particularly interesting town. We decided to go to on a daytrip to Naples and fell in love with the city. Each morning we took a boat to Naples, regretting that we could not spend the nights there rather than returning to our prepaid hotel in Sorrento. We hoped to get back to Naples and do the city justice, but somehow never managed to do so. My love for Ferrante's books was the impetus for a return trip to Naples. Combining literary analysis, with a study of the political and cultural history explored in the Neapolitan novels, has been a rewarding experience for me as a writer and, I hope, also for the reader seeking to deepen an understanding of Elena Ferrante's world.

1
Ferrante Fever

> *"Are Elena Ferrante's four Neapolitan novels even books? I began to doubt it when I talked about them with other people—mostly women. We returned to life too quickly as we spoke: who was your Lila, the childhood friend who effortlessly dazzled everyone? Or—a question not happily answered—were you Lila?... The usual distance between fiction and life collapses when you read Ferrante."*—Joanna Biggs, *London Review of Books*

I cannot recall any books that I have read in my adult life which have affected me as powerfully as Elena Ferrante's novels. I am not alone. "Ferrante Fever," as it has been dubbed, is a global phenomenon. According to Ferrante's publisher, her books have been sold in nearly fifty countries, and as of 2016, have sold about 5.5 million copies worldwide. The four Neapolitan novels have sold nearly two million copies in North America, with worldwide sales in English now topping three million.[1] Elena Ferrante was named by *Time* magazine as one of the "100 Most Influential People of the Year" in April 2016—not bad for a "fictional character."

Ferrante has found a receptive audience in places where women's lives are far more constrained than in Europe or North America. Pakistani writer Binah Shah sees the Neapolitan novels as very relevant to Pakistani women, noting that the social changes which took place in Italy from the 1950s to the 21st century are now occurring in Pakistan: "In the story of Elena and Lila, Pakistani women will see themselves navigating all the phases of life in the face of brutality and oppression, misogyny and violence. And they will realize that their lives, too, are all about possibility, with the sustaining force of female friendships to guide them along all the triumphs and pitfalls in their paths."[2] In an interview with the *New York Daily News*, Yooyeon Noh, who acquired the Neapolitan novels for Korea's Hangilsa Publishing, expects that Korean readers will embrace the books.

Citing the family orientation of Korean women, Noh states, "I've always thought Italian people and Korean people share some common character."[3] Ferrante has certainly tapped into aspects of women's experience that at least to some extent transcend class and cultural boundaries.

Adam Kirsch in the *Global Novel: Writing the World in the 21st Century* has included the Neapolitan novels among the books he considers examples of the global novel: Orhan Pamuk's *Snow*; Chimamanda Ngozi Adichie's *Americanah*; Mohsin Hamid's *The Reluctant Fundamentalist*; Margaret Atwood's *Oryx and Crake*; Haruki Murakami's *1Q84*; Roberto Bolano's *2666*; and Michel Houellebecq's *The Possibility of an Island*. Despite their diversity, Kirsch thinks "what unites all these various approaches is the insistence on the global dimension not just of contemporary experience, but of contemporary imagination ... it can start from the scale of a single neighborhood showing how even the most constrained of lives are affected by world-wide movements."[4] Although the Neapolitan novels are intensely local, Ferrante's narrator Elena Greco becomes increasingly aware of and part of a larger world. Elena's children become global citizens, living and loving across borders; two of her three daughters are living in the United States, with one married to an Iranian.

The global dimension is an integral part of Ferrante's perspective and may contribute to her rapidly growing international audience. Ferrante told *New York Times* interviewer Rachel Donadio that her worldwide success has come as something of a surprise: "I never asked myself how the women in my stories would be received outside Italy. I wrote first and foremost for myself, and if I published I did so leaving the task of finding readers to the book itself. Now I know that thanks to Europa Editions [Ferrante's English-language publisher], to Ann Goldstein [her English-language translator] and to James Wood and so many other reviewers and writers and readers, the heart of these stories has burst forth, and it is not only Italian. I'm both surprised and happy."[5]

This success is especially remarkable for books in translation. Michael Reynolds, editor in chief of Europa Editions, noted that Ferrante's success "is extremely unusual even for a book not in translation. For a book in translation, it is rather phenomenal."[6] The English language editions of Ferrante's work have been more successful than the original Italian; her greatest success to date has been in the Anglophone world. Perhaps for the Anglo reader there is the attraction of the exotic—and for many of Ferrante's readers the world of mid–20th century working class Naples is

1. Ferrante Fever

terra incognita. For these readers, there is both a sense of recognition—the experiences which women share across cultures—as well as the fascination of a different world.

According to Rachel Donadio, enthusiasm for Ferrante is much greater in England than in Italy. "Although she has a small cult following, I've been struck by the number of friends in Italy—intellectuals, journalists, readers—who had never heard of Ferrante until I mentioned her." Donadio noted that in fall 2014 the Turin daily *La Stampa* likened the Neapolitan novels to an Italian soap opera, suggesting that the Italian literary world has not taken Ferrante seriously.[7] Daniela Petracco, Ferrante's publisher at Europa Editions, noted in an interview with *The Telegraph* that Ferrante's three novellas were never major best sellers in Italy: "She really became a bestseller once the noise they were making in the UK and the US reached Italy." Petracco believes Ferrante is so popular in Britain because her novels are "similar to English 19th-century novels—works by Eliot or Dickens. The large cast of characters, the coincidences, the way people's lives intertwine—that, in particular, appeals to British readers."[8] This may also be part of the reason Ferrante appeals as well to so many American readers, many of whom grew up on a diet of 19th-century British fiction. Although Ferrante has her devoted readers throughout the Anglophone world in the United States, Canada, New Zealand and Australia, "Ferrante Fever" appears to burn most brightly in Britain. According to one British blogger, Ferrante readers are everywhere: "Fellow book lovers, by now I'm sure you've heard the term 'Ferrante Fever'—and by George, I've got it. In fact, glancing around the tube on my way to work, it seems everyone in London's got it—women, men, children (but realistically, probably not too many children)."[9] Rarely does an author attain such a high degree of critical and popular success.

The closest thing to "Ferrante Fever" I can recall is the cult of Jane Austen. The Janeites, as they are sometimes called, have themselves become the object of study as literary scholars such as Deidre Lynch trace readers' responses to Austen's novels.[10] As with the Janeites, it is striking the extent to which Ferrante's readers respond to her work on a deeply personal level. How to explain this? From *The Imaginary Book Club*, an online book club: "You leave the books knowing more about yourself than you did before, haunted by how the words written for another person can seem so entirely particular to you."[11] From writer Madeline Gressel, who began reading the Neapolitan Quartet based on a recommendation of a very close friend: "The friendship that is at the heart of the novels, she told me, reminded her of our own friendship. At the time I began reading, I was angry with this particular friend for continuing to live as roommates with an ex-boyfriend of mine…. Reading Elena Ferrante, I have the strange feeling that my own life is unfolding before me: past and present but, above all, future, and what's more, I understand it…. I can see that I won't miss the men that have left me…. I can see that I wounded my friend with my jealousy and punishment, and that it wasn't worth the satisfaction."[12]

Over and over again, Ferrante's readers relate that they experience her characters as real people, dealing with real difficulties and crises that mirror experiences in their own lives. As Joanna Biggs put it in her review in the *London Review of Books*: "Are Elena Ferrante's four Neapolitan novels even books? I began to doubt it when I talked about them with other people—mostly women. We returned to life too quickly as we spoke: who was your Lila, the childhood friend who effortlessly dazzled everyone? Or—a question not happily answered—were you Lila?… The usual distance between fiction and life collapses when you read Ferrante."[13] I am one of the many readers who have gleaned insights into my own life from reading Ferrante's books. The arc of the narrator's life in the Neapolitan Quartet generally corresponds with mine, with the tremendous social/cultural changes of the 1960s and 1970s affecting my life as it did the lives of Ferrante's characters. I was born in September 1944, a month later than Lila and Elena. Until recently, I was convinced that Ferrante was a real woman born in 1944, because throughout the Neapolitan quartet she had an unerring sense of what was happening in the world at each stage of Lila and Elena's lives. I was intensely interested in how the cultural changes of the 1960s–1970s played out in a world in many ways very different from my own, as well as any insights I might glean into my life's trajectory.

Some of Ferrante's (relatively few) male readers have also expressed the idea that she is speaking directly to their experience. Michael Reynolds, the editor for Europa Editions, the American affiliate of Ferrante's Italian publisher, responded to a question about his reaction to Ferrante's books when he read *The Days of Abandonment* for the first time: "I was floored. It was early in my time in Italy, I was separating from my ex-wife and I thought: how does she know that about me? Is she writing about me…. I saw myself in the husband and I saw myself in Olga, the wife. Elena Ferrante sticks her finger in our wounds."[14] Male readers like Reynolds are the exception. Ferrante's audience is largely female and booksellers such as Nicola Orichuia, co-owner of I AM Books, reported that nine out of ten buyers are women.[15] The most common response of Ferrante's male readers has been to view her novels as a unique window onto the female experience, generally unavailable to the male reader. From Damien's blog *Travel Readings*: "What seduced me most in those four books is to read a story in which a woman's point of view, a woman's voice is clearly audible." He states that he has rarely been "so completely given access to a female state of mind and perception."[16]

And there are those few male readers who deny that Ferrante's novels are focused on female experience, seeing them instead as a broad canvas delving into all aspects of the human experience in the vein of Tolstoy, Dickens, or Balzac. Journalist Anna Silliman interviewed her father, who had a very enthusiastic response to the Neapolitan novels but did not see them as particularly concerned with female experience: "I thought it was one of the best novels I've read since *War and Peace*. I thought it was on that scale. The way she integrated various subplots was just extraordinary. Every character was interesting.... Some women write novels that you would feel are designed for a female audience.... I don't think this was, not for a moment. I think this was meant to be a work on a grand scale. All human life is here. And that's what was so compelling about it."[17]

It's noteworthy how many of Ferrante's readers have compared her to Tolstoy, a comparison that occurred to me as well. When I finished the last of the Neapolitan novels, I experienced a feeling I hadn't felt since high school when I read voraciously—deep depression that a book I loved had come to an end. I recall this reaction to *War and Peace* but, I'm embarrassed to admit, also with *Gone with the Wind*. I loved big books with a large cast of characters and a vividly drawn social world. There is a further connection between Tolstoy and Ferrante in addition to the large canvas and narrative sweep. Ferrante shares Tolstoy's ability to convey characters experiencing contradictory emotions as well as characters like Elena Greco who can present one face to the world, the impression of a "good girl," while seething with resentment and jealousy on the inside. We share the most intimate thoughts of the great fictional characters, knowing them in a way we can never know our family, friends and colleagues whose innermost thoughts we are doubtless fortunate not to know.

The narrator of the Neapolitan novels is a woman in her late sixties trying to make sense of her life and this, no doubt, is part of the reason so many older women (myself included) are drawn to Ferrante. For older women, Ferrante recreates what it feels like to be young—the passion, the intensity, living in the grip of powerful, barely understood emotions. Like Ferrante's narrator, Elena Greco, older readers may be wrestling with the challenge of integrating their present-day selves with the overall trajectory of their lives.

Whatever their age, Ferrante's devoted readers tend to be very protective of her, generally reacting negatively to Claudio Gatti's "unmasking" of Ferrante and frequently expressing anger at her publisher's choice of book covers for the American and British editions. Some of these readers see the pastel colors, dreamy seaside scenes and women with their backs turned as iconography typical of "chick lit" and unworthy of a serious writer like Ferrante. *Slate*'s Miriam Krule interviewed Ferrante's publisher Sandra Ozzola Ferri about the outpouring of criticism of Ferrante's book covers. Ozzola, who appeared somewhat defensive, complained that "many people didn't understand the game we were playing, that of, let's say, dressing an extremely refined story with a touch of vulgarity." Perhaps revealing her own class prejudices, Ozzola noted that *My Brilliant Friend* concludes "with a scene of a very vulgar Neapolitan wedding. The wedding and Elena's impression of it ... is an extremely important moment in the book. That's why I intentionally searched for a photo that was 'kitsch'. This design choice continued in the subsequent books, because vulgarity is an important aspect of the books, of all that Elena wants to distance herself from." Ozzola also noted Ferrante approved the covers and "agreed with our choice to purposefully use 'low-class' images."[18]

Defenders of the covers have argued that the critics are devaluing literature associated with women. In "The Subtle Genius of Elena Ferrante's Bad Book Covers," Emily Harnett wrote: "But to despise the covers—and, by extension, the kind of novel they evoke—in the name of *good* literature is to buy into the destructive stigma that has long been attached to 'women's fiction' as a genre."[19] Romanian blogger Georgiana, creator of *Readers' High Tea*, has helpfully posted photos of the American, Norwegian, Dutch, Spanish, Romanian, German, Italian, Australian, and Chinese editions.[20] (My preference is for the Australian covers.) I don't recall another writer's book covers that have generated so much controversy.

Of course not everyone is enamored of Ferrante. There are the inevitable naysayers and the satirists who mock her fanatically devoted readers. Catherine Bennett's piece in the *Guardian*, "Modern Tribes; The Elena Ferrante Fan," is a hilarious spoof of "Ferrante Fever." Bennett describes the response of a member of the tribe when she meets someone who hasn't read Ferrante: "Really? Not even *My Brilliant Friend*? You're so lucky you've got the whole series ahead of you.... Look, take this one. I always carry a spare copy in case I find someone hasn't discovered her, though you must be the last person in London."[21] I recognized myself here. Novelist Claire Messud reports that she has "pressed Ferrante's novels on friends with mixed results." Some fall in love with the books, but others cannot see what all the fuss is about: "One woman said, of *My Brilliant Friend*, 'How's it different from Judy Blume? Just girls getting their periods.'" Messud thinks that those who don't recognize Ferrante's genius "are those who can't face her uncomfortable truths: that women's friendships are as much about hatred as love; that our projections determine our stories as much as does any fact; that we carry our origins, indelibly, to our graves."[22]

And truth be told, there is also an occasional extremely negative review such as Fernanda Moore's "Neapolitan Nonsense." According to Moore, "the overall plot, in which a melodramatic and humorless woman struggles to transcend her humble origins, is both overdone and ordinary." Moore thinks that the prose, "in Ann Goldstein's translation, is artless, repetitive, and stale. There are too many characters to keep track of.... The Neapolitan novels are not great literature; they're potboilers dressed in exotic Italian vestments. They have won their audience for the same reason highbrow soap operas such as *Downton Abbey* appeal to those who like their domestic melodrama to come with a patina of European refinement."[23] Literary critic Tim Parks can also be counted as among the naysayers. He reports: "Again and again I pick up her novels and again and again I give up around page fifty. My impression is of something wearisomely concocted, determinedly melodramatic, forever playing on Neapolitan stereotype."[24]

Moore and Parks represent a minority opinion, and there is every reason to believe that "Ferrante Fever" will spread as the Neapolitan novels are being adapted for an Italian television series. The *New York Daily News* reported that Ferrante insisted there be an Italian version before an English language version, that the series be filmed in Naples, and that the actress playing Lila be Neapolitan to be true to the dialect. Ferrante intends to maintain artistic control and will approve the scripts.[25] According to Michael Reynolds, editor in chief of Europa Editions, Ferrante "is very much involved in the project, nothing happens without her, and for me that's enough to be sure it will be good."[26] I admit to some trepidation. Without Ferrante's powerful prose, these books could so easily deteriorate into soap opera.

Involvement in a film adaptation of her books is nothing new for Ferrante. She worked with screenwriter Mario Martone on the screenplay for her novella *Troubling Love*. Martone sent Ferrante the third draft of his screenplay, telling her that he "tried to understand and respect the book, and at the same time filter it through my experiences, my memories, my perception of Naples."[27] Ferrante replied with very detailed comments, some of which support Martone, while others question his choices, suggesting Ferrante has some familiarity with screenwriting—perhaps the influence of Domenico Starnone, who was a successful screen writer. Ferrante's letters to Martone contain reactions to various changes Martone had made to the narrative, including very specific suggestions as to how she thought he should structure the film. One of the choices about which she had reservations was Martone's plan to include something of the political climate of the time. She cautioned: "I don't dislike the electoral updating, providing it remains 'landscape,' distant sound, not indispensable detail."[28]

Ferrante was especially attuned to the use of dialect and questions Martone's having the main character Delia speak in dialect at the very beginning of her story. She saw all the lines in dialect as potentially problematic—"the lurking stereotype of the recitation in a Neapolitan cadence, complaining, maudlin, tremulous, overdone, with a display of sentimentality that doesn't communicate sentiments."[29] She acknowledged that these characteristics are sometimes found in Neapolitan dialect, but cautioned against exaggerating it. Her comments suggest that she will be paying close attention to the use of dialect in the television version of the Neapolitan novels. Ferrante is well aware that although something is inevitably lost in a film adaptation of a novel, film has its own resources unavailable to a novelist. In a letter to Martone, after the film version of *Troubling Love* had been completed, Ferrante wrote that for her the strongest moments were those in which Martone found "great visual solutions for showing Delia's emotions." She told Martone that his film had rid her of "a series of prejudices [she] had concerning the limits of a filmed story."[30]

Ferrante fans will no doubt enjoy many iterations of the Neapolitan novels and many opportunities to ponder the relative merits of the novel vs. a theatrical production or a film adaptation. In addition to the upcoming television series, in 2016 BBC Radio 4 aired an adaptation of the Neapolitan novels by prize-winning playwright Timberlake Wertenbaker; reviews were mixed. I managed to hear some of it when it was available on demand from BBC radio. As someone who has never listened to audio books, I was not the right candidate for a radio dramatization; I want to consume books the old-fashioned way. Also, I found the English accents disconcerting and agreed with Kate Chisholm's review in *The Spectator*: "To me the background music was wrong in flavour, the child actors too English and stilted, the voices of Lena and Lila as grown-ups not distinctive enough. I wanted to be taken to the baking hot streets of Naples, but found myself rooted in London."[31]

However, Alex O'Connell, writing for *The Times*, had a different assessment: "Yet once you tune in to the accents ... the story possesses you. The precise dialogue, artful reduction and accomplished performances made me, a Ferrante addict, want to listen on and read the novels all over again." O'Connell asked Wertenbaker why she had the characters speak in Manchester accents: "I definitely didn't want them to be from London or the southeast—that would be like setting it in Florence or Milan. Liverpool was right, but too distinctive an accent and place. We wouldn't have dreamt of them speaking with Italian accents." So they settled on "around Manchester."[32]

Adaptations of beloved literary works are always controversial. The London stage production of the Neapolitan novels appears to have generated as much controversy as the BBC radio program. The commission for the first stage adaptation of the Neapolitan novels was not awarded to a major theatre, as might have been expected, but to the Rose Theatre. According to April De Angelis, the playwright who adapted the novels for the stage, the Rose Theatre in Kingston came to the project early, approaching Ferrante's publishers before "Ferrante Fever" became an international phenomenon: "When pitching, I just said things that I thought were true, like it had to be an ensemble, that it had so many wonderful opportunities for community scenes.... I thought that the neighbourhood is just so exciting on stage—you can bring the courtyard to life. And then there was this relationship between two women so the history of post-war Italy and the history of feminism and of class is all put through this complicated, truthful relationship between two women. That's really unusual ... it's still not the norm to have one woman at the centre of a play, but to have two."[33]

In response to an interviewer's question as to how the nearly 1,600 pages of the Neapolitan Quartet into could be compressed into just four acts over two evenings, the director of the Rose Theatre production, Melly Still, acknowledged the impossibility of doing so: "There's this strange, wonderful experience, which I think is particular to reading. It becomes personal and consummate." She thinks a television series could manage to convey the scope of the novel, but "theatre has a different role, somehow distilling the experience of reading. Of course you end up losing some of the characters who you've grown to know and love ... you exist in a distilled Ferrante world."[34]

Audiences and reviewers are often disappointed with adaptations of literary works. They bring their expectations based on their conception of the book, and mixed reviews are the usual result. The *Daily Mail*'s Patrick Marmion described the Rose Theatre production as a "wild goose chase in which the adapter, April De Angelis, demonstrates a tin ear for dialogue" and deplored the "cartoon characters and leaden dialogue."[35] Gary Naylor's lukewarm review in *Broadway World* questions whether a theatrical adaptation of the Neapolitan novels is possible: "By covering the 66 years time span of the four novels in one theatrical gulp, too many complexities are lost in the need to compress the narrative."[36] The *Guardian*'s Susannah Clapp has a very different response: "Against the odds, adapter April De Angelis and director Melly Still have pulled off their dramatization in *My Brilliant Friend.* There are absences and some awkwardness, but the essence of the books—intensity—wins through."[37] The responses to the television series may be even more divided than those to the radio program and to the stage production, as the audience will be much larger and will probably include many who have not read the novels. The television series will in all likelihood increase sales of the novels; "Ferrante Fever" shows no signs of abating.

2
Who Is Elena Ferrante? Does It Matter?

"I believe that books, once they are written, have no need of their authors. If they have something to say, they will sooner or later find readers; if not, they won't."—Elena Ferrante, *Frantumaglia: A Writer's Journey*

Ferrante's choice to write under a pseudonym has attracted more attention than any other aspect of her work. Up until Claudio Gatti's "unmasking" of Ferrante in October 2016, most Anglophone readers had no clue as to her real identity, although in Italian literary circles Rome-based translator Anita Raja and her husband novelist Domenico Starnone had long been identified as "prime suspects." Relying on financial records related to real estate transactions and royalty payments, Gatti identified Ferrante as Anita Raja and also speculated that Starnone might be her collaborator. Just about everyone who has written about the exposure of Ferrante's identity has supported her decision to remain anonymous and attacked Gatti's "unmasking," frequently describing it in terms of sexual violation. *The New Republic*'s Charlotte Shane, for example, argued that "Gatti's defense of his piece continues to echo the most chilling claims of men who physically violate a woman while claiming the resisting woman wanted it and had it coming."[1] Gatti had very few defenders, among them the *Washington Post* editorial board: "Ms. Ferrante (or Ms. Raja) is not a sacred deity; she is a gifted writer. As such, her identity is a legitimate subject of interest. Literary scholarship is rich with studies of Jane Austen, Leo Tolstoy, the Bronte sisters and others, including those who wished fervently to be left alone by devotees and the wide world, such as J.D. Salinger. If the Neapolitan quartet is an influential work on feminism, Italy or postwar history, and some readers and scholars want to delve into its origins, why should that be suppressed?"[2]

In her many interviews conducted by letters and email, Ferrante staunchly defended her decision to shield her identity. In an interview with the *New York Times*, she wrote that her desire for anonymity arose from anxiety about public exposure: "More than 20 years ago, I felt the burden of exposing myself in public, I wanted to detach myself from the finished story; I wanted the books to assert themselves without my patronage."[3] Similarly she told the *Paris Review*: "At first I was frightened at the thought of having to come out of my shell. Timidity prevailed. Later, I came to feel hostility towards the media, which doesn't pay attention to books themselves and values a work according to the author's reputation."[4]

Although Ferrante described her initial desire for anonymity in personal terms, over the years she began to develop a philosophical position defending anonymity, insisting that a literary work should stand on its own without biographical information or commentary from an author. She in all probability drew upon the work of Roland Barthes who in his 1968 essay "The Death of the Author" argued: "The image of literature to be found in contemporary culture is tyrannically centered on the author, his person, his history, his tastes, his passions."[5] According to Barthes, if the author disappears, then the reader is free to interpret the work as she chooses. Despite her insistence that the author's commentary is a distraction, Ferrante communicated her evolving explanation of her choice to write under a pseudonym through numerous interviews. The usual procedure was for the interviewer to submit questions through Ferrante's publisher and Ferrante would reply by email. She told the *Guardian* that she has no regrets about her decision not to reveal her identity: "Today I feel, thanks to this decision, that I have gained a space of my own, a space that is free, where I feel active and present. To relinquish it would be very painful."[6] She has argued that if her books "have something to say, they will sooner or later find readers; if not, they won't."[7] Anonymity allows a space of absolute creative freedom, essential because her books stick "a finger in certain wounds I have that are still infected."[8] What she fears the most is the loss of that creative space: if she should lose it, she insists she will no longer publish.

It has become received opinion, both among Ferrante scholars and among her enthusiastic fans, that there is something suspect about preoccupation with Ferrante's identity. In *The Works of Elena Ferrante: Reconfiguring the Margins*, an edited collection of essays intended for an academic audience, editors Grace Bullaro and Stephanie Love deliberately decided

2. Who Is Elena Ferrante?

to "ignore the vexed question of Ferrante's anonymity ... which seems to fascinate the general public as well as critics and scholars ... function[ing] more as a distraction from the work itself than as a way of deepening our understanding of it."[9] After a while I became more or less convinced by the arguments of Ferrante scholars and Ferrante herself that her books should stand on their own merits and should have no need for the biographical prop of an author. However, I still found myself searching for the biographical core in her novels and was not totally convinced that there was something illegitimate about an interest in an author's life story. Academics such as Tiziana de Rogatis have contended: "For the academy, it doesn't matter who the person Elena Ferrante is.... We don't need to know who the woman is who goes grocery shopping when she isn't writing. We are interested in other things, for example the influence that *House of Liars* ... had on her."[10] But certainly there are life experiences that might have as much influence on a writer's work as the books she has read.

There is considerable continuity from book to book: Delia in *Troubling Love*, Olga in *The Days of Abandonment*, Leda in *The Lost Daughter*, Elena in the Neapolitan novels are all variations on the same character—an educated woman from a poor neighborhood in Naples who has struggled to achieve middle class status, has literary ambitions, a failed marriage, a troubled relationship with her mother and with her children, and who is torn by guilt for putting her needs above her children's. Not all of the characters share all these characteristics: Delia, for example, does not have children and was not married; however, there is enough similarity in these four women that something like an image of the woman who created them seems to emerge. Many of Ferrante's readers became convinced they had a sense of the person through her books. From her translator Ann Goldstein: "I have started feeling that she is very present as a person in some way in her books. And so I don't feel any need to know the actual person, because this person's mind is so vivid."[11] Almost all of Ferrante's readers (at least pre–Gatti) assumed some connection between Ferrante's life and the lives of her narrators and believed that on some level the events described in her novels did in fact occur. As blogger Veronique Darwin wrote: "In any case, I find it hard to believe that whoever Ferrante really is, this all did not happen."[12]

Ferrante's readers generally accepted her decision to conceal her identity, seeing her as part of a tradition of female writers who chose to write anonymously or under a pseudonym. Some of her defenders drew upon John Mullan's *Anonymity: A Secret History of English Literature*, placing Ferrante's work within a long tradition of writers seeking a haven in anonymity. According to Mullan: "A good proportion of what is now English literature consists of works first published, like *The Rape of the Lock*, without their authors' names."[13] Women writers in particular have used pseudonyms or chosen anonymity to shield themselves from cultural biases against female authors; George Eliot, George Sand and the Brontë sisters all published under masculine pseudonyms. Ferrante apparently sees her choice of name in this larger context. In her introduction to Jane Austen's *Sense and Sensibility*, she wrote: "The fact that Jane Austen, in the course of her short life, published her books anonymously made a great impression on me as a girl of 15 ... I was past 20 when I returned to Austen. And from that moment not only did I love everything she had written but I was passionate about her anonymity."[14] Ferrante said she never considered using a male pseudonym like George Eliot or the Brontë sisters, telling the *Sydney Herald*: "The time to transform ourselves into men is over."[15]

Ferrante has forcefully denied the rumors that she is a man. Her devoted readers have long considered this an impossibility, both because of the authenticity of her rendering of female experience and, as Dayna Tortorici has claimed, "no man I know would write so well and not take credit for it."[16] I was among those convinced that Ferrante was a woman. In a classic example of confirmation bias, I chose to ignore the findings of scholars who analyzed Ferrante's books with text analysis software, concluding that there was a "high probability" that Domenico Starnone was the principal author. Similarly, I brushed off reports that Starnone's novel *Lacci* (*Ties*), has striking similarities to Ferrante's *The Days of Abandonment*. I simply dismissed evidence that did not fit my hypothesis.

However, when Claudio Gatti produced evidence that Raja and Starnone had some history of collaboration, I was forced to consider the possibility that Ferrante's novels may not be solely the work of a woman writer. Gatti noted that Raja translated German writer Christa Wolf into Italian, and both Raja and Starnone have acknowledged Wolf's influence. According to Gatti: "In a March 2009 article for the Neapolitan daily *Il Mattino*, the couple explained, "Every book by Christa that [Raja] translated into Italian led to months of intense discussions between the two of us, an opportunity to reflect, to learn. It wasn't just driven by literary passion, but by our desire to master a complex text ... and enhance the way we look at the world, and see how we can become better.... [Christa] immediately seduced us."[17]

I was assimilating this information at the same time I was reading *Frantumaglia: A Writer's Journey*, a collection of Ferrante's letters, essays, interviews, and material deleted from her early novels. Although some of the individual pieces are fascinating, *Frantumaglia* is a shapeless, repetitive compilation, more like a scrapbook than a book. The intriguing title, which Ferrante defines as her mother's word for "a disquiet not otherwise definable ... a miscellaneous crowd of things in her head, debris in a muddy water of the brain," does not bear much relationship to the book, which mostly consists of repetitive explanations/rationales for Ferrante's work.[18] I find it surprising that Ferrante, the author of such intricately structured books as the Neapolitan novels, would want to put her name to something as shapeless as *Frantumaglia*. According to Claudio Gatti, *Frantumaglia* was "the result of a smart P.R. move" by Ferrante's publishers, who urged Ferrante to respond to "the healthy desire of your readers to know you better."[19]

I might have had a somewhat more positive reaction to *Frantumaglia* if I had read it before Claudio Gatti's well-documented claim that Ferrante was Anita Raja, who, unlike Ferrante, did not grow up in an impoverished Neapolitan neighborhood, but rather left Naples at the age of three and lived in middle class comfort in Rome. Unlike Elena Greco whose parents had little formal education, Raja was the daughter of an Italian magistrate and a German Jewish Holocaust survivor who worked as a teacher. Throughout *Frantumaglia* there are numerous (clearly false) references to Ferrante's childhood and adolescence in Naples: her fears of growing up in a violent neighborhood; her relationship with her mother, who spoke the Neapolitan dialect and worked as a seamstress; her struggle for upward mobility, very much like that of Elena Greco's climb up the class ladder. Ferrante described Naples as "a space containing all my primary childhood, adolescent, and early adult experiences."[20] Ferrante's publishers apparently encouraged this deception. One of the first letters in *Frantumaglia* includes a reference to Sandra Ferri's request that Ferrante contribute to a book she was editing about growing up in Naples.

In *Frantumaglia* Ferrante implies that her narrators' emotional experiences were based on her own life, stating that it was frequently painful to delete certain sections of *Troubling Love* and *Days of Abandonment* "because what I was narrating was mine, I had struggled to dig it out and find a form for it."[21] What are we to make of this? The tangle of falsehoods (or fictional detail as some readers prefer to call it) makes disentangling "truth" from "fiction" impossible. We know that many of the biographical details purporting to describe Ferrante's childhood and adolescence in Naples are untrue. However, the description of her narrators' emotional lives may be true to the author's experience. Gatti suggested something like this when he wondered if Ferrante's "self-described attraction to what she called 'images of crisis' and to looking at 'what most terrifies us' is not in some way linked to the story of Raja's mother, Golda Frieda Petzenbaum ... [who] experienced the worst tragedy of the twentieth century as a young girl, emerging not as a victim but as a woman capable of the accomplishment that her daughter, Anita Raja, attributed to ... Christa Wolf's Cassandra: 'rebuilding an independent female self, able to move away from the life rhythms of an era of horrible butchers.'"[22]

Almost as if anticipating the criticism that would come her way if it became known that she does not share the background of her characters, Ferrante contended in a 2015 interview: "Writing—and not only fiction—is always an illicit appropriation. Our singularity as authors is a small note in the margin. The rest we take from the repository of those who have written before us, from the lives, from the most intimate feelings of others. Without the authorization of anything or anyone."[23] Ferrante may have been obliquely referring to the debate about cultural appropriation then raging in literary circles. With the exception of Adam Kirsch and Alyssa Rosenberg, none of the responses to Gatti's identification of Ferrante as Raja that I have read addresses this issue of what we now call "cultural appropriation." Adam Kirsch, in his *New York Times* essay, sees Ferrante's work as a response to those who question an author's right to tell stories about people unlike herself: "But now it appears that one of the world's best-loved writers is actually a sterling example of the power of appropriation. For it turns out that in telling the story of poor Neapolitan girls like Lila and Elena, Ms. Raja was claiming the right to imagine the lives of people quite unlike herself. In doing so, she was able to write books in which millions of people found themselves reflected—books about feminism and patriarchy, poverty and violence, education and ambition."[24]

Of course, very few people would question Ferrante's right to portray the lives of women living in poverty. What is problematic is Ferrante's encouraging readers to believe that Elena Ferrante, the author, shares the background of her character Elena Greco. Alyssa Rosenberg notes that "this literary kerfuffle about [Ferrante's background] comes at a moment of intense debate about cultural appropriation, and more specifically, whether authors have the right to create characters from communities not their own, and what their obligations are should they choose to do so."[25] This last point is the critical one: do writers have any obligation to let their readers know if their background is very different from the lives of their characters, particularly if the author is writing from a position of privilege with respect to the characters? If, as I now believe is most likely, Raja and Starnone are the co-authors of Ferrante's novels, we have one author who shares the working class Neapolitan background of Ferrante (and her narrator Elena Greco), but not her gender, and the other co-author who shares the gender of Ferrante, but not her working class background. Assuming this is true, the reader is faced with the questions: To what extent is this relevant to the debate about cultural appropriation? To what extent is this at all relevant to an analysis/assessment of Ferrante's novels?

From what I have read in many reviews and blog posts, most of Ferrante's readers do not appear to be concerned about Ferrante's falsely claimed Neapolitan background, viewing it as a literary device. Journalist Maria Laurino is one of the few reviewers who raised concerns about what some see as "lies" and others as "fictional detail" in *Frantumaglia*: "One can argue that fictional truths are grounded in falsehoods, that literary truth is, in Ferrante's words, 'released exclusively by words used well.' But in an age when facts are viewed as optional, when tragedies of history are denied, to purposefully lie in a nonfiction format is jarring. Why not simply remain in the silence of a chosen anonymity?"[26]

At the same time as they view Ferrante as a fictional character, many of Ferrante's devoted readers tend to see the wide-ranging reflections in *Frantumaglia* as the genuine beliefs of the author, presumed to be Anita Raja. But if some sections of *Frantumaglia* are clearly fiction, how can we be sure the rest is not? In *Frantumaglia*, Ferrante argues that literature itself is in some sense a lie. She admits to lying at times but claims not to tell "petty lies ... except to avoid danger, to protect myself."[27] Certainly Anita Raja did not have to weave a web of falsehoods about her biography in order "to avoid danger." She did not need to construct the increasingly elaborate literary persona of Elena Ferrante to shield her identity; she could simply have remained silent about her biography, as Maria Laurino has suggested. Could the creation of Elena Ferrante have been a marketing strategy—perhaps devised by her publishers? Clearly many readers were eager to believe that the author of the Neapolitan novels was writing from lived experience.

Ferrante, when explaining her choice to publish under a pseudonym, claims over and over again that her books should stand for themselves, that there is no need of any explanation or information beyond the text. However, the very existence of her collection of interviews and letters in *Frantumaglia* undermines that claim. As Michiko Kakutani observed in her *New York Times* review: "It's a padded, often self-indulgent volume that undermines her stated belief that 'books, once they are written, have no need of their authors.' In fact, this book is a 384-page repudiation of Ferrante's assertion that the text is 'a self-sufficient body, which has in itself, in its makeup, all the questions and all the answers.'" Kakutani has noted that Ferrante's "self-conscious and stilted statements [in *Frantumaglia*] stand in stark contrast to the visceral immediacy of Ms. Ferrante's novels."[28] Like Kakutani, I noticed that much of the writing in *Frantumaglia* was very different from that that of the novels—much more abstract, more academic. Of course, changes in style do not necessarily mean two authors, although Claudio Gatti's revelations have certainly encouraged speculation, perhaps implicit in Kakutani's review, that Anita Raja and Domenico Starnone are the co-authors of Ferrante's novels and essays.

Gatti's revelations have challenged the belief that there are aspects of the female experience that can only be fully understood and described by a woman writer, and have also challenged the widely held assumption that great literature must be the work of one mind, one visionary genius. Recent Shakespeare scholarship suggests that a work of genius can be a collaborative effort. Using computerized tools to analyze texts, the New Oxford Shakespeare's team of international scholars have concluded that *Henry VI*, Parts One, Two and Three are among as many as 17 Shakespeare plays that they now believe contain writing by other people.[29] In some sense all works of art are collaborative, and Ferrante in her interview with *Paris Review* makes this point: "And yet there is no work that is not the result of tradition, of many skills, of a sort of collective intelligence."[30] References to joint authorship abound within the *Neapolitan Quartet*: Lila and Elena dream of writing a novel together and Elena credits Lila as the inspiration for much of her writing. What Elena refers to as the "play of shared creation" is a major theme of the novels.

There are allusions to both gender bending and collaborative authorship scattered throughout Ferrante's work, almost as if she is providing clues to the authorship of her novels. In *Frantumaglia*, Ferrante tells the story of Ariadne, suffering because she believes her lover Theseus has abandoned her on the island of Amathus. In order to console her, the women of Amathus write love letters to her, pretending the letters are from Theseus. Ferrante focused on "the women's effort to enter the head, the words of a man" and "the women's collaboration—a true harmonious group project—to feign a man's psychic and lexical makeup."[31] In her many interviews, Ferrante returns again and again to the idea of collaborative authorship and the belief that "a good writer—male or female—can imitate the two sexes with equal effectiveness."[32]

Tiziana de Rogatis has argued that it "doesn't matter whether the 'real' Ferrante is a woman, a man or transgender; whether she is heterosexual or homosexual; an individual human being or a collective. What matters is that in the years when she wrote her first three novels ...when her readers were few and success unpredictable, she chose to identify as a woman writer" and wrote from the perspective of a woman. De Rogatis assumes the existence of a unitary female gaze that can be identified as such but does not necessarily require a life lived in a female body. According to de Rogatis, for a long time, Ferrante consciously chose to contend with gender bias: "She's had fewer opportunities for publication; she's been labelled as a writer of sentimental novels aimed at a female readership; and she's been ignored by cultural reviews."[33] However, in a world where women are the primary consumers of novels, identification as a woman is in all likelihood going to increase sales. Ferrante's publishers clearly pursued a wildly successful strategy of appealing to women readers, choosing cover designs that clearly signaled that the intended audience was female.

Many of Ferrante's readers expressed relief that at least Gatti identified a woman as the author of the Neapolitan novels; however, despite mounting evidence to the contrary, many readers ignored Gatti's suggestion that Domenico Starnone might have played a role in their creation. Gatti reported that after analyzing Ferrante's books with text analysis software, in 2006 a group of physicists and mathematicians at La Sapienza University in Rome concluded that there was a "high probability" that Starnone was the principal author.[34] In 2016 with ten more years of linguistic data to analyze, the Swiss start-up OrphAnalytics provided more evidence pointing to Starnone's authorship.[35] In February 2017 Expert

System, using Cogito semantic technology, compared Ferrante's style with those of four of the writers considered the most likely candidates behind the Ferrante pseudonym; they concluded: "Domenico Starnone is most similar to Elena Ferrante from a linguistic and stylistic point of view."[36] And most recently, in September 2017, Patrick Juola and a team of computer scientists at the University of Padua analyzed 150 novels by 40 different authors in the past 30 years to identify the author with a style most similar to Ferrante's. Juola noted that everyone working on the project identified Starnone as the likely author.[37]

Yet the insistence that Ferrante's novels must be solely the work of a woman persists. In response to the announcement that Saverio Costanzo would direct the HBO adaptation of *My Brilliant Friend*, Julie Kosin in a 2017 article in *Harper's Bazaar* argued that "placing a man in charge of telling the HBO adaptation undermines the politics of gender oppression that are inextricably woven into Elena Ferrante's Neapolitan Novels.... As a man, it's almost impossible for Costanzo to identify with Lenù and Lila's struggles."[38] Kosin seems not to have considered the possibility that a man might have been involved in writing *My Brilliant Friend*.

Unlike Kosin, I can no longer so easily dismiss the possibility that Starnone had a hand in the Neapolitan Quartet. Starnone, like the fictional Ferrante, did grow up in a working class Neapolitan family, and like Ferrante his mother was a seamstress. The mother who worked as a seamstress recurs in Ferrante's work. Both Olga in *The Days of Abandonment* and Delia in *Troubling Love* have mothers who were seamstresses, and like Ferrante in *Frantumaglia*, they recall specific details of their mothers' working lives—the kind of detail that feels like it is based on direct observation. There are many such details about growing up in poverty in Naples that suggest an author familiar with this world. Elena describes the daily ritual of dismantling the dining room furniture, making up the beds at night and unmaking them in the morning, so the dining room could double as a bedroom. In the Greco family's small apartment, the few rooms had to serve more than one purpose. Elena's parents lacked money for anything beyond the basic necessities; they never bought newspapers and, until her high school teacher Professor Galiani passed along her newspapers to her, Elena had never read one. Elena also noted that she hadn't grown up brushing her teeth; "it was a recent habit acquired in Pisa" (TWL, 81). Certainly Starnone was more likely to have had (or known people who had) such experiences than was Anita Raja with her middle class Roman upbringing.

Also, Delia's father in *Troubling Love* is similar to Starnone's father as he has described him in interviews with the Italian media—a jealous, abusive, frustrated railway worker who dreamed of being an artist: " 'My mother was dazzled by this domineering, persuasive, charming, violent man,' he told *Io Donna*, an Italian women's magazine. 'He never hurt us, but he beat her up before our very eyes. And always for the same reason—jealousy.'"[39] The frustrated railway worker who saw himself as an artist also occurs in the Neapolitan novels in the figure of Nino Sarratore's father, Donato, although without the physical violence. Donato's abusive behavior, like Nino's, took the form of chronic infidelity. Such similarities between Starnone's family history and that of the characters in Ferrante's novels have fueled the belief that Starnone had a hand in Ferrante's novels. The suspicion has grown with the publication of the English language translation of his novel *Ties*, which bears a striking resemblance to Ferrante's *The Days of Abandonment*. The conversation has shifted from Ferrante's anonymity to the possible role of Starnone. Although there are certainly many Ferrante fans, who would be deeply disappointed to learn that the books were not solely the work of a woman, there are others (and I include myself here) intrigued by the collaboration of a man and woman on books that so powerfully explore issues of gender.

For some time, I have tried to suppress the impulse to extract a biographical core from Ferrante's novels, but the desire persists. Ferrante's insistence on a shield of anonymity probably has had the perverse effect of making at least some of her readers all the more curious about the author behind the books they love. Now after Gatti's revelations suggesting that Domenic Starnone may have had a hand in Ferrante's work, I find myself re-reading the novels with an eye to what parts may have been written by Raja, what parts by Starnone. I am reluctant to confess reading the novels this way, but must admit that it actually adds to the enjoyment. My guess is that Starnone is the principal author of the Neapolitan Quartet, that Raja is the principal author of *Frantumaglia* and that the publishers encouraged the fictional creation of Elena Ferrante; they certainly have a stake in the image of Ferrante as a powerful woman writer.

As of this writing only two of Starnone's thirteen novels have been translated into English. The first of these, *First Execution*, is what is often called an experimental novel or metafiction.[40] Unlike the Neapolitan Quartet with its traditional structure, in *First Execution* Starnone breaks the illusion of a fictional world and allows his narrator to analyze the authorial choices he made when developing his characters and structuring the plot. The novel ends with a presentation of five possible endings; presumably, it's up to the reader to decide which ending works best. Despite these structural differences, I saw many stylistic similarities to Ferrante, including long stretches of dialogue without any of the usual markers to indicate the speaker, as well as a dramatic opening and conclusion which leaves much unresolved. In addition, there are thematic similarities between *First Execution* and the Neapolitan novels; the exploration of the ethical implications of political violence is the major theme of *First Execution* and one of the thematic strands in the Neapolitan novels. The central character of *First Execution* is a former teacher, a man of the left, who agonizes over whether his teaching has led one of his former students to engage in political violence. In both Starnone's brief novel and Ferrante's Neapolitan novels, the characters' willingness to condone political violence and their belief in the possibility of revolution change dramatically over the course of time.

Ties, which appeared in English translation in March 2017, is closer to conventional narrative structure than *First Execution*; there is no attempt to call attention to the text as fiction. There are striking similarities between *Ties* and Ferrante's novella *The Days of Abandonment*; both novels begin with a man abandoning his wife and children for a much younger woman, leaving his wife distraught, angry and unwilling to accept what has happened. However, *The Days of Abandonment*, set in the 1990s, takes a different turn from *Ties*, in which the husband's decision to abandon his family occurs in the 1970s. In *The Days of Abandonment*, Olga soon develops a life and identity of her own. In *Ties*, Vanda, who came of age in a more traditional era, is more focused on getting her husband to return.

Ties spans a much longer arc of time than *Days of Abandonment* and continues the story into the 21st century. Whereas *The Days of Abandonment* is told from Olga's point of view, *Ties* offers three different perspectives on Vanda and Aldo's troubled marriage. The first part of *Ties* consists of Vanda's letters to her husband Aldo, demanding an explanation of his decision to leave her, letters very reminiscent of Olga's insistence that her husband explain himself. The second part gives Aldo's, perspective—an outlook very similar to that of Olga's husband, Mario, who believes he is entitled to pursue happiness with a younger woman. Unlike Mario, Aldo, ridden with guilt about his children, eventually returns to his wife. He must endure Vanda's anger at his betrayal—an open wound after many years.

The third part of the novella is narrated by their daughter Anna who describes the impact of her parents' conflict-ridden relationship on their children—a legacy of pain, which leads Anna and her brother to take shocking revenge on their parents. *Ties* is a cautionary tale for those who believe that parents in an unhappy marriage should stay together for the sake of the children.

Ties has the intense, almost claustrophobic quality of Ferrante's novellas. The changes in gender relations that began in the wake of the sexual revolution of the 1960s and 1970s, and traced over a roughly fifty year period in the four Neapolitan novels, are compressed into the 149 pages of *Ties*. The marital breakdown explored in *Ties*, in Ferrante's novellas and in the Neapolitan Quartet, all have their origins in the sense of a new world in the making in which all established institutions are being challenged. In the third volume of the Neapolitan novels, Elena Greco describes her desire to be free of her marriage: "I wanted to break the rules as the entire world was breaking the rules" (TWL, 258). Aldo's desire to break free of his marriage is expressed in similar terms, but he is painfully aware of the persistence of traditional values: "The new era has only spread out a flashy veil over the old one, archaic impulses fester under the rouge of modernity."[41] By the time of the next generation—Elena's and Aldo's children—the changes in gender roles have taken root. Elena, reflecting on her daughters' lives, notes: "The time of faithfulness and permanent relationships was over for men and for women" (SLC, 393). Aldo's daughter Anna reflects sarcastically on her brother's life: "He's convinced naturally that the right road is the one he's been on: multiplying mothers, multiplying fatherhood, multiplying the nucleus of love and sex. And a confusion of roles. The end in other words of the traditional concept of the couple: no monogamy, various women, all of them loved, various children, all of them adored."[42]

As I become more familiar with Starnone's work, the conviction grows that he had a hand in Ferrante's novels and may have been the principal author of the Neapolitan Quartet. Starnone's explorations of changes in Italian society on a personal level (*Ties*) and on a political level (*First Execution*) are echoed in the complex interplay of themes in the Neapolitan Quartet. However, neither Ferrante's novellas nor the two Starnone books in English translation prepare the reader for the broad canvas, wide range of compelling characters, and the rich tapestry of interrelated themes of the Neapolitan Quartet. Starnone is a powerful writer, and I hope that more of his novels will be translated, and not just because I enjoy looking for traces of Ferrante in his work. I also hope that Raja and Starnone will acknowledge what I believe is their joint creation of Elena Ferrante and her works. The story of their collaboration would surely be fascinating. As *New Yorker* critic Aaron Bady described the relationship between *Ties* and *Days of Abandonment*: "*Ties* is one half of a collaboration far more intriguing than co-authorship of individual books: a riveting dialogue on marriage conducted, on the page, between one novelist and another." In an interview with Bady, Starnone vociferously denied any connection between *Ties* and *Days of Abandonment*. But apparently trying to have it both ways, in the same interview, "Starnone coyly pointed out that both *Ties* and *Days of Abandonment* contain the precise detail of a glass vessel, which each wife breaks in response to her husband's faithlessness."[43]

I cannot help but think of Dayna Tortorici's comment as to why she did not think the author behind Ferrante was male: "No man I know would write so well and not take credit for it."[44] The decision to publish under the pseudonym of Elena Ferrante was made over two decades ago, before Ferrante became an international publishing sensation. Could Starnone at this point in his life want recognition for his contribution towards the creation of the fictional character Elena Ferrante and her powerful novels? The veil of anonymity has been lifted, but the saga of Ferrante, Raja, and Starnone has yet to play itself out. But in the last analysis does authorship of the Neapolitan novels matter? On one level, yes. It is currently received opinion among many academics that there is something suspect about an interest in biography or that anyone at all troubled by Ferrante's falsely claimed Neapolitan background is lacking in sophistication and just doesn't understand how literature works. However, an analysis of the extent to which an author's life may have entered her literary works is a legitimate area of inquiry; this has certainly been the case with many female authors who have sought to conceal their identity—for example, Jane Austen, the Brontës, George Eliott, and George Sand.

However, on another level, it may not matter if Starnone turns out to be the principal author of the Neapolitan novels. I question whether we will read the novels differently if we know that the author is not a woman drawing on her own experience of class and gender discrimination. In my recent re-reading of the Neapolitan novels, I forgot all about Anita Raja, Domenico Starnone and Claudio Gatti and became once again totally immersed in the world of Lila and Elena. This is what counts.

3

Ann Goldstein and the Challenges of Translation

> *"There's an essay by an Italian writer called Cesare Garboli where he talks about the translator as an actor, a performer, and no one's ever going to perform the same way."*—Ann Goldstein

The thoughts that Anglophone readers encounter in reading Elena Ferrante's works are Elena Ferrante's; the actual words they read are Ann Goldstein's. Goldstein is Ferrante's English-language translator, and it is generally acknowledged that she is highly skilled. Together with Ferrante, she was shortlisted for the 2016 Man Booker International Prize. In addition, she has won the PEN Renato Poggioli Award as well as awards from the American Academy of Arts and Letters and the Italian Ministry of Foreign Affairs. Her first translation of Ferrante's work was *The Days of Abandonment* published in 2005; since then she has translated all of Ferrante's novels as well as *Frantumaglia: A Writer's Journey*, a collection of letters and essays. In addition, she has translated other major Italian writers, such as Pier Paolo Pasolini, Jhumpa Lahiri, and Primo Levi, whose complete works she edited.

Ferrante's novels appeared on the world stage at a time of an increasing interest in literature in translation. In 2016, the *Guardian* reported that although the market for literary fiction has stagnated during the past 15 years, sales of translated fiction have grown by 96 percent.[1] The recent publication of so much literature in translation has been greeted enthusiastically by readers and by critics such as Adam Kirsch in The *Global Novel: Writing the World in the 21st Century*. Kirsch has argued, that despite fears of critics troubled by the hegemony of English, world literature has not become increasingly deracinated, with local languages replaced by "an easily consumable style preferably in English." He cites the Neapolitan novels as an example of a literature that "is not thinly generic but richly particular; not international in scope but localized on the scale of a single neighborhood, not about isolated individuals traveling through a featureless world, but about the thick web of social and economic relationships that determine the course of individual lives."[2] The heightened interest in literature in translation has led to a greater appreciation of the art of the translator. Starting in 2016, the Man Booker International Prize, given for a translation into English of a work of fiction written in another language, will be shared equally between the author and the translator. Launched in 2017 with the goal of addressing the gender imbalance in translated literature, the Warwick Prize for Women in Translation is also divided between the writer and her translator(s). Honoring the translator alongside the author is a measure of the increased recognition currently given to translation.

Interest in women in translation has grown dramatically, aided by WiT (Women in Translation), a global collaborative project dedicated to increasing the number of publications of works written by women and translated into English. According to WiT, "only a tiny fraction of fiction published in English is translated, and only about a quarter of that translated fiction was originally written by women."[3] To remedy this situation, WiT has declared every August as Women in Translation month to promote existing titles written by women in translation as well as to pressure publishers to commission more translations of works written by women. The recent feature length *New York Times* magazine article on Emily Wilson's translation of *The Odyssey* into English is a testament to the surge of interest in translations by women. Wilson, the first woman to translate *The Odyssey* into English views all translations as interpretations and states, "I do think that gender matters" and says she approaches the task of translation with "whatever I have linguistically, sonically, emotionally."[4]

Goldstein has welcomed recent recognition for translators and in her many interviews has discussed the rewards and the difficulties inherent in the art of translation. She sees the acknowledgment of the translator's role as a "gratifying development" and notes, "Certainly all translators have had this experience of a review, where long passages from the book are quoted without reference to them, or to the fact that these passages have been translated from another language."[5] Ferrante's Anglophone readers have the good fortune to have a translator who has provided them with considerable insight into the process of translation. In addition to numerous interviews, Goldstein has spoken at many events about the choices she has made as a translator, functioning almost as a surrogate for the elusive author(s).

Given Goldstein's reputation, I could not help but wonder who is responsible for the powerful phrasing—Ferrante or Goldstein? Gabriel Garcia Marquez famously said that his novel *One Hundred Years of Solitude* was better in its English version, as translated by Gregory Rabassa, than in its original Spanish. Through reading, side by side, the Italian and English editions of the third volume of the Neapolitan novels, *Those Who Leave and Those Who Stay*, I tried to determine whether something similar was the case with Goldstein and Ferrante. Admittedly my reading knowledge of Italian is not really up to the task, but it appears to me that the power of the prose stems from the original, which Goldstein has faithfully followed. Fidelity to the original is central to Goldstein's philosophy of translation. In response to a question from the *Los Angeles Review of Books*, "What makes a translation bad?" Goldstein responded, "I think probably every bad translation is bad in its own way. I think it's bad when it tries to rewrite the book, the original. Of course, as a reader you might not know this has happened. But you can tell if it sounds stilted."[6]

There will almost certainly be general agreement that the translator's first and most important task is to be faithful to the author—the translator's motto, in almost everyone's opinion, should be *Semper fidelis*, "always faithful." There will be rather less agreement, however, as to what that means. Richard Bojar has described the extreme view taken by Russian-American novelist Vladimir Nabokov, who believed that a translator should be absolutely and literally faithful to an author's words, ignoring everything else. His translation of Pushkin's *Eugene Onegin* is utterly faithful to this opinion; it is a literal, pedestrian, almost word-for-word prose translation. It completely ignores that *Eugene Onegin* is a poem in iambic tetrameter with a very complicated rhyme scheme. In fact, it ignores everything about the poem except for the literal meaning of the words. Is this fidelity to the original? Most critics have thought not. Almost the opposite view was taken by Richard Pevear and Larissa Volokhonsky who have translated a large part of classic 19th-century Russian literature, including Tolstoy's *War and Peace*. Pevear and Volokhonsky consider that fidelity demands that obvious stylistic features be retained in translation. Maintaining fidelity to the author's literal meaning and conveying a sense of the author's style are not easily reconcilable goals. Numerous translators have struggled with the issue of fidelity to the original and arrived at very different conclusions.[7]

Richard Bojar's comparison of the titles of the Neapolitan novels in Ferrante's Italian and Goldstein's English illustrates some of the difficulties of translation. The first Neapolitan novel is entitled *L'Amica Geniale*:

> *L' Amica Geniale*
> The female-friend brilliant
> My Brilliant Friend

The first line above is the Italian title, the second an attempt at a literal word-for-word translation, and the third idiomatic English. The first word in the Italian is *L'*—The. In English, the phrase "The Brilliant Friend" sounds more like a generic title than a reference to a particular friend, rather as though the author were writing a psychological treatise on brilliant friends. Since the narrator of the novel is Elena, who is describing her friend Lila as *geniale*, the word "my" seems the most natural translation of the definite article. Lila at one point describes Elena as her brilliant friend, so there is some ambiguity as to which one (or both?) is the brilliant friend.

The second Italian word, *amica*, means a female friend. There is no way in Italian to say "friend" without specifying the sex of the friend—*amico* for a male friend, *amica* for a female. (The masculine plural, *amici*, is used both for groups of male friends and for groups of friends of both sexes; the female plural, *amiche*, is used for only for groups of female friends.) In English, on the other hand, the word friend is unisex. We have the words girlfriend and boyfriend, but they are subject to misinterpretation. In English, it seems impossible to specify the sex of the friend without emphasizing it, which the Italian definitely does not do. Given the difficulty of specifying a female friend in English, Goldstein correctly decided simply to omit the reference to gender. The reader will find out soon enough who the *amica* is.

Finally, note that *geniale* does not mean genial. It comes from the word *genio*, meaning genius. Goldstein could have entitled her translation *My Friend the Genius*, but preferred the much more idiomatic *My Brilliant Friend*. A pair of words like *geniale*/genial is often called a pair of "false friends"—two words which look as though they ought to be the same, but aren't.

3. Ann Goldstein and the Challenges of Translation

Even for good translators like Goldstein, "false friends" can occasionally create problems. In *Storia di chi fugge e di chi resta*, we encounter the clause *mi colpi la sua notorieta*. The narrator is Elena Greco; she is speaking with approbation of Nino Sarratore's extensive knowledge of the people of the district in Florence through which they were walking. Elena was surprised by how many people Nino knew, by how many greeted him by name, including a well-known historian. She was struck (*mi colpi*) by how well known he was (*la sua notorieta*). Unfortunately, in translating this, Goldstein was betrayed by the pair of false friends, *notorieta*/notoriety; her translation reads, "I was struck by his notoriety." As translations of *notorieta*, *Langenscheidt's Standard Italian Dictionary* gives "general knowledge; affidavit; notoriety." The Italian word is much broader than its English false friend. In English, the word notoriety is derogatory, thus we cannot speak of Nino's notoriety in the Florentine neighborhood where they were walking. In English, notoriety is the kind of fame one gets for doing something evil or tabooed, not for being well regarded.

The Italian title of the second Neapolitan novel is *Storia del nuovo cognomen*:

> Storia del nuovo cognome
> Story of the new family-name
> The Story of (a) New Name

Goldstein seems to have felt that the English "Story" demanded a definite article, and supplied one. Interestingly, she did not do this with the titles of the third and fourth novels, both of which also begin with "Story of"; with the third she also omitted "Story of." The Italian *del* means "of the," but for some reason Goldstein preferred "of a." Perhaps she felt that "of the new name" implied that there was only one new name, while in fact there were two—both Elena and Lila married and took new family names. Finally, the word *cognome* means specifically family name, and is a not uncommon Italian word. The word cognomen exists in English, but it is a formal, unusual word, a technical term, borrowed from Latin, and used almost only to refer to the last names of ancient Romans—the Caesar in Gaius Julius Caesar, or the Cicero in Marcus Tullius Cicero. Clearly, using a formal term to translate an everyday word would be a false note, and so Goldstein avoided cognomen and was satisfied simply with name. She could of course have entitled the second Neapolitan novel *The Story of a New Family Name*, but that would have meant lengthening the title for little reason, which she may have been reluctant to do.

The title of the third Neapolitan novel, *Storia di chi fugge e di chi resta*, called for more intervention on the translator's part:

> *Storia di chi fugge e di chi resta*
> Story of those who flee and of those who remain
> Those Who Leave and Those Who Stay

This time, Goldstein decided to suppress "(The) Story of," perhaps again for the sake of brevity. The Italian relative pronoun *chi* (who) can stand without antecedent to mean "those who" or "the one who." English, on the other hand, prefers to express antecedents and demands "those who" or "the one who." A literal translation of the title "Story of Who Flees and Who Stays" is at best awkward. If "Storia" is used, Italian demands that the preposition *di* be repeated. Goldstein's decision to omit "Story of" made it unnecessary to use any preposition, thus shortening the title. Unexpectedly, in this title Goldstein decided to translate the verb *fuggire*, meaning "flee" or "run away" as "leave." Perhaps she felt that leave and stay are natural antitheses, like come and go or black and white, and thus combine to make a more natural title.

The title of the fourth Neapolitan novel, *Storia della bambina perduta*, caused the least difficulty:

> *Storia della bambina perduta*
> Story of the child-feminine lost
> Story of the Lost Child

Once again, faced with a short title, Goldstein keeps "Story of." And once again, as with the word *amica* in the title of the first novel, the word *bambina* is gender marked, while its English equivalent is not. For some reason, while Goldstein gave the word story a definite article in the title of the second novel, she decided not to do so in the title of the fourth.[8]

My experience of reading the English and Italian versions of *Those Who Leave, Those Who Stay* side by side certainly gave me a greater appreciation of the multitude of difficult choices a translator faces. As Goldstein noted, there are always words for which there are no exact equivalents. I found myself at times disagreeing with her word choices but at the same time thinking: who I am to disagree with this renowned translator? But given that the translator must chose among several possibilities for each word, an occasional unfortunate choice is inevitable. Given the range of options for just about every word, I wonder how a translator ever manages to finish the job. As Goldstein put it: "you're always making a choice that might not be the one somebody else would make. You're choosing from a range of meanings. When Ferrante uses a word in Italian, it has a certain resonance in that language. You're probably not going to find a word in English that has the same resonance, but you have to find the one that you think is the most important."[9]

When comparing the English and Italian translations I became aware of some linguistic resources available to a writer in Italian, but not available in English. Italian is not a highly inflected language like Latin or Russian, but it is a more highly inflected language than English, and often conveys by word-endings information that in English is conveyed by word order. Since Italian is less bound by word order than is English, Italian offers the writer more options for the structure of the sentences. For example, when Lila and Elena, now in their early sixties, find their childhood friend Gigliola Spagnuolo dead in a church flowerbed Elena reflects on those who could not escape the cruel net of abuse:

> How many who had been girls with us were no longer alive, had disappeared from the face of the earth because of illness, because their nervous systems had been unable to endure the sandpaper of torments, because their blood had been spilled [TWL, 24].

Compare the Italian translation:

> *Quante personae que erano state bambine insieme a noi non erano piu vive, sparite dalla faccia della terra per malattia perche la nervatura non aveva retto alla carta vetrata dei tormenti, perche era stato versato il loro sangue [Storia di chi fugge e di chi resta, 16].*

Ferrante's sentence strikes me as far more powerful, ending with the emphasis on blood. For Goldstein a literal translation, "because had been spilled their blood," is not an option.

In the interviews with Goldstein I have read, she does not address the word order issue per se, but does speak of the resources available to those who write in Italian, unavailable to their English translators. Goldstein values both fidelity to the author's meaning and to the emotional resonance of her language, which she considers a much more difficult feat. She has frequently noted that the greatest challenge was maintaining the intensity of the sentences while respecting the rules of English syntax: "[Ferrante's] intensity is difficult; you have to be sure to get it, to capture it. She uses run-on sentences in Italian, and to deal with the run-on sentences in English is more complicated than in Italian, because English doesn't like run-on sentences that much. But you don't want to lose the power of what she's building up in those sentences."[10]

As Richard Bojar has noted, the problem, fortunately, is really a problem only of punctuation—essentially a pseudo-problem. Ferrante's run-on sentences are sequences of paratactically adjoined clauses separated by commas. The punctuation separating them, however, is essentially irrelevant. Goldstein might well have translated the passage quoted above as follows:

> How many who had been girls with us were no longer alive? How many had disappeared from the face of the earth because of illness? How many had disappeared because their nervous systems had been unable to endure the sandpaper of torments? How many had disappeared because they had been murdered? [TWL, 17].

This translation makes full sentences of Ferrante's clauses. Doing so requires giving each verb a subject and signaling the end of each resulting sentence with a question mark. The repetition makes this translation a few words longer than Goldstein's. To be more succinct, Goldstein might have tried:

> How many who had been girls with us were no longer alive? Or had disappeared from the face of the earth because of illness? Or because their nervous systems had been unable to endure the sandpaper of torments? Or had disappeared because they had been murdered? [TWL, 17].

These translations have much the same impact as Ferrante's. They do not give as strong a sensation as Ferrante's of a flood of language pouring out. On the other hand, their repetitions give them a hammering-like effect at least equally strong. Goldstein, however, would seem to be a fairly conservative translator, and decided to keep Ferrante's sentences and punctuation as they were precisely because they were Ferrante's. She wanted, to the extent possible, to retain Ferrante's sentence structures, and so simply translated them, clause by clause, as they came.[11]

Goldstein speculates as to how she might have handled Ferrante's run-on sentences differently: "I'm not saying that I would take away the run-on sentences, because I do think they serve a purpose and they're certainly there in the Italian. They are somewhat modified in the English—it's just too hard in English. I don't know, it's hard to say what I might have done differently. I might have done fewer or more, I might have changed the pace. It's always a hazard of translation—you're constantly second-guessing yourself, and at a certain point it loses its usefulness."[12] I have yet to encounter a reader who complained about Ferrante's run-on sentences. Much more common is praise for their emotional power. From the

3. Ann Goldstein and the Challenges of Translation

Guardian's Megan O'Rourke: "[Ferrante's] style is immersive, its intensity a cumulative effect of her bracing run-on sentences, which whip forward with muscular rigour."[13]

In response to a question as to whether it was difficult to convey the emotional intensity of Ferrante's prose in English, Goldstein acknowledged that English lacks "the color and cadence of Italian," and continued, "Obviously, I am trying to do it in the same way to keep something of the Italian structure because I think it is very effective.[14] According to Goldstein, "Italian is a naturally beautiful language. It's very mellifluous. In terms of the sound, it's very expressive. English can be very beautiful, but not in the same way—it's not this kind of flowing, fluid thing." Goldstein thinks Ferrante doesn't want to be a "beautiful writer," constructing "elaborate, beautiful, flowery kinds of sentences." Rather, Ferrante writes directly about her characters' experiences: "The fact that she's describing things that are not usually described in those terms in Italian literature means that the language she uses is often a little cruder, more raw. I don't mean vulgar. I just mean it's more direct, really. And kind of brutal."[15]

Ferrante's graphic sex scenes posed particular problems for Goldstein: "Getting the right tone with body parts is very hard. The language is pretty plain. But it's not slangy.... Goldstein thinks that physical scenes like sexual intercourse are especially difficult, both because of the vocabulary and "because it's such a sharp physical picture, and specific physical pictures— I don't know why—are really hard to get right because it's hard to describe the positions of the bodies."[16] Ferrante is known for her scenes of bad sex. Certainly among the most grotesque is the scene in *The Story of the Lost Child* when Elena discovers her lover Nino having sex with her housekeeper in the bathroom. As Goldstein noted, the physical image is compelling, conveying Nino's stunned surprise, the housekeeper's fear and Elena's horrified disbelief.

With the Neapolitan Quartet, Goldstein faced the additional challenge of translating four books in a series. When she worked on *My Brilliant Friend*, the first of the Neapolitan novels, the other three books had not yet been published: "I didn't have the advantage of having read the whole thing first, or of being able to go to the end and then come back to the beginning. A word like *smarginatura*.... I never remember how I ended up translating that, I think it's 'dissolving boundaries.' But if I had known that that was going to come up again in book three or four with the earthquake where [Ferrante] really talks about it at much greater length, I might have chosen a different phrase."[17] Goldstein believes that you have to know the ending of a novel—or in this case a series of novels—to be true to the beginning. She thinks that if she were to translate the Neapolitan novels again with knowledge of the ending, she would probably do certain things differently.

Goldstein is thankful that she did not have the further challenge of translating Neapolitan dialect: "Luckily Ferrante doesn't write in dialect.... I'm grateful.... I think a lot of Italians are grateful, too. I think this was one of her reasons ... people wouldn't understand it. It's really like another language."[18] Although Ferrante for the most part does not use actual dialect, the indication in the text "in dialect" is an important indicator of a character's social status or emotional state. Professor of Italian Studies Rebecca Falkoff has noted that although spoken Italian is widely understood among Neapolitans from all walks of life, "for a native speaker of dialect who did not complete secondary schooling and had little experience beyond his or her local community, it might be very difficult to produce grammatically correct standard Italian."[19] Failure to master standard Italian had consequences for employment opportunities and for social mobility. For those characters fluent in both Neapolitan dialect and in standard Italian, shift into dialect is usually an indicator of intense emotion or of close personal and familial ties. It's always worth noting when Ferrante indicates that one of the characters has shifted to dialect.

The complicated interplay between Italian and dialect is especially important in the first volume, *My Brilliant Friend*. Italian was the language of the schools; as a consequence, the expansion of primary education in the 1950s had consequences for working class Italians. Children from poor families had the opportunity to learn the language of upward mobility, whereas their parents, like those of many of the children in Lila's and Elena's elementary school, had few years of schooling and thus little exposure to standard Italian. In *My Brilliant Friend*, the tensions between those who were bi-dialectal in both Italian and Neapolitan and those who spoke only Neapolitan played out within families and among friends, with those who had mastered Italian enjoying greater status and opportunities.

In response to an interviewer's question as to how she approached conversation in dialect, even if the dialect itself wasn't present in Ferrante's writing, Goldstein replied that she "didn't consciously do anything, but as a translator following the lead of the author, I think [the dialect] might've come out a certain way. I've heard Italians say that the language is slightly different, that you can hear echoes of the dialect" when Ferrante indicates the language is in dialect. "Not of the words, but the sound or the feeling of it."[20] If there are indeed echoes of dialect in the language marked as "in dialect," it may be further evidence that Starnone, who grew up speaking Neapolitan dialect, was co-author of the novels. Certainly the frequency with which Ferrante uses the marker "in dialect," to indicate a speaker's status, relationship to others in the conversation, or emotional state suggests that the author of the Neapolitan Novels is quite familiar with the norms governing the use of Neapolitan dialect.

Anthropologist Jillian R. Cavanaugh notes that expressions in Neapolitan dialect appear occasionally in the Italian version of the Neapolitan novels, but there was only one instance in which Goldstein decided to incorporate Neapolitan dialect in the English translation. On the way to Capri for their honeymoon, Lila insisted that her husband Stefano take her home; she was enraged because he had given the shoes she had designed to her archenemy, Marcello Solara. Stefano defended himself by claiming it was Lila's brother who had decided to give the shoes to Marcello; Lila demanded: "You piece of shit ... repeat what you just said in front of those other two shit men. And only when she had uttered that expression in dialect, shit men, *uommen'e mmerd....* Stefano struck her in the face with his strong hand, a violent slap..." (SNN, 33). Perhaps Goldstein decided to include the dialect expression in this one instance because in this case the dialect is very close to standard Italian, or perhaps she wanted to underscore the close connection between dialect use and strong emotion, particularly negative emotion. The reader may not have the opportunity to learn many words in Neapolitan dialect, but certainly will develop a sense of what a shift from Italian into dialect might signify. As Cavanaugh has observed: "Readers may not begin the Neapolitan Novels with a knowledge of what dialect means in Italy, but they will certainly finish them with it due to how frequently Ferrante metalinguistically directs their attention to the language in which a character speaks or an interaction occurs, forging links, as she goes between the two languages and various modes of being, feeling and acting."[21]

There are surely many sentence level nuances that are inevitably lost in the English translation. However, Goldstein has provided Ferrante's Anglophone readers with considerable insight into the process of translation, along with her sense of Ferrante the author. Many translators have written about the challenges they faced translating particular works; among the more famous, Eleanor Marx and Lydia Davis have written about their experiences translating *Madame Bovary* (separate translations),[22] and Gregory Rabassa has published a book-length study of his career as a translator of such luminaries as Jorge Amado, Julio Cortazar, Clarice Lispector, and Gabriel Garcia Marquez.[23] However, with Goldstein we have something to my knowledge never before available—a running commentary on the process of translating the Neapolitan novels appearing in major newspapers and periodicals during the same time frame as the publication of the novels. I look forward to reading her translation of Primo Levi's collected works and hope that she will again provide her readers with insights into challenges of translation, in this case a work very different from Ferrante's.

4

The Novellas

> "My women are strong, educated, self-aware and aware of their rights, just, but at the same time subject to unexpected breakdowns, to subservience of every kind, to mean feelings. I've also experienced this oscillation. I know it well, and that also affects the way I write."—Elena Ferrante, *Frantumaglia: A Writer's Journey*

Before the Neapolitan quartet, Ferrante published three short novellas: *Troubling Love*, *The Days of Abandonment*, and *The Lost Daughter*. All three have a narrator at a crisis point in her life—the death of a mother, the dissolution of a marriage, the emergence of buried memories of abandoning her children. All three have a narrator who is in some sense deeply disturbed in contrast to Elena Greco, the narrator of the Neapolitan novels, whose voice is much more measured. Elena is not a consistently reliable narrator but is more so than the narrators of the novellas. She also has the perspective that comes from narrating events that transpired over the long arc of sixty years.

The three novellas share a kind of claustrophobic intensity with the reader trapped in the mind of the troubled narrator, sharing her pain and confusion. Many readers who come to the novellas after reading one or more of the Neapolitan novels find them difficult, disturbing. James Wood, whose *New Yorker* review introduced many readers to Ferrante, confessed he struggled to connect "the old work" with the later series, which in contrast was "like water, really, it has a lovely, fresh easiness about it."[1] Although not as immediately engaging as the Neapolitan Quartet, the novellas are powerful works that deserve to be read in their own right rather than as preparatory studies for the Neapolitan novels. However, it is difficult not to read the novellas as a foreshadowing of the later works, as they all contain variations on themes and characters that dominate the Neapolitan novels—but without the densely populated social world. All three novellas explore the struggles of women who want more from life than what was allowed to their mothers, and who live in fear of turning into their mothers. All three narrators are from a working class Neapolitan background, which they have managed to escape through education. They grew up in a world in which casual violence against women is the norm; yet as Ferrante has described them, they are women who "don't submit.... Instead they fight, and they cope.... I feel them not as women who are suffering, but as women who are struggling."[2]

In an interview with Rachel Donadio for the *New York Times*. Ferrante has emphasized the continuity between the novellas and the Neapolitan novels, describing her characters as reminiscent of real women she has known who, because of the pain they have endured and the battles they have waged, have stirred her imagination: "my mother, a childhood girlfriend, acquaintances whose stories I know. In general I combine their experiences with my own and Delia, Amalia, Olga, Leda, Nina, Elena, Lenù are born out of that mix." Ferrante describes her women as "strong, educated, self-aware and aware of their rights, but at the same time subject to unexpected breakdowns, to subservience of every kind, to mean feelings." She identifies with her characters because she too has "experienced this oscillation" between strength and unexpected weakness and believes it has influenced the way she writes.[3] Here Ferrante alludes to shared values and psychological experiences rather than to the shared class background she has claimed in many interviews.

Troubling Love

I found *Troubling Love*, Ferrante's first published work (1992 in Italian, 2006 in English translation), by far the most difficult, the most disturbing of the three novellas. It has been described by literary critic Dayna Tortorici as an experimental novel: "The conflation of past and present challenges basic comprehension, and unmarked shifts in subject send the reader flipping back in search of a pronoun's referent. This is standard fare for an experimental novel, which a generous reader would say *Troubling Love* is."[4] Elena Greco, the narrator of the Neapolitan novels, describes the Italian literary world in the 1980s as a "complicated moment in the literary market [with] writers of my age, hesitating between the avant-garde and traditional story telling" (SLC, 290). It may be that Ferrante is describing her own narrative choices, with *Troubling Love* as to some extent avant-garde and her later works as a shift to something more closely resembling traditional story telling.

Troubling Love is also in a sense a mystery story with the mystery not fully resolved. The central character Delia, a single woman in her 40s, like all Ferrante's narrators grew up in working class Naples, acquired an education, and left the old neighborhood. Her mother Amalia, with whom she has a complicated relationship, is still living in Naples and visits Delia regularly. Delia both loves and is irritated by her mother. Whenever Amalia visited her daughter, now living in Rome, she would set about rearranging the objects in Delia's apartment; when she departed, Delia would rearrange "everything according to my taste that she had arranged according to hers" (TL, 12). After receiving several disturbing phone calls from her mother who was travelling to Rome ostensibly to visit her, Delia learned that her mother drowned at a beach resort where she and a male companion had stopped on their way to Rome. Delia became obsessed with understanding what led to her mother's death: was it a suicide or an accident? Delia began to unravel, a dissolution underscored by her fear that her "whole body would be unleashed against [her]" (TL, 41).

A major theme running throughout Ferrante's work is life in a female body. I had largely forgotten what it was like to be surprised by an unexpected period, to have to take that monthly flow of blood into account. Ferrante brought it all back. At her mother's funeral, Delia experienced a sudden heavy flow of menstrual blood, accompanied by dizziness and nausea. She escaped to a filthy bathroom where she appeared to have a hallucination of her dead mother, also menstruating and removing "some bloody linen rags." Repellent physical detail runs throughout the novella. At one point, Delia heard (or perhaps imagined) she heard a man yelling obscenities in dialect at her—"a soft river of sound that involved me, my sisters, my mother in a concoction of semen, saliva, feces, urine, in every possible orifice" (TL, 19).

Such graphic physical detail characterizes Ferrante's sex scenes. Delia's sexual encounter with Antonio, the son of the man her mother spent her final days with, is one of Ferrante's most disturbing. Antonio had been Delia's childhood "playmate" and their games usually consisted of mimicking adult sexual behavior; as adults, they were reenacting those awkward childhood games. While having sex with Antonio, Delia found herself "paralyzed by a growing embarrassment because of the copious liquids spilling out of [her]"—a response to sexual intercourse she has had many times in the past. Antonio "pulled back abruptly with a gesture of repulsion as he felt [her] soaking wet" (TL 91–93). Descriptions of sexual experiences throughout Ferrante's work are often similarly characterized by embarrassment, disgust, and lack of sexual satisfaction.

The experience with Antonio awakened Delia's deeply buried memories, as does her confrontation with the abusive father her mother was forced to flee from decades ago. The reader, like Delia, is a detective trying to piece together the clues and understand Delia's response to an experience of sexual molestation many years ago. Delia's gradual recovery of the experience is so powerfully rendered that if *Troubling Love* had been the first of the Ferrante's books I had read, I would have expected sexual abuse of children to be a major theme in her work, similar to the way the theme runs through Toni Morrison's work from her first novel *The Bluest Eye* to her most recent, *God Help the Child*. However, *Troubling Love* is the only book in which this becomes a major theme, although the sexual molestation of a teenage Elena Greco by Donato Sarratore, the father of the young man she loved, in some ways recalls the experience of the young child Delia in *Troubling Love*. Delia had "felt pleasure and pain at the same time" (TL, 132); similarly, when Donato touched Elena's vagina she was terrified by his behavior and horrified by the "pleasure that [she] nevertheless felt" (BF 232). As a teenager with emotional and intellectual resources, Elena did not suffer the severe trauma that the child Delia experienced. Delia's adult life was marked by the trauma of childhood sexual abuse—both her inability to form loving relationships and her troubled relationship with the mother she thought failed to protect her. Delia's recovery of the long buried memory of sexual abuse and her belated reconciliation with her deceased mother suggest that she might finally be able to move beyond childhood trauma.

Another theme that emerges in *Troubling Love*, but does not recur in the other Ferrante novels, is the deeply troubled relationship between father and daughter. Delia's father is a violent, pathologically jealous man; his abusive behavior toward his wife Amalia terrified Delia and her sisters. Eventually Amalia managed to leave him and build a new life for herself and her daughters. In her attempt to uncover the mystery of Amalia's death, Delia decided to visit the father she has not seen for many years. She asked him why he had not come to Amalia's funeral; he replied by asking her if she would come to his. When she answered no, he punched her, shouting that she was a whore just like her mother. Still consumed with rage and jealousy, he told Delia he had wanted to kill Amalia "because she thought she could enjoy her old age, leaving me to rot in this room." They quarrel about the lie Delia told to her father forty years ago, that her mother had been involved with another man. Her father replied: "You were repulsive even as a child. It was you who pushed your mother to leave me." He struck her again, in the chest. As she left, he yelled after her, "You're old, too." And referring to a menstrual stain on her dress, "Take off that dress. You're revolting" (TL, 116). This is probably the ugliest, most disturbing scene between a father and daughter I have ever read.

It is surprising that a theme so powerfully rendered is not one of Ferrante's recurrent themes. There are other father figures in Ferrante's books capable of abusive behavior but their relationship with their daughters is not totally defined by it. In *Troubling Love*, like all Ferrante's novels, there is an intricate interplay of related themes: mother/daughter relations; violence against women; the harassment of women in public space; the dissolution of a marriage; women on the verge of slipping into mental illness; sexual relations deformed by rigid gender roles. Childhood sexual abuse and pathological father/daughter relations, however, are major themes only in *Troubling Love*. Interestingly, Domenico Starnone has told Italian interviewers that his father was a violent man, whose abusive behavior towards his wife was (like Delia's father's) fueled by obsessive jealousy.

The class anxieties that emerge as a dominant theme in the Neapolitan novels are present only as an undercurrent in *Troubling Love* and the two other novellas. The narrators are mature women who have managed to enter the middle class; their climb up the class ladder with its attendant anxieties is, for the most part, behind them. All the themes (to varying degrees) of the Neapolitan novels are present in *Troubling Love* and the other two novellas, with one notable exception—the theme most associated with Ferrante, the power and complexity of female friendship. The friendship theme may be absent form the novellas, but stylistically, the novellas prefigure the later works, sharing with them such features as: Ferrante's signature run-on sentences, building to a crescendo; the often shocking physical detail; the structural pattern of reverie and recollection punctuated by powerful scenes that define characters and clarify major themes. Ferrante's style has frequently been described as cinematic and many of these fully realized scenes lend themselves to a film script.

Troubling Love also shares a narrative frame similar to that of the Neapolitan Quartet; both open with the narrator trying to unravel the mystery surrounding the disappearance of a woman in her sixties. For Delia in *Troubling Love* the woman is her mother Amalia, who disappeared en route to visiting her daughter and whose body was found washed ashore on a beach in a resort town near Naples; for Elena in the Neapolitan Quartet, the woman is her life-long friend Lila who has disappeared without a trace. In yet another link between Delia and Elena, both were deeply ambivalent about their mothers, but ultimately came to terms with their mothers' legacy. Each one had feared turning into a woman like her mother, but after their mothers' deaths, both Delia and Elena accepted the extent to which they were indeed their mother's daughter; both embraced the physical resemblance, with Elena acquiring her mother's characteristic limp and Delia altering her photo on her identity card to more closely resemble her mother.

Some critics such as Dayna Tortorici consider *Troubling Love* the weakest of Ferrante's novellas and contend that "Delia's breakthrough offers little reward for the reader's efforts."[5] If I had read this critique after a first reading of *Troubling Love*, I would probably have agreed. But on a second reading the story comes into sharper focus, and the power of the novella emerges. *Troubling Love* demands that the reader work harder than in Ferrante's other books, but this reader is convinced it is worth the effort.

The Days of Abandonment

Ferrante is a master of the compelling opening and *The Days of Abandonment* begins with one of her best: "One April afternoon, right after lunch, my husband announced that he wanted to leave me. He did it while we were clearing the table; the children were quarreling as usual in the next room" (DA, 9). Olga, the narrator, is a well-educated woman, depressed by the loss of her dreams of becoming a writer, torn between love for her children and anger at the constraints of domestic life. Her initial denial that her husband was leaving her was soon replaced by an all-consuming rage. Many of Ferrante's readers have contended that a story as powerfully told as *The Days of Abandonment* must be rooted in the author's own experience. Ferrante provides some support for this, telling *The Paris*

Review: "Quite naturally, everything settled around an experience of mine that had seemed to me unspeakable—the humiliation of abandonment."[6] Once again we are confronted with the question: Is this the author developing the fictional character of Ferrante or is the author (or one of the authors) alluding to her own painful experience?

Ferrante treats marital breakdown in all of her novels, but with the exception of *The Days of Abandonment* it is the woman who leaves the man. Amalia in *Troubling Love* and Lila in the Neapolitan novels leave their abusive husbands; Leda in *The Lost Daughter* and Elena in the Neapolitan novels leave their basically decent husbands in search of a more fulfilling life. Only in the searing account of desertion in *Days of Abandonment* does Ferrante portray a woman abandoned by her husband. Olga in *The Days of Abandonment* may be the least sympathetic of Ferrante's narrators. Ferrante told the *Paris Review* that she enjoys "breaking through [her] character's armor of good education and good manners. I enjoy upsetting her self-image, her will, and revealing another rougher soul underneath, someone raucous, maybe even crude."[7] Although Ferrante is here making a general statement about all her narrators, it applies most of all to Olga. All Ferrante's narrators have a dark side that the reader sees, but for the most part the world does not. They are well-educated women, generally behaving according to social norms; however, in their inner lives they reveal hostilities and jealousies, which they do not act upon. Olga is different in that her inner turmoil leads to ugly, sometimes violent actions.

At first Olga hoped she could convince her husband Mario to return. In one of Ferrante's most memorable scenes, Olga prepared a special dinner for Mario who had come to discuss arrangements for their two children. She made a sauce that he liked very much, but not fully in control of her emotions, she cooked distractedly and broke a bottle of wine. During the tense dinner, Mario admitted his involvement with another woman, when "suddenly something cracked in his mouth ... he groaned. Now he was spitting what was in his mouth into the palm of his hand, pasta and sauce and blood, it was really blood, red blood" (DA, 19). Mario pulled a sliver of glass out of his mouth, stormed out of the apartment, shouting that Olga frightened him, that she had put glass in his pasta. Olga hadn't intentionally done so, but Ferrante leaves open the possibility of subconscious aggression.

A ghost from her childhood in Naples returned to haunt Olga—a woman consumed with grief because her husband had abandoned her for another woman: "The woman lost everything, even her name ... for everyone she became the *poverella*" (DA 16). As her own mind began to crumble, Olga was tormented by hallucinatory images of the *poverella*. For three decades Olga had feared becoming like her. As a young woman, she was determined to conquer this fear and not become like those women who were destroyed by their lovers' abandonment. Now, faced with her husband's betrayal, Olga finds herself descending into a grief akin to the *poverella's*; however, on the verge of losing her mind, she somehow finds the inner resources to step back from the abyss. It is not an easy read.

Many of Ferrante's readers, including her publisher and translator, have reported that they had to stop reading *The Days of Abandonment*. Translator Ann Goldstein said that there were moments when she just had to walk away from the book. She cites one moment in particular: "Just the part about the dog [in *The Days of Abandonment*]—actually, as it happens, I had a dog who died shortly before that, but I had to stop. I was thinking, 'I don't think I can read this part again.' Those things have an intense effect on your emotional self."[8] Ferrante's publisher Sandra Ferri reported that that when she read the manuscript of *The Days of Abandonment*, she had to put it down mid-way: "I was so frightened, I called (Elena) and said, 'Tell me nothing will happen with the children!'"[9] Given Olga's Medea-like rage and desire for vengeance, one can understand Ferri's fear.

Literary critic Stefania Lucamante has observed: "When speaking about abandoned wives in literature ... it becomes difficult not to deal with myth, with the Ur-abandoned wife Medea." Lucamante notes that both Medea and Olga left their native city to follow their husband to a city which was in many ways another world: "In the transition from Colchis to the rich and advanced Corinth, from crime-ridden Naples to industrialized Turin, the situations appear to be strikingly similar."[10] Olga is most reminiscent of Medea when roaming the streets of Turin searching for her ex-husband and his new lover. One afternoon, Olga saw Mario on the street with his lover, Carla, their former babysitter, with whom he had been having an affair for the past five years. Using an image from the ancient Mediterranean, from Medea's world, Olga attacked Mario striking him "like a battering ram." Consumed by "a black mania for destruction," she rips "the sleeve from his shirt, knocking him to the ground, kicking him as he covers his face, his nose bleeding." Then she turned to Carla, who was wearing earrings that had once belonged to Mario's mother, earrings he had given to Olga: "I wanted to rip them off her, together with the ear.... I wanted to drag them with me as if with a hook I'd snagged her garment of flesh" (DA, 70–72). If Mario had not pushed her away, Olga would have ripped the earrings from Carla's earlobes. Jewelry in Ferrante's novels often carries considerable symbolic weight. Mario's gift of the earrings to Olga was an emblem of her membership in his family and of what he had once believed would be his enduring love for her. When after their separation, Mario entered their house to take back the earrings, Olga viewed it as an indication he intended to remove her completely from his life. His gift of the earrings to his new lover was the ultimate blow, resulting in Olga's violent response. *The Days of Abandonment* inverts a major theme found throughout Ferrante's work: male violence against women. Here, rage and grief leads to a woman's violent attack on her husband and his lover.

In *Frantumaglia*, Ferrante included a section she had decided to delete from her harrowing tale of a woman abandoned by her husband. The section omitted from *The Days of Abandonment* describes Olga's flirtations with other men; over the years these flirtations occurred more frequently. Thanks to these casual relationships, Olga felt less oppressed by her role as a wife whose life was confined to household duties and childcare and who no longer dreamed of becoming a writer. The most serious relationship was with one of her husband's associates. Olga aggressively pursued him: "If he had wanted to make love I would have done it. If he had asked me to leave Mario and the children, I wouldn't have hesitated."[11] Many of Ferrante's readers have viewed *The Days of Abandonment* as a feminist *cri de coeur* from a woman wronged. The deleted section complicates the narrative and at least to some extent undermines sympathy for Olga. When an interviewer suggested that Ferrante's male characters are part of a pattern in Italian literature in which men are cowards and scoundrels, Ferrante replied: "In my intentions, Mario, Olga's husband, is neither cowardly nor a scoundrel. He's just a man who has stopped loving the woman he lives with and comes up against the impossibility of breaking that bond without humiliating her, without hurting her."[12]

Ferrante portrays both her male and female characters as prisoners of gender, their lives constrained by the expectations of a deeply sexist society. The deleted section is consistent with Ferrante's nuanced view of marital breakdown. Unfortunately, Ferrante does not provide a convincing explanation of her reasons for the deletion. She utilized this material in

Those Who Leave and Those Who Stay where Elena's dissatisfaction with her husband takes the form of similar flirtations. This is one of the great pleasures of Ferrante's work—observing how she weaves some of the same material into different situations, a theme and variations approach to narrative structure.

Probably many readers can sympathize with Olga when her rage is directed at Mario and his lover—at least the rage is directed towards the guilty party. However, there are times when her anger is directed at the innocent and the reader's sympathy can quickly turn to horror. When a woman complained to Olga that her dog Otto was out of control, Olga ordered him to stop barking. When Otto refused her command, Olga began to beat him mercilessly: "I was lashing and lashing and lashing, as he huddled, yelping, his body hugging the ground, ears low, sad and motionless under the incomprehensible hail of blows." As the woman hurried away from her, Olga noted she "was frightened now not by the dog but by me" (DA, 54).

Ferrante allows us to see Olga's mental deterioration from the perspective of those she encounters in her daily rounds—the passersby in the streets, the locksmiths working in her home, the Greek chorus to Olga's Medea. Olga's cruelty towards the children she loves stops far short of Medea's murder of her children, but certainly falls within what most readers would consider child abuse. At one point irritated with her children's games in a park, Olga realized that she wanted to wound her children, especially her son. She saw her son Gianni as a little Mario, speaking like Mario with a Turinese accent, growing up "foolish and presumptuous, and aggressive" (DA, 65). Angry with him for hiding from her in a cannon in the park, Olga grabbed her son, shook him hard, telling him if he did that again, she would kill him. She described herself as "like a lump of food that my children chewed without stopping." Like the *poverella*, who believed that her husband left her because she bore the "odor of motherhood," Olga also thought that "the stink of motherhood" was one of the reasons that Mario abandoned her (DA, 91–92).

Desperate for validation that she is still attractive to men, Olga turned to her neighbor Carrano, a gentlemanly cellist in his early 50s. Their graphically described sexual encounter is perhaps the most disturbing of Ferrante's scenes of bad sex. Despite his attraction to her, Carrano had difficulty maintaining an erection and then ejaculated prematurely. Olga treated him cruelly: "'Never mind,' I said, with a dry explosion of laughter in my throat, and I tore the rubber off his already limp penis, threw it away, it stained the floor with a viscid yellow stripe. 'You missed the target'" (DA, 87).

The next day, demoralized by the encounter with Carrano, seething with rage at Mario, and exhausted by the burdens of daily life, Olga came perilously close to total mental breakdown. Olga's unraveling culminated in what she characterized as "the hardest day of the ordeal of my abandonment" (DA, 88). Her son was ill with an intestinal virus and a frighteningly high fever, her apartment invaded by a plague of ants, her dog Otto poisoned perhaps by insecticide or perhaps by poisoned dog biscuits left in the park by a hostile neighbor. Her apartment was reeking with odors from the dog's diarrhea and her son's vomit. She could not remember how to operate her new lock, and was unable to open the door of her apartment. Her telephone line was not functioning and her cell phone broken, leaving her with no way of calling for help. As Wood memorably described Olga's traumatic experience: "Ferrante turns ordinary domestic misery into an expressionistic hell; she can pull a scream out of thin air."[13] Olga saw herself on the edge of a precipice, on the verge of falling into an abyss of intolerable grief from which she would never recover. After an agonizing struggle, her dog died in her arms, and the dam finally burst. She began to cry, "an uncontrollable lament, unlike any other crying of those days" of abandonment (DA, 146). The fever breaks and Olga realizes she no longer loves her husband. No longer imprisoned by grief, she managed to unlock the door.

Olga has banished the ghost of the *poverella*; the man responsible for so much suffering does not have the power to hurt her. After a meeting with Mario about childcare arrangements, she looked at him and understood "there was no longer anything about him that could interest me. He wasn't even a fragment of the past, he was only a stain, like the print of a hand left years ago on a wall" (DA, 186). Ferrante knows how to depict the long, painful process of falling out of love; her description of Olga's growing disaffection from Mario is as convincingly rendered as Elena Greco's ability to finally see her lover Nino as the callous, self-absorbed man he had become, or perhaps always was. Yet the rupture could never be total: Olga realized that her children embodied aspects of Mario, traits that over the years "would explode suddenly from inside their bones" (DA, 164). She wondered how much she would be forced to continue loving Mario without even recognizing it, simply by virtue of loving her children.

After so much suffering, Olga finds equilibrium. As Ferrante described her: "Olga is a woman of today who knows that she can't react to abandonment by breaking down."[14] The novella ends with a rapprochement with the kindly cellist Carrano—"we loved each other for a long time, in the days and months to come quietly" (DA, 188). This is a story that has been told many times before in novels, plays, films—the abandoned wife, torn by grief, who manages to come to terms with her loss, eventually finding solace with another man. But never in my experience has this familiar tale been told with such power. Ferrante's incandescent prose transforms what might have been just another sad story of an abandoned wife coping with betrayal. The best description comes from Ferrante herself: "I tend toward an expansive sentence that has a cold surface and, visible underneath it, a magma of unbearable heat."[15]

The Days of Abandonment has been viewed as Ferrante's response to Simone de Beauvoir's *Les Femmes Rompues*, known as *The Woman Destroyed* in the English translation.[16] Ferrante does explicitly refer to Beauvoir's novella. Olga's high school French teacher had given it to her when she told her teacher she wanted to become a writer. Olga returned the book with "an arrogant statement," calling Beauvoir's women stupid. She characterized them as "cultured women, in comfortable circumstances, they broke like knickknacks in the hands of straying men" (DA, 21). Olga wanted to write about women with emotional and intellectual resources, not about abandoned wives unable to come to terms with the loss of their husbands' love. Beauvoir was writing a cautionary tale, describing the psychological deterioration of a traditional woman, Monique, when her husband left her for another woman. Monique had lived only for her husband and children and could not withstand the loss of her identity as a wife. Olga did have an identity as an aspiring writer, which she struggled to regain in the aftermath of her husband's betrayal. Both women try to understand what has happened to them. Monique records her reactions in her diary; Olga does so in letters she writes to her husband. But Monique is unable to resign herself to the loss of her husband, and the novel ends with Monique in a downward spiral while Olga manages to emerge from the depths of an overwhelming depression.

Although *The Days of Abandonment* was clearly in some sense a response to *The Woman Destroyed*, I question whether Beauvoir's novel was the actual inspiration for *The Days of Abandonment*, which certainly feels like it originated in deeply personal experience. Now with the publication of Domenico Starnone's *Ties*, *The Days of Abandonment* has become part of an intertextual drama—a response to Beauvoir which itself has inspired a response by Starnone.

The Lost Daughter

The Lost Daughter shares much thematic material with the other novellas, themes also central in the Neapolitan novels. In all three novellas motherhood is a major theme: in *Troubling Love*, Delia's complicated love/hate relationship with her mother; in *The Days of Abandonment* and in *The Lost Daughter*, Olga's and Leda's love for their children warring with their anger about the constraints of motherhood. Marital breakdown occurs in all three novels: in *Troubling Love*, Delia's mother Amalia leaves her abusive husband; in *The Days of Abandonment*, Olga is abandoned by her husband; and in *The Lost Daughter*, Leda abandons her husband. *The Lost Daughter* (which appeared in English in 2009) is the novella that focuses the most on the social dimension, on the wider world with its class tensions and the struggle for upward mobility, which emerges as a major theme in the Neapolitan novels. All three narrators of the novellas have managed to get an education and escape their impoverished backgrounds; in *The Lost Daughter*, more so than in *Troubling Love* and *The Days of Abandonment*, we have a glimpse of the world the narrators of the novellas have left behind.

Like *The Days of Abandonment*, *The Lost Daughter* begins with a riveting scene. Leda, a divorced university professor is in the hospital after losing control of her car. She told her doctor and family members that drowsiness had caused the accident, although she "knew that drowsiness wasn't to blame. At the origin was a gesture of mine that made no sense." She decides not to speak of it to anyone because "the hardest things to talk about are the ones we ourselves can't understand" (LD, 10). *The Lost Daughter* explores the painful memories that led to that senseless gesture. Leda, now freed from daily responsibilities for her children, had decided to take a seaside vacation on the Ionian coast. When her daughters moved to Toronto, she was surprised by her reaction. For the first time in twenty-five years, she no longer experienced the anxiety of having to care for her children. She felt "miraculously unfettered as if a difficult job, finally brought to completion, no longer weighed me down" (LD, 10–11).

Leda found herself sharing the beach with a noisy Neapolitan family similar to the family she had escaped, and soon became absorbed in watching a young woman and her daughter, who although they belonged to the Neapolitan family, remained apart, playing with a doll, "talking to each other peacefully as if they alone existed" (LD, 17). Leda's interest in the mother and daughter soon became an obsession, stirring up memories of her own mother, of her mother's discomfort with her husband's relatives who were much like the Neapolitan family, and Leda's memories of her conflict-filled relationship with her own daughters.

Although Ferrante's novellas stand alone as powerful literary texts, they also prefigure much that is contained in the Neapolitan novels. The characters on the beach in *The Lost Daughter* in some ways resemble the characters on the beach on Ischia in *The Story of a New Name*, the second of the Neapolitan novels. One of the pleasures of reading Ferrante is seeing similar characters/situations/themes recur in different iterations. Before Gatti's revelations, I was convinced that Elena Ferrante had a background similar to that of her narrator, Elena Greco, and couldn't resist tracing the common elements in these recurring themes searching for the biographical core. We now know that Ferrante is not a woman from an impoverished Neapolitan background and that whatever biographical core may exist is a much more complicated matter.

The characters in *The Lost Daughter* who resemble those in the Neapolitan novels include Nina, the young woman on the beach, who resembles Lila (called Lina by everyone other than the narrator) of the Neapolitan novels, but without Lila's dazzling intellect. Ferrante describes Nina in terms very similar to her physical description of Lila: her "slim body ... her slender neck, the shapely head and long wavy glossy black hair" (LD, 17). The description of Nina's husband is very like that that of Lila's husband Stefano, "a heavy thickset man, at least four inches shorter than his wife" (LD, 22). Like Stefano, he comes to the beach resort on the weekends to be with his wife Nina who, like Lila, spends the week at the beach. Like Lila, Nina develops a romantic attachment to a young student Gino and spends time with him when her husband is absent. Gino looks very much like Lila's lover in the Neapolitan novels, Nino Sarratore. Like Nino, Gino is tall, thin and dark although without Nino's intellectual intensity. Even their names are similar—Lina/Nina, Nino/Gino. Both Nina and Lila/Lina are alienated from their husbands' families, but in the Neapolitan novels, Ferrante creates a much more emotionally charged triangle with a very different outcome. In *The Lost Daughter* Nina toys with the idea of having an affair and leaving her husband; in *The Story of a New Name*, Lila has a passionate affair with Nino and eventually does leave her husband. In *The Story of a New Name* Ferrante is in some sense returning to the narrative in *The Lost Daughter* but dramatically reshaping, transforming it.

Although the present day story of Leda's beach vacation contains elements of Lila's story, Leda's half-buried memories, emerging as she watches the drama unfolding on the beach, recall Elena's story. The heart of *The Lost Daughter* is not the story of Nina's unhappiness with her marriage, but rather the emotions stirred in Leda as she watches Nina and her daughter, playing with a doll. Transfixed by the closeness of their relationship, Leda found painful memories rising to the surface of her consciousness—her abandonment of her young children for her lover and the pursuit of her intellectual ambitions, a theme that recurs in the Neapolitan novels when Elena leaves her solid but unexciting husband and the chains of domesticity for Nino and the pursuit of her dreams of becoming a writer. Leda in *The Lost Daughter* and Elena in the Neapolitan Quartet share the desire to shake off the shackles of motherhood at the same time harboring fear of harming/losing their children.

One day on the beach Nina's daughter disappeared. Leda remembered losing her young daughter on the beach and the terror she felt. She was running along the beach frantically searching for her daughter, looking in every direction but toward the sea, recalling that she "didn't dare even to glance at the water." Leda realized that Nina was behaving the same way, desperately searching everywhere but keeping her back to the sea; she remembered her reaction when her daughter Bianca was found—crying with happiness, relief and also screaming with rage "because of the crushing weight of responsibility, the bond that strangles" (LD, 38). Leda found Nina's daughter on the beach crying because her doll was lost; the child was inconsolable. Leda also found the lost doll and for reasons she didn't understand, took the doll home with her, intending to return it the next day; however, inexplicably she held onto the doll.

She began to recall disturbing memories of her treatment of her daughters, memories bound up with a doll. Worn out by the stress of caring for two young daughters, frustrated by her inability to realize her academic ambitions, Leda had directed her anger towards her children. Enraged that her daughter Bianca did not appreciate Mina, the doll from

Leda's childhood that she had given to her daughter, Leda described her reaction: "I gave her a nasty shove; she was a child of three, but at that moment she seemed older, stronger than me. I tore Mina away from her and finally her eyes showed fear" (LD, 44). Throughout Ferrante's work, dolls appear at key moments, a proxy for the bonds between mothers and daughters, for female friendships and in the Neapolitan novels becoming a frame for the entire quartet. *My Brilliant Friend* opens with Elena and Lila searching for their lost dolls and the final volume, *The Story of the Lost Child*, ends with Elena receiving a mysterious package, presumably from Lila, containing those long lost dolls.

The doll that Leda cannot make herself return destroys whatever hope she may have had for a relationship with Nina. She doesn't understand her reasons for keeping the doll or her reasons for impulsively telling Nina and her sister-in-law that she had abandoned her children. Leda responded to their shock and their question as to why she did this, by saying only that she had been very tired. When Nina asked Leda if she returned for love of her daughters, Leda rejected the culturally venerated ideal of self-sacrificial motherhood: "I returned for the same reason I left: for love of myself." Leda had never spoken to anyone of that time in her life, not even to herself. She now tried to justify to herself why she abandoned her children: "All the hopes of youth seemed to have been destroyed, I seemed to be falling backward toward my mother, my grandmother, the chain of mute or angry women I came from. Missed opportunities. Ambition was still burning, fed by a young body, by an imagination full of plans" (LD, 64).

The desire for a life unlike their mothers is a driving force for all Ferrante's narrators, but with Amalia and Elena the rejection of their mothers' world is intermingled with some degree of attachment, some positive feelings towards their mothers. With Leda there is only cold detachment. When she abandoned her children for three years, Leda acknowledged that her mother had worn herself out taking care of them. However, she expressed no gratitude for her mother's devotion to her children, nor for any thing else her mother had ever done; instead, "the secret rage I harbored against myself, I turned on her" (LD, 79). Like Olga and Elena, Leda raged against the bonds of motherhood, but only Leda completely severed ties with her children for three years. Yet the guilt Leda felt about abandoning her daughters continued to torment her many years later and was in some tangled way the motive force behind her theft of the doll.

Leda, like Delia and Olga, initially appears rational and self-contained but as the story develops she, like them, is revealed as deeply disturbed, struggling to cope with turbulent and contradictory emotions. She cannot bring herself to return the doll and appears strangely unmoved by the suffering she has caused Nina and her daughter; distancing her self from the emotional turmoil, she refers to her actions as merely "complicating [Nina's] existence" (LD, 120). Her much greater degree of detachment and self-absorption than that of Ferrante's other narrators is in all probability the reason some readers have found Leda the least sympathetic. Literary critic Lisa Mullenneaux finds Leda "annoying" and the plot of *The Lost Daughter* "opaque." Mullenneaux also argues that "one of the novel's weaknesses is that much of the drama takes place in Leda's head."[17] For some readers, the broad canvas and densely populated world of the Neapolitan novels comes as a relief after the often claustrophobic novellas. If Ferrante had continued writing in the vein of the novellas—brief, emotionally charged novels about moments of extreme tension in a woman's life—she would have had her devoted readers, but I doubt that she would have become an international sensation.

5

The Neapolitan Novels: Women's Friendship

"God only knows what goes on in the mind of a friend. Absolute trust and strong affections harbor rancor, trickery, and betrayal."— Elena Ferrante, *Frantumaglia: A Writer's Journey*

The Neapolitan novels are an intricately structured series of four novels. As Margaret Drabble has noted, Ferrante's "acclaimed quartet abounds in cleverly deployed postmodern devices such as alter egos, lost texts, recurrent motifs and destroyed manuscripts, but the human interest is so overwhelming that we read on, volume after volume, hardly noticing the sophistication of the narration."[1] The complicated interplay of themes does not fully emerge until a second reading. Also, it was only on a second reading that I noticed the extent to which Ferrante complicates what at first reading may seem like straightforward chronological story telling. The first volume of *My Brilliant Friend* begins with a sixty-six-year-old Elena learning about the disappearance of her childhood friend Lila, who she believes wants to disappear without a trace. To forestall this, Elena intends to capture Lila in writing, including all the details of their decades long friendship, all that remained in her memory. The four volumes of the Neapolitan Quartet are the result of this effort, and from this point on the narration largely proceeds in chronological order, beginning with the friendship that develops between Lena and Lila in elementary school.

However, Ferrante at several key points departs from chronology and uses a narrative strategy that serves to reinforce key scenes. Ferrante will begin an episode, such as the story of the lost dolls in the beginning of *My Brilliant Friend*, drop the story after a few pages, only to continue it again about thirty pages later, returning to it once again in the fourth volume,

Story of the Lost Child, when we finally learn how the dolls disappeared. Similarly, Lila refers to an experience of disorientation she called "dissolving margins" at a New Year's party. After a few pages, the description of the New Year's party is dropped, but returned to again in expanded form—a scene crucial for understanding the machismo of the male characters and the pervasiveness of the culture of violence. Another example of this narrative strategy occurs in the second volume, *The Story of a New Name*, which begins with Elena's shocking destruction of papers Lila had entrusted to her; jealous of Lila's superior writing ability, Elena threw the box containing Lila's notebooks into the Arno River. After a few pages, Ferrante drops this scene and returns to a chronological account of the lives of Elena and Lila, but returns to the unforgettable scene of the destroyed notebooks at the end of *The Story of a New Name*. Other instances of this technique occur, no doubt used to underscore the importance of these scenes and also perhaps to mimic the non-linear process of memory. Ferrante's narrative technique, for the most part, does not employ the temporal dislocations of the experimental novel, but neither is it straightforward chronological narration.

The complicated narrative structure of the Neapolitan novels encompasses many thematic strands: the extent to which class and gender constrain women's lives: the complexities of women's friendships over time; the enduring bonds of mother/daughter relationships; the increasing fragility of relationships between men and women; the difficulty of ever erasing the imprint of one's background; and an exploration of the social and economic divisions in Italy. Ferrante has placed her story of the friendship of Elena Greco and Lila Cerullo within the context of a fully realized social world, with language that is nuanced, powerful, that makes the reader want to linger over her sentences. Elena Greco is the narrator of the series of novels; at times her voice seems fused with the author's; at other times there is clearly a critical distance between Elena Ferrante, the author, and Elena, her character.

The major themes of the novellas reappear in the Neapolitan Novels: the burdens and joys of motherhood; marital breakdown; sexual betrayal; male violence against women. However, the friendship theme that looms so large in the Neapolitan Quartet is not present in the novellas, and in the Quartet the complex orchestration of themes occurs within a densely populated social world, far different from the novellas' intense concentration on the inner life of the principal character. Ferrante helpfully provides an index to the large cast of characters that recur throughout the Quartet, along with the various names and nicknames used to refer to them. Elena's family and old friends from the neighborhood often refer to her as Lenu or Lenuccia; Lila, whose given name is Rafaella, is referred to by everyone other than Elena as Lina.

The broad canvas of the Neapolitan novels and the emphasis on women's friendships that extend over a lifetime are the new elements in Ferrante's work. Granted, in *Frantumaglia* Ferrante refers to the relationship between Leda and Nina in *The Lost Daughter* as a "budding friendship."[2] Perhaps in some sense this relationship could be seen as an anticipation of the theme of friendship between women, but Leda appears to be seeking a surrogate daughter, not a friend. Unable to communicate with her daughters, Leda hopes for some form of connection with Nina. She speculated: "Nina could even see me as a future. Choose for your companion an alien daughter" (LD, 72). Friendship does not seem to be what Leda is searching for.

Judging from the reviews and blog posts, female friendship is the theme that resonates most with Ferrante's readers. From novelist Claire Messud: "Part social tapestry, part feminist Bildungsroman, this tetralogy shines above all because of its vibrant, unflinching study of friendship."[3] Few reviewers have questioned the centrality of friendship to the Neapolitan novels. One of these few, Cary Knapp, has noted: "Shift your focus, and the friendship becomes less the story's center and more of a premise and framework for Elena to review her life."[4] Like Knapp, I have begun to see friendship not so much as the central theme of the Neapolitan novels but rather as the framework for exploring the choices available to women whose options are constrained by gender and class. Ferrante's comments in *Frantumaglia* also suggest that the theme of friendship is a narrative device to explore women's lives over the long arc of time. Ferrante has said she had intended to tell the story of an old person who wanted to disappear without a trace. Then she introduced a childhood friend who would bear witness to every event in the life of the person who would disappear. Ferrante finally realized: "What interested me was to dig into the lives of two women, full of affinities and yet divergent. That's what I did."[5]

Thus the life-long friendship of Elena and Lila provides the narrative frame for the novels. The intricate structure, the careful patterning never seem forced and for many of those reading rapidly, consumed with desire to find out what happens next, the patterning is not fully apparent on a

5. Women's Friendship

first reading. *My Brilliant Friend* begins near the end of Elena and Lila's story. Elena, a writer in her 60s, learned about the disappearance of her life-long friend Lila. Determined to preserve something of Lila, she began to record the story of their friendship. The first incident Elena relates, the attempt to recover the lost dolls the girls believed had been stolen from them, prefigures much of their relationship—the close connection and the sometimes bitter rivalry.

For Elena, Lila is a rival but also a role model, an inspiration and a protector. Armed with her father's knife, Lila vowed to protect Elena against the overlords of the neighborhood, Marcello and Michele Solara. Elena and Lila were taking their usual Sunday walk, with Elena wearing her best dress and her mother's silver bracelet when the Solara brothers offered to take them for a ride in their new car. Accepting the invitation would have been unthinkable given the rigid gender mores in their world. Marcello then grabbed Elena's wrist; she abruptly pulled her arm away and broke the bracelet. Seeing her dismay at having damaged her mother's jewelry, Marcello got out of the car to retrieve the bracelet, vowing to fix it. When he tried again to touch Elena's wrist, Lila pushed him against the car, pulled out her knife and held it against his throat. Elena was convinced Lila would not have hesitated to cut Marcello's throat; Michele also realized it and told Marcello to get back in the car and apologize. Marcello then recovered the bracelet and repaired it by squeezing the link that had broken, apologized to Elena and drove away. The bracelet has become bound up with Elena's emerging sexuality and the potentially dangerous attention it attracts. Like the dolls, the bracelet reappears at key points in the narrative, accumulating further associations and serving as a symbol of the bonds between women, of the experiences women share. With such recurrent motifs, Ferrante weaves the intricate tapestry of the Neapolitan novels.

Elena and Lila's paths diverged when Lila's parents could not or would not pay her school fees and she was denied the educational opportunities open to Elena. Her options limited by lack of an education, Lila then made a disastrous marriage at the age of sixteen; *My Brilliant Friend* concludes with Lila's realization on her wedding day that she had made a terrible mistake. The second volume, *The Story of a New Name*, focuses on the love affair between Lila and Nino Sarratore. Lila and Elena's friendship was tested by their love for the same man—the dazzling, seductive and ethically challenged Nino Sarratore. Lila left her husband for Nino, but the relationship ended in disaster. At the conclusion of volume two, Lila, pregnant and abandoned by Nino, was at her lowest point. Volume three, *Those Who Leave and Those Who Stay*, focuses on the up and down career trajectory of Elena, now a writer, married with two children. Like Lila, Elena also left her husband for the feckless Sarratore. Eventually Nino disappeared from both their lives. The fourth volume, *Story of the Lost Child*, returns to a focus on the friendship between Lila and Elena. Elena has returned to Naples; and she and Lila became pregnant at the same time and raised their children side by side. Their paths diverged once again when Lila, devastated by the loss of her daughter, retreated from the world and Elena, worn out by the daily struggle of living in Naples, realized she could no longer remain in the city. The Neapolitan Quartet ends where it began, with Lila's disappearance without a trace; she has finally left Naples, destination unknown. Her final parting gift to Elena, the long lost dolls left by Elena's mailbox in Turin, may be an indication that although their friendship has ruptured, Lila has reached out to Elena with a gesture of reconciliation.

Ferrante's publisher Sandra Ozzola has noted that before the Neapolitan novels, there were few works of literary fiction that placed female friendship at the center of the narrative. Ozzola refers to "the novelty of female friendship as a theme" stating that before the Neapolitan Quartet there wasn't a literary tradition to draw on."[6] I can think of only one example (pre–Ferrante) of a novel that has as its central theme a troubled, lifelong friendship between two women—Toni Morrison's *Sula*, which traces the friendship of Nel Wright and Sula Peace from childhood through late middle age.[7] The time period in *Sula* stretches from the 1920s to the 1960s, whereas the Neapolitan novels cover the 1950s to early 2000s. *Sula* and the Neapolitan novels are in many ways quite different in historical period and in structure; Sula is a relatively short novel whereas the Neapolitan novels span approximately 1600 pages. However, there are striking similarities; both *Sula* and the Neapolitan novels are carefully structured with key scenes paralleling and echoing earlier scenes. In both books, the characters' lives are constrained by class and gender, although in *Sula* race is the greatest limitation on the characters' dreams and ambitions. In both cases there are gaps in their friendship, but for far longer periods with Nel and Sula. As with Elena and Lila, Nel and Sula both love the same man. Elena is angry and depressed that Lila has taken the man she loves; Nel is devastated when Sula takes her husband. In consequence, the rupture between Nel and Sula is far greater than that between Lila and Elena.

Sula, like Lila, is the rebel—extraordinarily talented but because of the constraints of race and class unable to find a creative outlet. For both Sula and Lila, the absence of opportunity to develop their exceptional talents leads to self-destructive behavior, what other characters sometimes view as "evil." Nel, like Elena, is the "good girl" seeking respectability by making conventional choices. Nel doesn't have Elena's drive for upward mobility but what was possible, albeit very difficult, for a poor Southern Italian girl in post–World War II Italy was impossible for a poor African American girl in pre–World War II America. Ferrante's comments about Elena and Lila's relationship to the historical background in the Neapolitan novels could easily be said about Sula and Nel: "I felt Elena and Lila were alienated from history in all its political, social, economic, cultural aspects—and yet they were part of history in everything they said or did. I wanted the historical period to be a faintly defined background, but also to emerge from the characters' lives, from their uncertainties, decisions, actions, language."[8] In both *Sula* and the Neapolitan novels, the focus is not on major historical figures or events, but rather ordinary people, those not part of the historical record but whose lives were impacted by larger forces and whose everyday choices, in the aggregate, played a part in changing roles and expectations for both men and women. Given that women's friendship has not been a central theme of books by and about women before Ferrante, I find it striking that no one (to my knowledge) has noted the many similarities between the Neapolitan novels and *Sula*.

Apparently post–Ferrante there has been an increase in books about women's friendship, most notably Zadie Smith's *Swing Time*, which depicts the friendship of two biracial girls growing up in a working class neighborhood in London.[9] There are a few striking similarities to the Neapolitan novels; the two girls in *Swing Time* share a passion for dance and dream of becoming dancers just as Elena and Lila share a passion for literature and dream of becoming writers. In *Swing Time* the unnamed narrator is the "good girl" who like Elena goes to college and leaves the neighborhood; her friend Tracey is "the bad girl" who like Lila has real talent, but makes poor choices, never realizes her ambition to become a successful dancer, and remains in the neighborhood. Like the friendship between Elena and Lila, the relationship between the two girls in *Swing Time* is marked by misunderstanding and long breaks in their friendship. The similarities in the two books suggest that Zadie Smith may have influenced by Ferrante. *My Brilliant Friend* was published in 2012, probably the time period when Smith was working on *Swing Time*, which was published in 2016.

Certainly, the recent spate of books about female friendship can't all be attributed to Ferrante. According to Alex Clark, "recently, there has been a growth in the literary depiction of a particular type of friendship, one that has in the past found itself vulnerable to dilution and deflection by the ostensibly more powerful imperatives of heterosexuality and motherhood. Fictional female friends are suddenly all around us, from Elena Ferrante's Lila and Elena to Emma Cline's group of murderous California adolescents in *The Girls*."[10] Claire Messud's *The Burning Girl* is among the latest contribution to the increasing number of novels about female friendship. Like *Sula*, *Swing Time* and the Neapolitan novels, *The Burning Girl* follows the familiar pattern of the friendship novel, tracing the intense relationship between two childhood friends who grow apart—the "good girl" Julia who does well in school and goes off to college and the more troubled girl Cassie who remains in the small town where they grew up. The friendship plot appears to be overtaking the marriage plot and the mother/daughter drama in novels about women's lives, perhaps reflecting the consequences of divorce and weakening of family ties, with longtime friendships offering the continuous relationships that family, lovers, and spouses may no longer provide.[11]

Except for her relationship with her daughters, Elena's friendship with Lila is the only relationship she has maintained over a lifetime. Her brothers vanish from her life, as does her younger sister Elisa with whom she was once close. Their relationship became strained when Elisa married the leader of an organized crime syndicate, Marcello Solara. Elena thought that the sister she once knew had disappeared forever, subsumed into the role of Signora Solara. Elena insisted she tried to be loving with her sister and with her little nephew Silvio, despite disliking Silvio because of his resemblance to Marcello. Elisa recognized her sister's insincerity and accused her of loving Lila's child more than hers. Long aware that Elena valued her friendship with Lila more than her relationship with her, Elisa complained that Elena went to live near Lila, not near her or their widowed father. Elisa bitterly lamented the breakdown of family ties, which she once thought were strong, but now realizes are fragile. After her husband was murdered, Elisa left the neighborhood and remarried, but did not invite Elena to the wedding. Elena did not appear to be at all upset by the estrangement from her sister, in sharp contrast to the anguish she felt when Lila severed all ties with her in old age, a time when she was "in need of closeness and solidarity" (SLC, 465). However, the final scene when

5. Women's Friendship

Elena finds the long lost dolls Lila has left by her mailbox holds out the hope that in some sense the friendship may endure.

What appears to have resonated most with Ferrante's readers is the complicated portrayal of female friendship, laced with envy and hostility, what Ferrante has referred to in one of her many interviews as the "disorderliness of female friendship."[12] The ambivalence and rivalry which characterized Elena's and Lila's long relationship is evident from the very beginning. When they were in elementary school, Lila convinced Elena to skip school and explore the world beyond the confines of the neighborhood. They were well on their way to the sea, when Lila, realizing that a thunderstorm was on the horizon, insisted they turn back. Elena's mother was furious when she learned about Elena's foray outside the neighborhood and demanded that her father beat her. The next day, when Lila saw the bruises on Elena's arm, she was surprised that her only punishment had been a beating, and that Elena's parents were still sending her to middle school. Elena wondered if Lila, envious of Elena because her parents were allowing her to continue her education, had encouraged the trip, hoping that Elena's parents would punish her by refusing to allow her to continue her schooling. Or perhaps, Lila had insisted they go back to avoid that very punishment. Years later, looking back at the incident, trying to disentangle Lila's motives, Elena speculated that perhaps Lila had at different times wanted both outcomes. In contrast to male friendship, which Ferrante sees as having "developed a rigorous code of conduct," female friendships are "a terra incognita ... a land without fixed rules. Anything and everything can happen to you, nothing is certain.... God only knows what goes on in the mind of a friend. Absolute trust and strong affections harbor rancor, trickery, and betrayal."[13]

Ferrante's readers (at least pre–Gatti) assumed some biographical basis for the story of the friendship/rivalry between Elena and Lina. Ferrante, perhaps sensing readers' desire for this, told the *Paris Review* that there was some connection between the friendship of Elena and Lila and her relationship with a childhood friend whom she had written about in the Milan daily newspaper *Corriere della Sera*, several years after her death. According to Ferrante that newspaper piece was "the first written trace of the friendship between Lila and Elena."[14] Asked by *Vanity Fair* whether the friendship between Lila and Elena described in the Neapolitan novels was based on an actual friendship, Ferrante replied that "it comes from a long, complicated, difficult friendship that began at the end of early childhood."[15] In several interviews Ferrante similarly suggests that this friendship had a real life basis. However, we now know that many of the biographical details in Ferrante's numerous interviews are fictional, part of the creation of the persona of Elena Ferrante, a shield for the real identity of the author(s). Is this suggestion of a real-life basis for the story of Elena and Lila's friendship just another fictional detail? In another interview, Ferrante suggests that Lila is a composite character: "I have had friends and acquaintances that are not too dissimilar, unruly and yet at the same time overwhelmed by the struggle of living in opposition to the world. Lila owes much to them. They were uncomfortable women, uncomfortable most of all with themselves. Living in opposition is not easy."[16]

Perhaps if Lila is a composite character, there is a trace of Elsa Morante. On numerous occasions, Ferrante has acknowledged Morante's influence on her writing, and she was no doubt familiar with the details of Morante's life. Ferrante, who apparently has a reading knowledge of English, may very well have read Lily Tuck's biography of Morante, *Woman of Rome: A Life of Elsa Morante*, published in 2008, around the time Ferrante was probably beginning the Neapolitan novels. Morante, like Lila, was a child prodigy who, according to Tuck, learned to read and write at a very early age. Tuck reports that Morante claimed she composed her first poem at the age of two and a half and, at the age of five, collected her poems in a blue-lined school notebook: "Her handwriting is sure and tidy, her letters are perfectly formed." Her poems "scan and rhyme perfectly and are illustrated with colorful and intricately drawn little figures of people and animals."[17] Lila in elementary school wrote a novel that Elena described as "ten sheets of graph paper, folded and held together with a dressmaker's pin. It had a cover drawn in pastels and the title ... was *The Blue Fairy*. How exciting it was, how many difficult words there were" (BF, 71).

Like Lila's teacher Maestra Oliviero, the headmistress in Elsa Morante's middle school recognized her genius. At a school performance of a play Elsa had written, the headmistress told the audience members that the words "they were about to hear were written by a child who was in the room and that they ... were in the presence of a genius."[18] Like Lila, Elsa was first in her class and as with Lila, the other children resented her intellectual superiority. Morante's biography may have provided some of the inspiration for the depiction of Lila as a child, one strand in what Ferrante has characterized as a composite character.

Elena and Lila have some times been described as the two halves of a divided character. Novelist Rachel Cusk has argued: "In Elena and Lila, Ferrante's modern woman is bisected and given two faces; where in her other works the divided woman speaks to and wrestles with herself, the Neapolitan series externalizes and literalizes those politics to show their almost insurmountable complexity."[19] Cusk may be over-complicating here. Lila and Elena are two well-developed characters with their own fully realized individual histories and traits. Initially, I had a hard time believing in Lila. This is no doubt partly because everything we know comes from Elena's perspective. In response to *The Sydney Morning Herald's* question as to whether she ever wrote any pages from Lila's point of view, Ferrante acknowledged that in the first draft, there were sections written by Lila at several points in the narrative, "but then it seemed right to me that Elena should remain the sole source of the story."[20] Similarly in response to a *Guardian* interviewer who asked if she would ever be tempted to let Lila tell her own story, Ferrante again insisted that the Quartet "can only be Elena's tale: outside that tale she would probably be unable to define herself."[21]

However, Elena's first person narration is not the only reason I had some difficulty believing in Lila. I have never personally known anyone with Lila's genius. It was easier to believe in the reality of Elena, a far more familiar type. Lila was spectacularly intellectually gifted, mercurial, unpredictable. As a child, Lila learned to read at three, dazzled her teachers, and was totally fearless. Elena was the "good girl," intelligent, hardworking, eager to please who struggled to keep up with that "brilliant dazzling girl" (BF, 47). Lila mentions that people are afraid of her, while Elena has a talent for making herself liked. Yet under the surface Elena is far from the good girl. She at times expresses a degree of awareness of what the "good girl" mask has cost her, wondering why she always had ready a pleasing smile, a cheerful laugh when things went wrong. Why did she "always find plausible excuses for those who made her suffer" (SNN, 237)?

Ferrante in *Frantumaglia* describes herself in terms reminiscent of Elena Greco: "So I taught myself to be silent, I apologized for everything, I reined in my tongue, I was polite and compliant. Yet secretly I was bad."[22] When Lila was devastated that her parents would not pay her school fees, Elena admitted that in some hidden part of herself she looked forward to attending a school where Lila would never enter, where without competition from Lila, she would be the best student, and that she might sometimes tell Lila about her experiences, boasting about her success. Elena's feelings about Lila are inextricably bound up with envy, sometimes with the desire to see her harmed. At times Elena wished that Lila would die—once motivated by jealousy when Lila became involved with Nino, and again when despite her academic success, Elena could never free herself from the feeling of being inferior to Lila. Despite not seeing Lila for years, with their connection continuing only through intermittent telephone calls, Elena confessed that the wish that Lila would die persisted, and despite her struggle to suppress that wish, it wouldn't go away.

Since we see Lila almost entirely through Elena's perspective we don't know to what extent Lila resents Elena. We have Lila's notebooks that she entrusted to Elena for safe-keeping and in which she expressed the bitter anger she felt when accompanying Elena to a party with people from the educated elite. Lila felt diminished by the experience and felt the need to mock Elena's aspirations, deriding her for wanting to be "a puppet from the neighborhood who performs so [she]can be welcomed into the home of those people" (SNN, 163). We also have the observations of other characters, who warned Elena that Lila has harbored ill will towards her. Nella Incardo, an elderly woman Elena stayed with during a vacation on Ischia told her that Lila was well aware that Elena is a better person; as a consequence, Lila doesn't love Elena in the unambivalent way Nella thinks Elena loves Lila. Nella has apparently not detected any of the envy and resentment Elena harbors toward Lila. When Elena asked Nella if she thought Lila hated her, Nella replied, that she didn't know, but that Lila "knows how to wound, it's written in her face, it's enough to look at her forehead and her eyes" (SNN, 286).

In the fourth volume, *Story of the Lost Child*, Pietro, now Elena's ex-husband, tells her that Lila may hate her, that it must be very difficult for Lila to see every day that Elena is free, while she has remained trapped: "If there's an inferno, it's inside her unsatisfied mind" (SLC, 395). In response to Pietro, Elena categorically denied that Lila hated her. However, whether or not Lila experiences moments of hatred towards Elena, she is clearly painfully aware of her limited options compared to Elena's. Frustrated with the daily demands of caring for a young child and overcome with bitterness, Lila once angrily announced that Elena would become a writer while she would be condemned to a life of domestic drudgery.

Although at times Elena appears to be in denial about the tensions in her relationship with Lila, at other times she expresses opinions very similar to Nella Incardo's observation that Lila knows how to wound: "Lila was malicious.... She had shown me not only that she knew how to wound with words but that she would kill without hesitation." Elena resorts to words like "evil" or "devilish" to describe her friend and recalled that it gradually became evident, not only to her, who had been observing Lila from elementary school, but to everyone in the neighborhood, "that an essence not only seductive but dangerous emanated from Lila" (BF, 143).

My Brilliant Friend begins with an epigraph from Goethe's *Faust*, which appears to refer to this devilish aspect of Lila:

> THE LORD: Therein thou'rt free, according to thy merits;
> The like of thee have never moved My hate.
> Of all the bold, denying Spirits,
> The waggish knave least trouble doth create.
> Man's active nature, flagging, seeks too soon the level;
> Unqualified repose he learns to crave;
> Whence, willingly, the comrade him I gave,
> Who works, excites, and must create, as Devil.

Elena recalled that since she was a child Lila seemed to her like a devil, "but in a good way" (SNN, 286). Throughout the Neapolitan novels, there are frequent references to a supernatural dimension to Lila's intellectual gifts. Rumors had spread throughout the neighborhood that Lila was capable of casting an evil spell, that her miscarriage was intentional, that she destroyed the "creatures in her belly" (TWL, 239). Despite her education, Elena at times succumbed to fears that from afar Lila was casting an evil spell on her. In the frequent references to evil spells and "the evil eye," Ferrante may be drawing on Neapolitan folk traditions. According to historian Tommaso Astarito, at the end of the 18th century most Neapolitans, not just the poor and uneducated, began to believe in a practice know as jettatura, the ability of some people (the *jettadori*) to harm others simply by looking at them with an "evil eye." The *jettadori* themselves might be unaware of their powers.[23] Belief in such supernatural forces was a way of making sense of psychological depths and inchoate fears that Ferrante's characters do not fully understand. Elena frequently resorts to references to devilish behavior and evil spells to describe what she saw as Lila's extraordinary powers. If Lila's creativity is laced with a streak of the demonic, this may be the inevitable outcome when a very gifted woman is denied an outlet for her talents.

For Elena, Lila was both a rival and a source of inspiration. What Elena did by herself did not excite her; only what Lila touched mattered to her. When Lila became obsessed with designing a pair of shoes that she hoped would make her family rich, Elena developed an all-consuming interest in shoes; when Lila, no longer attending school appeared to lose interest in academic subjects, Elena felt her own interest waning. She needed Lila to unlock her own creative potential and she both valued and resented Lila's superior talents. Yet despite the rivalry and jealousy, Elena and Lila were there for each other when it mattered. Elena returned to Naples to nurse Lila back to health when she was seriously ill; Lila was always ready to take care of Elena's children when she had to travel to advance her career. Love and mutual support coexisted with hostility and jealousy. Elena described their relationship as "tangled"; the four Neapolitan novels are her attempt to disentangle that knot.

Although deprived of the opportunity to continue her education, Lila continued studying on her own; in middle school, Elena thought that Lila was still ahead of her in everything, "as if she were going to a secret school." Lila fell in love with Virgil's *Aeneid* and managed to read all twelve books in a few days, while Elena was still in Book Two. Based on her reading of the *Aeneid*, Lila made the observation that "when there is no love, not only the life of the people becomes sterile, but the life of cities"—a concept that Elena used as the basis for a school essay (BF, 160). The essay is much praised by Elena's teachers; rationalizing her unacknowledged appropriation of Lila's ideas, Elena convinced herself that although the ideas for the essay had come from Lila, she was the one who developed them.

The inspiration Elena drew from Lila's writing was always intermingled with envy. When she received a letter from Lila, Elena was reminded of the novel *The Blue Fairy* Lila had written soon after she was forced to leave school. Elena was struck by Lila's ability to write naturally as if she were speaking, to leave no trace of effort, so that the reader wasn't aware of the "artifice of the written word" (BF, 227). Elena was embarrassed by the letters she had written to Lila with their exaggerated tone, their superficiality, the false cheerfulness, the false sorrow. She was convinced that with her, school had made a mistake; the proof was there, in the sharp contrast between her writing and Lila's letter. Despite her success in school, Elena is haunted by the fear that Lila is the truly brilliant one and that she is an unworthy impostor. She sees her success as something achieved through sheer persistence rather than through talent; the old fear of being overshadowed by Lila never disappeared.

Lila had entrusted Elena with a box filled with her notebooks, which she feared her husband would destroy. Elena immediately started reading the notebooks even though she had sworn to Lila that she would not. She was convinced that every word of Lila's diminished hers; in Elena's mind, every sentence of Lila's, even those written when she was still a young child, underscored the emptiness of Elena's own writing. Compared to Lila's, Elena saw her own writing as insignificant. Consumed with jealousy of Lila's talent and tormented by self-doubt, Elena threw the box with Lila's notebooks into the Arno. Elena, the "good girl" was capable of real malevolence. Yet despite destroying Lila's writing, Elena could never free herself from her sense of inferiority and couldn't keep the wish at bay that Lila would die. Elena's preoccupation with Lila's writing ability continued into old age; increasingly doubting the value of her life's work, Elena feared that Lila would some day write something much better.

What Elena referred to as "the play of shared creation" is yet another aspect of the central role writing played in Elena's and Lila's friendship (SNN, 122). Inspired by Louisa May Alcott's success with *Little Women*, which Elena and Lila loved and read together, Lila proposed that they co-author a book together. Although they never managed to co-author a book, over the years there were many projects of shared creation. Elena's essay about the *Aeneid* was certainly one, with Lila providing the conceptual framework and Elena the well-formed sentences. Lila's analysis of the *Aeneid* helped Elena to impress her teachers and advance her academic career; also, Lila's gift for literary analysis might have contributed to Elena's winning a scholarship to the prestigious University of Pisa.

When Elena took the rigorous exam for the scholarship, one of the professors interrogating Elena realized that at one point she appeared to be losing confidence in herself. Instead of expecting Elena to answer his questions, he asked her to talk instead about a book she had read recently. Elena recalled how on the beach at Ischia, Lila had dazzled both Nino and Elena with her interpretation of Samuel Beckett's work; she responded to the professor by drawing on Lila's interpretation of Beckett's plays. The professor had previously told Elena that she tended to rush headlong into subjects about which she had little knowledge. After hearing her critique of Beckett, "the professor's ironic expression changed slowly to bewilderment" (SNN, 326). Ferrante appears to suggest that Elena's analysis of Beckett surprised and impressed the professor and was to some extent responsible for winning the scholarship that transformed her life. Still another echo of Lila's conversation came to Elena's rescue at an awkward moment. At her first meeting with her future husband's cultured family, Elena was intimidated by their knowledge of world affairs; feeling she must somehow enter the conversation, she recalled and uttered verbatim a remark of Lila's: "The Americans, after Hiroshima and Nagasaki, should be brought to trial for crimes against humanity" (SNN, 410). The sentiment was well received by her future in-laws who were impressed by what they saw as Elena's knowledge of history and politics.

When Elena was struggling to write an article she hoped to publish with the help of Nino, she asked Lila for help. After Lila's revisions, the page reflected what Elena had written, but it was clearer, more persuasive. When, Elena gave the revised article to Nino, she did not acknowledge Lila's contribution to the essay. Nino was impressed by the quality of the writing and obviously annoyed that it was better than his writing. In response to Elena's questions about when her article would be published, he told her that the journal didn't have room for it. We don't find out what actually happened with Elena's article until much later in the fourth volume of the Neapolitan novels. Elena and Nino at that point are a couple and Nino asked for her help in editing his writing. Then as if to convince her of his need for her assistance, he revealed what he described as the "most shameful thing" he had ever done (SLC, 68). Envious of what he saw as Elena's superior skill, he threw away the article she had entrusted him to submit to a magazine. He admitted that he was unable to tolerate that her writing was so much better than his. Elena failed once again to acknowledge Lila's contribution to the essay.

When Elena wrote an article on labor unrest for the Communist Party newspaper *L'Unita*, she based it on Lila's account of abominable working conditions in the factory where she worked, once again without crediting Lila. When Elena was trapped in a loveless marriage with two young children and unable to focus on a book project, Elena began telephoning Lila every day hoping Lila would inspire her, setting her imagination in motion. When Lila began to talk about the neighborhood, Elena found her subject—the web of violence that had long dominated and deformed life in Naples. Her mother-in-law thought the novel was unpublishable; "all that hatred was unpleasant" (TWL, 268). Elena acquiesced and put the novel in a drawer; years later, under pressure from her publisher to produce a novel, Elena submitted the novel she had written about the neighborhood in the 1970s. She discovered that Italy in the 1980s was ready for her novel. As with the essay about religion and the article about labor relations, Elena did not acknowledge that her novel about life in the neighborhood had been inspired by Lila.

As Elena's career took off again in the mid-1980s, she grew increasingly comfortable admitting, at least to herself, the debt she owed to Lila. When Elena was struggling with an article she had been commissioned to write, she called Lila, and found that as usual a brief remark of Lila's was enough to inspire her. At one time, Elena had hidden from herself that she needed the stimulation Lila provided: now she could admit, without anxiety, that talking to Lila generated ideas. However, the old fear of being overshadowed by Lila, the fear that everything she had accomplished was due to Lila's influence, never completely disappeared, returning at points when Elena was beginning to lose confidence in the value of her life's work.

Not all Elena and Lila's shared creation took the form of Elena appropriating Lila's words. Furious with her husband for displaying a photo of her in the store where she worked, Lila decided to transform the photo into an image of violation. She enlisted Elena's help: "We suspended time. We isolated space, there remained only the play of glue, scissors, paper, paint: the play of shared creation" (SNN, 122). Similar delight in collaborative effort occurs when Lila in the early 1980s teaches Elena how to use a word processing program. Elena and Lila were assembling documents incriminating the neighborhood's organized crime bosses, the Solaras, in various illegal activities. As they organized and summarized the materials, Elena noted that it had been many years since they had undertaken something together. Lila then showed Elena a new computer, which Elena described as "a kind of television with a keyboard." Lila pressed the power button and began to type on the keyboard. Elena was astonished to see the writing appear "silently on the screen, green like newly sprouted grass." Ferrante conveys the wonder many people experienced when they first used a personal computer, "dazzling, hypnotic segments began to lengthen, sentences that I said, sentences that she said, our volatile discussions were imprinted on the dark well of the screen.... Lila wrote, I would reconsider" (SLC, 311–312). Elena marveled that with one key Lila erased all she had written, that she could reposition entire paragraphs, making them reappear higher up or lower down in a second. Then Lila changed her mind and in a second everything was altered again. Elena was amazed that there was no longer any need for pen, or pencil, and that the lines of text were all perfectly straight.

Elena and Lila's attempt to expose the crimes of the Solara brothers was to be their last collaborative effort. However, the dream of shared creation persisted into late middle age as Elena fantasized about Lila calling one day to request Elena's help editing a text she had written about the history and culture of Naples. The recurrent theme of the play of shared creation is especially interesting in that there is evidence suggesting that Ferrante's novels are themselves shared creations. Ferrante frequently refers to the collaborative nature of art: "The media simply can't discuss a work of literature without pointing to some writer-hero and yet there is no work of literature that is not the fruit of tradition, of many skills, of a sort of collective intelligence. We wrongfully diminish this collective intelligence when we insist on there being a single protagonist behind every work of art."[24] The "play of shared creation" characterizes the friendship of Elena and Lila as well as (in all probability) the collaboration between Anita Raja and Domenico Starnone.

For a relationship as intense as that between Lila and Elena, the word friendship seems inadequate; a love affair seems a better description of their relationship with its passionate intensity, turbulent quarrels, separations and reconciliations. But love affair is a phrase we reserve for relationships with an erotic dimension. There is the suggestion of such a dimension in the scene before Lila's wedding when she asked Elena to come to her house to help her wash and dress. Elena had never seen Lila naked and experienced the "embarrassment of gazing with pleasure at her body." Elena describes her emotional turmoil, her heart "agitated, [her] veins inflamed" (BF, 312–313). Although there are erotic undertones, Elena's agitation was more a response to her fear of losing her friendship with Lila now that she was about to become Signora Caracci than to the emergence of sexual feelings towards Lila.

The only other suggestion of a possible erotic dimension occurs much later when, in response to Elena's daughter erotic play with Lila's son Gennaro, Elena wondered if she had ever played games like that with her friends in the neighborhood. Had she and Lila ever touched each other? Elena admitted that she had admired Lila's body, but ruled out any sexual contact. They would have been much too afraid; if discovered, they would certainly have been beaten to death. The absence of an overt sexual dimension may preclude the use of the phrase "love affair," but Elena's and Lila's intense life long relationship is surely more of a love affair than the relatively brief and ultimately disastrous affair they each had with Nino Sarratore.

6

The Neapolitan Novels: Mothers and Daughters

"The task of a woman writer today is not to stop at the pleasures of the pregnant body, of birth, of bringing up children, but to delve truthfully into the darkest depth."—Elena Ferrante, *Frantumaglia: A Writer's Journey*

Motherhood, both its joys and constraints, has been a major theme in feminist theory and literature. Charlotte Perkins Gilman's harrowing semi-autobiographical short story "The Yellow Wallpaper" (1892), based on her experience of severe post-partum depression, was among the earliest and most influential texts. Gilman's doctor advised her to give up her literary ambitions and "live as domestic a life as possible.... And never touch pen, brush, or pencil as long as you live."[1] Ferrante may be deliberately echoing "The Yellow Wallpaper," when a doctor tells a physically exhausted Lila, "In your condition pregnancy would help, there is no better medicine for a woman" (TWL, 194).

The belief in the therapeutic value of pregnancy has no doubt declined in the wake of the feminist movement, but the tension between motherhood and the writing life persists. Adrienne Rich in *Of Woman Born: Motherhood as Experience and Institution* explores this conflict in language very similar to Ferrante's: "My children cause me the most exquisite suffering of which I have any experience. It is the suffering of ambivalence: the murderous alternation between bitter resentment and raw-edged nerves, and blissful gratification and tenderness.... I love them. But it's in the enormity and inevitability of this love that the sufferings lie."[2] Rich wrote poetry "jotted in fragments during children's naps ... or at 3:00 A.M. after rising with a wakeful child ... despair[ing] of doing any continuous work at this time."[3] Working class writers like Tillie Olsen have written about the struggles of women without economic resources who are trying to combine motherhood and writing. Olsen, who raised children and simultaneously worked outside the home, did not publish until she was fifty years old. Although in late middle age time for writing opened up, "the habits of a life time when everything else had to come before writing are not easily broken ... habits of years—response to others, distractibility, responsibility for daily matters—stay with you, mark you, become you."[4]

The list of women authors who have written variations on the theme of motherhood is a long one including Kate Chopin, Doris Lessing, Toni Morrison, Grace Paley, and Sylvia Plath. More recently Rachel Cusk has written about the dark side of motherhood in *A Life's Work: On Becoming a Mother*. Cusk emphasizes the loss of freedom and the doubts, with scant words about the joys of motherhood. Ferrante, in the vein of Adrienne Rich, explores the complicated intermixture of love and resentment that characterizes her narrators' experience of motherhood. She sees the theme of motherhood as central to her work: "Sometimes I think I haven't written about anything else. Every single one of my anxieties has ended up there. To conceive, to change shape, to feel inhabited by something increasingly alive that makes you feel ill and gives you a sense of well-being is both thrilling and threatening.... Children always remain an inescapable knot of love, of terrors, of satisfactions and anxieties."[5] Given that so much feminist literature about motherhood has been written, why does Ferrante's seem in some ways new? It is certainly in part due to the intensity of her language but also because no one else—to my mind—has so powerfully captured the anxiety that comes with the territory of motherhood: the fear of neglecting one's children and the potentially dire consequences of a moment's inattention; the fear of all the external forces which can threaten one's child. The final novel in the Neapolitan Quartet dramatizes the primal fear—so often in the back of a mother's mind—the fear of losing her child.

Ferrante explores mother/daughter relationships primarily from Elena Greco's perspective, as a daughter as well as a mother, in the context of the dramatic changes in the roles of women in post–World War II Italy. Elena is painfully aware of the burdens motherhood imposed on poor women of her mother's generation. One day a seventeen-year-old Elena looked with horror at the mothers of the old neighborhood: Sometimes they were screaming horrible insults at the children who were tormenting them; other times they maintained a grim silence, their lips tightly closed, their shoulders sagging. "Extremely thin with hollow eyes and cheeks, or with broad behinds, swollen ankles, heavy chests, they lugged shopping bags and small children who clung to their skirts and wanted to be picked up. And good God, they were ten, at most twenty years older than me" (SNN, 102). For Elena this was a cautionary tale, the inevitable consequence of early marriage and multiple pregnancies. Although she had very briefly considered such a marriage with her first boyfriend Antonio, Elena was now focused on carving out a future radically different from her mother's.

Lila does not appear to share Elena's deep fear of becoming like her mother and her relationship with her mother is not as fraught with conflict. One of the limitations of Ferrante's decision to use first person narration is that we learn relatively little about Lila's experience as a daughter or about her mother's life. Lila's mother is referred to as Nunzia; she is just one among many of the Neapolitan novels' large cast of characters. Elena never refers to her mother by her given name Immacolata; she is simply "my mother" and her larger than life presence takes center stage throughout the Neapolitan Quartet. Lila's relationship with her mother is far less troubled than Elena's epic struggle with her mother, who was torn between intense love for and deep resentment of her eldest daughter. Both mothers wanted their daughters to have opportunities unavailable to women of their generation. Lila's mother Nunzia told Elena that she wanted Lila to go on to middle school, but didn't know how to oppose her husband: With tears in her eyes, she admitted that Lila should have continued her education; "it was her destiny" (SNN, 234). Although unable to convince her husband that Lila should continue her schooling, Nunzia was protective towards her daughter and passionately defended her against Lila's husband's accusations of infidelity.

The relationship between Elena and her mother is far more tension filled, complicated by Elena's determination to leave the world of her family. Elena recalled that her mother was initially against letting her continue her education, but when Elena was not doing well in school her mother encouraged her to keep trying, telling her daughter: "Nowhere is it written that you can't do it" (BF, 105). As Elena became more successful, her mother became more invested in her success and was moved to tears as she watched her daughter unwrap the schoolbooks that a now prosperous Lila had bought for her. When Elena became seriously ill during her first year at the University of Pisa, her mother, who had never been outside of

Naples, travelled all night to Pisa to bring Elena food she hoped would make her well. Rather than being appreciative of her mother's help, Elena discovered that in her weakened state, she was more sensitive than ever to everything she detested about her mother. Elena was convinced her mother only cared about her success in school because it gave her something to brag about—she did not want to lose her status as the most fortunate mother in the neighborhood. Torn between pride in her daughter's success and rage at the growing estrangement between Elena and her family, Elena's mother accused her of having no loyalty to and no feelings for her family. She told her daughter she should not feel superior because of her education, warning her: "You came out of this belly and you are made of this substance so don't act superior" (TWL, 47). She insists that she is just as intelligent, maybe more so, than her daughter and would have done as well if she had had Elena's opportunities.

Despite the growing chasm between them, Elena's mother came to her aid once again when Elena was expecting her second child. As soon as her mother set foot in the house, Elena listed rules, including forbidding her mother to touch anything in her study or in her husband's, and most insulting of all, ordered her to stay in the kitchen or in her room if Elena had guests. Elena cruelly treated her mother like a servant, who "as if the fear of being sent away modified her nature, ... became a devoted servant who provided for every necessity of the house" (TWL, 259). Elena's ugly behavior can in part be explained by her class anxieties and in part by her fear of becoming like her mother.

She feared that she would acquire her mother's limp, the result of some long ago illness. Her mother's limping gait is used so often as a descriptor that it functions almost like a Homeric epithet. As a girl Elena saw modeling herself after Lila as the only way to escape becoming like her mother. However, her mother's limp seemed as if it were lying in wait for her, destined to emerge in Elena's body. When Elena was pregnant with her first daughter, she experienced a sharp pain in her leg. Realizing that she was beginning to limp all the time, she consulted a doctor who told her that the weight of her unborn child was causing a slight sciatica. Elena, displaying a tendency to superstition that occurred at times despite her education, did not accept the doctor's explanation, thinking instead that her mother's limp had settled in her body and would cause her to limp forever. Before her mother's death, Elena reconciled with her mother and the limp became a part of her, a symbol of that reconciliation. Lila accused Elena of having invented the limp in order to keep her mother alive within her and noted that the invention had become a reality; Elena now really did have a limp.

The inevitability of parental figures deeply buried in their children's flesh, emerging when least expected, is a recurrent theme throughout the Neapolitan novels. Seeing Lila's husband Stefano consumed by a jealous rage, Elena realized that the ghost of his father Don Achille was becoming visible. Elena had wondered if her childhood friend Alfonso, the youngest son of Don Achille, despite his delicate appearance, somehow also concealed the body of his father. Years later Alfonso, despite his efforts to transition to a woman, found that something of his father Don Achille was indeed appearing in his face. When Elena discovered her lover Nino having sex with her housekeeper Silvana, Elena saw in his face the expression of his father Donato, a serial womanizer like his son. The emergence of Elena's mother's limp is thus part of a pattern, suggesting a kind of biological determinism, an ironic counterpoint to Elena's story of transformation through education.

Much of the conflict between Elena and her mother was bound up with changes in social mores and Ferrante once again skillfully interweaves changes in the larger society with the lives of her characters. Elena's mother came from a generation in which divorce was uncommon and women thought they had no choice but to accept an unsatisfying marriage. She could not understand her daughter's choices, especially her decision to leave Pietro, her well-educated husband from a prominent family. When her mother told Elena never to show up in her house again if she left Pietro, Elena remonstrated that Italian society was not like it used to be; it was now possible to be a respectable woman, even if you leave your husband, even if you decide to live with another man. The generational conflict occurring throughout Europe and the Americas in the wake of the sexual revolution of the 1960s and 70s was especially intense in the deeply traditional culture of Southern Italy.

During the period of the most intense conflict in her relations with her mother, Elena began to see her cultured, well-educated mother-in-law as a surrogate role model. Elena describes her self as "mesmerized" by Adele's way of speaking, of dressing, her hairstyles, her jewelry (TWL, 99). When Elena became dissatisfied with her marriage to Pietro and disillusioned with the world of the Airotas, she no longer imitated Adele's style. As she was falling deeply in love with Nino Sarratore and on the brink of an affair with him, Elena recalled that when dressing to go to dinner with Nino, the only jewelry she wore was her mother's old silver bracelet. Once again, the bracelet appears at a key point in the Neapolitan novels as an emblem of sexuality and its dangers, and of Elena's conflict ridden relationship with her mother. After the dissolution of her marriage, Elena broke with Adele, telling her that for years she had seen Adele as the mother figure she thought she needed; now realizing she was wrong, she tells Adele, "My mother is better than you" (SLC, 89).

Despite her frequent cruelty toward her mother during the period of her marriage to Pietro, Elena came to her mother's assistance when it mattered. She did not regret that the full weight of her mother's illness fell largely on her and wanted her mother to realize, that even though their relationship had been deeply troubled, that she still loved her. When the tangled relationship between Elena and her mother finally came to an end, rather than feeling relief, Elena struggled to come to terms with her mother's death. The time they spent together during her mother's long illness had led to a reconciliation, and the day her mother died, Elena put on her mother's silver bracelet. No longer preferring the jewelry her former mother-in-law wore, from then on Elena often wore her mother's bracelet.

Elena's relations with her daughters were almost as ambivalent, as conflict-ridden as her relationship with her own mother. Laura Benedetti, in *Tigress in the Snow*, her groundbreaking study of the theme of motherhood in 20th-century Italian literature, has argued that prior to the 1980s women who had written about motherhood had done so almost exclusively from the perspective of daughters. According to Benedetti, "It was only in the 1980's that the complexity deriving from women's position as both daughters and (at least potentially) mothers became the focus of attention."[6] Ferrante's work, particularly the Neapolitan Quartet, is part of the post–1980s focus Benedetti has identified.

Elena's struggles with her role as a mother appear to have resonated most with Ferrante's readers who, judging from reviews and blog posts, are more likely to be at the stage of life where they are juggling responsibilities for children and the challenges of a career, rather than dealing with unresolved issues with a dying parent. Ferrante had covered this ground in *The Days of Abandonment* and *The Lost Daughter* but the scope of the Neapolitan Quartet allowed for fuller development and for placing these conflicts in the context of changing social roles of the tumultuous 1960s and 1970s. Men were changing more slowly than women. Despite his left wing politics, Elena's husband Pietro was quite conservative when it came to sexual politics. Elena had not wanted to get pregnant so soon after marriage, but her well-educated, socialist husband did not believe in contraception. The radical rethinking of gender roles emerging from the nascent Italian feminist movement had not yet penetrated Pietro's consciousness, and Elena became pregnant before they could resolve the issue.

Ferrante has written brilliantly about the shock of pregnancy. Perhaps the most chilling example is Leda's description of the experience of the birth of her second child in *The Lost Daughter*. Leda described the birth of her first daughter Bianca as the most intense pleasure she had ever experienced in her life, but her second pregnancy was torture. Her younger daughter Marta attacked her body, "forcing it to turn on itself, out of control. She immediately manifested herself, not as Marta but as a piece of living iron in my stomach ... a violent polyp so far from anything human that it reduced me, even though it fed and grew, to a rotting matter without life" (LD, 110). In the Neapolitan novels, Ferrante contrasts Elena's relatively easy pregnancies with Lila's harrowing experiences, very similar to Leda's experience with her daughter Marta. Lila described her pregnancy with her second child as her own body becoming angry with her and rebelling against her until she experienced the most terrible pain imaginable: "For hours she had felt in her belly sharp cold flames, an unbearable flow of pain that hit her brutally in the pit of her stomach and then returned, penetrating her kidneys" (SLC, 216). Passages like these led *New Yorker* critic Joan Acocella to the conclusion that "these books were written not just by a female but by one who has been pregnant."[7] However, just because one section appears to have been written by someone who experienced pregnancy, it does not follow that the entire Neapolitan Quartet must have been written by someone who has been pregnant. The idea that only one creative mind can be behind a work of art is a persistent unexamined assumption in much of the critical commentary on Ferrante's work.

For Elena, problems began after her relatively easy first pregnancy. Her initial reaction to the birth of her daughter was euphoric. When she first saw her daughter, a "black-haired, a violet organism that, full of energy writhed and wailed, [she] felt a physical pleasure so piercing" that she never again experienced any other pleasure comparable to it. But soon after, she found that her daughter had become "troublesome" (TWL, 237–38). Elena soon became pregnant again and for a time lost her ability to write, increasingly torn between her daughters and her literary ambitions. When Nino re-entered her life, her desire for him and the freedom he represented proved far more powerful than her ties to her children.

This is the point at which some readers lose sympathy for Elena. When she left her husband for Nino, her little girls begged her not to leave. In one of the most frequently quoted passages from the Neapolitan novels, Elena wrote: "I couldn't bear it. I knelt down, I held them around the waist, I said: All right, I won't go, you are my children, I'll stay with you. Those words calmed them" (TWL, 414). Then she packed her suitcase and a few days later, left the girls with a neighbor and joined Nino to fly to a conference in France. In the period soon after her separation from Pietro, Elena left her daughters with Pietro's mother, so she could be with Nino in Naples. She visited her children at her in-laws' house, trying to repress awareness of her daughters' pain at the separation. Once when her children saw that she was about to leave for a book tour, they began to cry, holding on to her dress and begging her to let go of her suitcase. She had to tear herself away from them as "their cries pursued her to the street" (SLC, 37). Elena's story recalls that of Leda in *The Lost Daughter*, but Elena maintained contact with her daughters during the period after her separation from Pietro, whereas Leda did not see her daughters for three years. Ferrante presents an uncomfortable truth—the needs of parents and children often conflict, with parent's happiness often coming at the expense of the child.

Responses to Elena's decision vary from horror at her selfishness to applause for her resolve to put her needs first and do what men have been doing since time immemorial—abandoning their wives and leaving them with the sole responsibility for their children. Elena's and Leda's desire to break free from the chains of motherhood alternates with overpowering love for and fear of losing their children. In *The Lost Daughter*, Leda remembered losing her young daughter on the beach and the terror she felt as she frantically searched for her. When her daughter was found, Leda experienced both tears of joy and screams of rage at the powerful bonds of motherhood, which were preventing her from realizing her literary ambitions.

As the years progressed, Elena, like Leda, also continued to feel torn between her daughters and her career aspirations. Ferrante provides the reader with the necessary information to see the consequences of Elena's neglect of her daughters, although Elena herself generally does not have eyes to see. Her two daughters become sullen adolescents who grow to hate each other and blame much of their unhappiness on their mother's neglect. Elena's oldest daughter Dede tells her mother that she doesn't understand her: "All you think about is yourself and that crap that you write" (SLC, 406). Elena's husband Pietro is aware of his and Elena's failures as parents, telling his former wife that children need stability and continuous affection which neither he nor Elena had been able to provide for their daughters. Elena avoided taking responsibility for her daughters' troubles and at one point blamed Lila for her difficulties. When Lila told Elena that they weren't meant to have children, Elena insisted on seeing herself as a good mother who wore herself out trying to do her work without neglecting her daughters. She saw both herself and her daughters through rose-colored glasses.

At one point Lila's partner Enzo told Elena that she must look at her daughters as they truly are. Elena protested that she does that all the time, but Enzo replied that she doesn't do it well. As Lila once remarked on Elena's capacity for denial: "Each of us narrates our life as it suits us" (TWL, 237). At times, such as these conversations Elena has with Lila and Enzo about her daughters, the reader sees clearly that Elena is an unreliable narrator and that Ferrante is viewing her narrator ironically. As Ferrante observed in an interview with *Vanity Fair*, "It has always fascinated me how a story comes to us through the filter of a protagonist whose consciousness is limited, inadequate, shaped by the facts that she herself is recounting, situations that she neither sees clearly nor understands."[8]

Elena's troubled relationship with her daughter Elsa came to a head when Elsa decided to run away with Lila's son Rino, the man her sister Dede loved, thus alienating not only her sister but also her mother, who saw uneducated, unemployed Rino as an unsuitable partner for her daughter. To add further insult to injury, after running out of money, Elsa took refuge with her grandmother Adele, thus revealing Elena's failures as a parent to her former in-laws. To finance her fling with Rino, Elsa had stolen money and jewelry from Elena, including Elena's mother's silver bracelet, which returns to center stage, once again implicated in a troubled mother-daughter relationship. When Elena arrived at Adele's house, she found Elsa wearing the stolen rings and silver bracelet. She demanded the return of her money, rings, and the bracelet, which had become a symbol of her reconciliation with her own mother. She immediately put on the bracelet, insisting that her daughter never touch her things again. Enraged,

Elena pushed her daughter against a wall, threatening to hit her. Elsa responded by telling her mother she hated her, never wanted to see her again, and that she "would never return to Naples, "that shitty place where you made us live" (SLC, 415).

Elena restored good relations with her daughters when the storm of their adolescence passed. Her two oldest daughters, Dede and Elsa, now living in the United States and embarked on academic careers, return every year to spend time with Elena, now living in Turin. During the Christmas holiday of 2002 when Elena was fifty-eight, Dede, Elsa, and Elena's youngest daughter Imma, along with their male partners, returned to stay with Elena for an extended period of time. Elena relished the time with her daughters and with her first grandchild, Dede's son Hamid. Underscoring a central theme of the Neapolitan Quartet—the impermanence of relationships between men and women—Elena's children's fathers (Pietro and Nino) were long gone from her life, but her relationships with her daughters have remained intact and have strengthened over time. However, the tensions had not totally disappeared. Her daughters started looking through copies of Elena's published works and began reading aloud lines from her books. Elsa, the daughter with whom Elena had the most troubled relationship, was reading from Elena's books with a particularly mocking tone. Only Elsa's boyfriend seemed to realize that she was hurting her mother and he interrupted her, took away the book, and changed the subject. Elena's rapprochement with her daughters was incomplete and the scars from the years of conflict were still apparent.

During the time Elena had become embroiled in bitter conflict with her daughters, Lila had become the good mother, who devoted herself to her daughter Tina, as well as the trusted friend who took care of Elena's daughters when Elena was traveling to promote her work. It is the good mother who suffers a tragic loss. On a crowded Neapolitan street, Lila looked away for a few minutes and her daughter disappeared without a trace, never to be found. The tragedy of *Story of the Lost Child* recalls Ferrante's first exploration of the fear of losing one's child in *The Lost Daughter*. In the earlier work, Leda remembered losing her young daughter on the beach and the terror she felt as she frantically searched for her. When her daughter was found, Leda alternated between tears of joy and screams of rage because of "the crushing weight of responsibility, the bond that strangles" (LD, 38).

There was no happy ending for Lila whose daughter Tina disappeared from the streets of Naples one Sunday afternoon. An exhaustive search failed to turn up any leads, but Ferrante provides a clue as to what may have happened to Tina. Ten years after the loss of Tina, Lila told Elena that she has often thought that "they" might have taken Tina because they thought she was Elena's daughter. A photograph of Elena and Tina, that misidentified Tina as Elena's daughter, had appeared along with a newspaper article about Elena's recent book on organized crime. Ferrante is relying on her readers' (at least her Italian readers') knowledge that the Camorra, the organized crime syndicate that controlled Naples, was known to sometimes kidnap and murder the relatives of its enemies— including writers who exposed the inner workings of the Camorra and its impact on Neapolitan life. Elena refused to entertain the idea that Tina had been taken in the mistaken belief she was Elena's daughter, in revenge for Elena's book and newspaper articles about the Camorra. She attributed Lila's belief in this possibility to her troubled mind, still stricken with grief for her lost daughter.

Motherhood is never easy for Ferrante's women and Lila experiences the worst that can happen. In response to an interviewer who asked if Ferrante thinks women would be stronger if they didn't have to bear the burdens of motherhood, Ferrante replied that the problem is not motherhood, but "what we tell ourselves about motherhood and child-rearing.... The task of a woman writer today is not to stop at the pleasures of the pregnant body, of birth, of bringing up children, but to delve truthfully into the darkest depth."[9] The darkest depth contains those inchoate fears that for Lila were realized in the tragic loss of her child. The theme of loss is all pervasive in the Neapolitan Quartet—loss of children, of parents, of stable family ties, of friendships, lovers, and husbands. In her powerful depiction of the mother/daughter relationship—its joys, sorrows, conflicts and the inevitable loss of the mother, Ferrante has made an unforgettable contribution to a major theme recurring throughout feminist literature.

7

The Neapolitan Novels: Love, Sex, Betrayal

> *"The time of faithfulness and permanent relationships was over for men and women."*—Elena Greco, Story of the Lost Child

In the late 1960s and 1970s, Italy underwent dramatic changes in social mores and in laws relating to marriage and the family. In 1968 laws were passed abolishing the criminalization of adultery and concubinage and placing husbands and wives on an equal footing in separation trials. In 1970, the Italian Parliament passed a law granting divorce after five years of separation. According to anthropologist Amalia Signorelli, by establishing equal rights and duties for husband and wife, the 1970 law "questioned the Italian monogamous nuclear family and the supremacy of the husband-father within it." Building on these victories, in 1974 voters overwhelmingly supported a referendum to repeal the divorce law requiring a five year waiting period. In 1975, the Italian Parliament passed a comprehensive reform of family law that gave women an equal say in all decisions regarding residence and the care and education of children; the law further recognized children born out of wedlock, granting them the same rights as children born within marriage.[1]

These legislative victories were all the more remarkable given that only three decades earlier, Italy under Mussolini was living under laws which sharply reduced educational and employment opportunities for women, encouraging them to devote their lives to having ever more children. Under Mussolini's fascist regime, women's wages were reduced to half those of men, and women's employment in government was limited to ten percent of all workers. Women were prohibited from teaching literature and philosophy in secondary schools or serving as administrators in middle schools. In order to discourage women from pursuing a university education, tuition for women was raised to twice that for men.[2] Given this horrendous history, the victories won by Italian women in 1970s must have been especially sweet.

The saga of Nina and Lila plays out against this background of cultural and institutional change. Their childhood was spent in a time of rigid gender roles and limited possibilities for girls of all socio-economic backgrounds, but especially for Southern Italian girls from working class backgrounds. To my mind, no one has charted the transition from childhood to young womanhood as powerfully as Ferrante, and this is especially the case for women growing up in poverty. There are universal aspects that all female readers can relate to, but also experiences specific to Elena and Lila's world. Most women can readily relate to Elena's discomfort about her changing body; she felt herself expanding like "pizza dough" while on her forehead, chin, and around her jaws "archipelagos of reddish swellings multiplied, then turned purple, finally developed yellowish tips" (BF, 120). Lila matured later than Elena, but her spectacular beauty altered the dynamics between the two girls as all the boys in the neighborhood became enamored of Lila. The young men sensed an energy emanating from Lila's maturing body that overpowered them, "like the swelling sound of beauty arriving" (BF, 143). For young women in Elena's and Lila's world, sexual maturity was fraught with increased surveillance and danger, as men saw themselves as responsible for protecting their female relatives' "honor." Elena refused a ride in the Solara brothers' car because if her father had found out he would have beaten her to death, while at the same time her little brothers would feel obligated to try to murder the Solaras. Everyone in the neighborhood knew the unwritten code and understood what was expected.

The traditional values that governed Elena and Lila's childhood had begun to break down in their adulthood and the Neapolitan Quartet is one long tale of broken marriages and failed relationships between men and women. As Elena reflected: "the time of faithfulness and permanent relationships was over for men and women" (SLC, 393). The first volume, *My Brilliant Friend*, begins in the 1950s with Lila and Elena growing up in a traditional patriarchal society—a world with early marriage, a world without divorce, a world in which a woman's identity was subsumed in her husband's. Lila's mutilation of her wedding photo becomes an image of her loss of identity, itself symbolized by the loss of her family name. In the altered photo Rafaella [Lina] Cerullo, was overwhelmed, her image was losing its shape and dissolving inside the body of her husband Stefano, "becoming a subsidiary emanation of him: Signora Caracci" (SNN, 124). Elena wondered if Lila's family name would disappear from her signature altogether and if she would no longer identify herself as Rafaella Cerullo Caracci, but simply as Rafaella Caracci; if her children would have difficulty remembering their mother's family name and her grandchildren would have no knowledge at all of the name Cerullo.

The theme of loss of identity when a woman assumes her husband's surname recurs throughout the Neapolitan novels. When Elena became engaged to Pietro Airota, her mother asked her, if she should write another book, whether her name would appear on the cover as Elena Airota. Elena replied that it would not because she preferred the name Elena Greco. Her mother readily agreed. In the final volume of the Neapolitan Quartet, Ferrante returned to the implications of a woman's surname. When Elena's daughters, Dede and Elsa, were young children, their paternal grandfather Guido Airota asked them if their surname was Greco or Airota; the girls without hesitation answered "Airota." Later when the girls were adolescents, Dede reported on a conversation she had with Lila who said that the rules governing surnames were stupid. Lila had noted that Rino emerged from her stomach, and lives with her, but despite this, he's called by his father's surname, Carracci. Dede noted that she and her sister emerged from Elena's stomach and spend more time with their mother than with their father, but are nonetheless known know as Airota. Dede further observed that anyone referring to Lila's stomach, doesn't refer to it as Stefano Carracci's stomach, nor does anyone referring to Elena's stomach refer to it as Pietro Airota's stomach. With impeccable logic, Dede concluded Rino should be called Rino Cerullo and she should be called Dede Greco. Dede's argument that female identity should not be submerged in male identity became the subject of Elena Greco's well-received second book, as well as one of major themes of Ferrante's novels.

Lila had experienced the trauma of loss of identity and agency when at the age of sixteen, she married Stefano Caracci, a prosperous grocer in a desperate attempt to escape marriage to Marcello Solara, a Camorrist who had been aggressively pursuing her. The marriage was a disaster. When Stefano tried to beat Lila into submission, there wasn't anyone in the neighborhood especially among the women, who had not thought for a long time that "she needed a good thrashing" (SNN, 45). Lila alternated

7. Love, Sex, Betrayal

between resistance and resignation, slipping into a deep depression. She emerged from despair during a summer vacation in Ischia when she fell in love with Nino, an intense intellectual who had rejected the machismo of the neighborhood. Lila confided to Elena (who suffered from unrequited love for Nino) that he had "snatched her away from death ... had restored to her the capacity to feel" and most of all "brought back to life her sense of herself" (SNN, 295).

Ferrante brilliantly conveys the process of falling in love, a story told from Elena's perspective. In perhaps the most powerful segment in the Neapolitan Novels, the narration slows down and Ferrante delves deeply into lives of her characters. Lila's family had taken her to a doctor to try to find out why she had not become pregnant. The doctor noted that Lila was very young and needed to become stronger; to that end, he prescribed a seaside vacation. Lila's husband Stefano, desperate for a child, rented a cottage on the island of Ischia and the drama begins with Lila and her husband, mother, brother, and sister-in law disembarking on Ischia. Elena had contrived to join them, motivated by her desire to see Nino who she had learned would be on Ischia for the summer. The narrator, the mature Elena, describes her younger self's comic misunderstanding of what she believed were Nino's overtures to her. The narrator's ironic tone is one of the ways Ferrante from time to time reminds the reader that these are the recollections of an older woman viewing her younger self from the vantage point of maturity. Blinded by her own desire for Nino, at first Elena could not see what was unfolding before her eyes. She finally realized that Nino's real interest was not her but Lila. The narrator's' ironic tone disappears and the mood shifts from the comic to lyric and then to tragic when it becomes apparent that there is little chance of a happy ending to this love affair.

Nino and Lila courted each other through intellectual discussions, sharing ideas and books. Although he had previously professed no interest in literature, Nino was mesmerized by Lila's interpretations of Samuel Beckett's plays; he borrowed the book, shared his interpretation of Beckett and they continued an emotionally charged discussion inspired by Beckett's ideas. When Elena finally realized that Nino and Lila were falling in love, she was overcome by a jealousy that she could not understand because "[she] felt at the same time jealous of Lila who was giving herself to Nino, of Nino who was giving himself to Lila" (SNN, 285). Elena was also torn with envy because of Lila's capacity for an all-consuming passion, an emotion Elena feared she was incapable of experiencing. Lila, apparently oblivious of Elena's feelings for Nino, told Elena she hoped that one day Elena would experience the kind of love she feels for Nino. Witnessing the deepening love between Lila and Nino was intensely painful for Elena and at one point, while watching Nino and Lila swimming, she wished that they would drown and "that death would take from them the joys of the next day" (SNN, 278).

The relationship between Lila and Nino is the great love affair of the Neapolitan Quartet; they are the Dido and Aeneas of the second volume, *The Story of a New Name*. Both Elena and Lila's imaginations were shaped by Virgil's *Aeneid*, and Ferrante herself refers to Dido, the Queen of Carthage, as one of the "characters who molded me ... a crucial female figure of my adolescence."[3] For a brief shining moment, Lila and Nino's love for each other rises above the grim world of the neighborhood. Elena noted that when Lila spoke of her love for Nino, she used that verb amare [to love], that they had encountered only in books and was not used in the neighborhood where everyone preferred *volere bene*. Lila eventually left her husband for Nino, something inconceivable in her world, placing herself at considerable risk. After twenty-three days, Nino abandoned Lila thinking (as Elena reconstructed his story), that Lila was not right for him, that she was pregnant, and that what was in her womb frightened him. Like Aeneas who left Dido to pursue his destiny to found Rome, Nino left Lila when he began to realize that his relationship with her was incompatible with his ambitions. Like Aeneas, Nino put his quest for advancement before love.

An echo of the love affair of Dido and Aeneas recurs in in the mad passion of widowed, mentally unstable, Melina Cappuccio for the married philanderer Donato Sarratore. Melina waged a war against Sarratore's wife Lidia, hoping to break up their marriage so that Donato would be free to live with her. Fearful of losing Donato, Melina began to deteriorate mentally and was seen walking along the *stradone* eating soap flakes. Most people in the neighborhood identified with Sarratore's wife; only Lila identified with her distant relative Melina, seeing something of her own mental fragility in Melina. Just as Elena feared turning into her mother, Lila feared turning into Melina. After an episode of murderous rage when the Sarratore family left the neighborhood, Melina's madness subsided, only to descend into insanity again when Sarratore reentered her life, sending her a copy of his recently published volume of poems inscribed to Melina who he said had encouraged his poetry. Melina began manically singing with happiness, her children trying to calm her to no avail.

Lila, then enthralled by the *Aeneid*, drew a connection between Melina's deterioration and Dido's when abandoned by Aeneas. Elena also saw Donato and Melina as overwhelmed by passion like Dido and Aeneas. An adolescent Elena rationalized Donato's affair with Melina, idealizing the mad passion despite Melina's broken mind. Melina recalls "the poverella" whose tragic fate haunted Olga, the narrator of Ferrante's *The Days of Abandonment*. As Lila feared turning into Melina, Olga feared becoming like the poverella. Consumed with grief because her husband abandoned her for another woman, the poverella, like Dido, committed suicide. Dido, Melina and the poverella all succumb to the destructive force of an obsessive love for a man who abandoned them. However, Melina's children cared for her and presumably saved her from the fate of Dido and the poverella. As they grew older, Lila's and Elena's romantic references to Dido disappeared, the realism of age replacing the idealism of youth. Lila, when she is in her late fifties, sees herself as "a crazy old woman like Melina," in her case undone not by unrequited love but by the tragic loss of her daughter (SLC, 453).

Unlike Dido, abandoned by Aeneas, Lila survived Nino's cruel abandonment, but the story of their love—at least on Nino's part—is never quite over. In some sense Lila remained the love of his life. For years Elena had sensed his continuing attraction to Lila and once when observing them together in the neighborhood wondered if they were trying to repress their never quite extinguished feelings for each other. When her mother was seriously ill, and Elena needed help tending to her mother and caring for her children, she observed that when she asked Nino for his help during the times when she was alone with her daughters, Nino was always busy. However, he "miraculously" managed to carve out time to help Lila when she was taking care of Elena's daughters. Elena feared arriving home and finding Nino and Lila together, "talking about everything under the sun as they used to do in Ischia" (SLC, 214–15). Elena's suspicions turned out to be well founded; at the time of her break-up with Nino, Elena learned that during the time that he was involved with her, he had tried to resume his relationship with Lila. Elena's chagrin at Nino's continued attraction to Lila far outlasted her own love for Nino. Years later when Elena met with Nino, now a member of Parliament, to get information about the charges filed against her old friend Pasquale, Nino mentioned Lila. Elena noted bitterly that despite so many years having passed, Nino never missed an opportunity to bring up Lila. Jealousy, hostility, hatred—these are emotions that so often persist the longest.

Elena saw Nino's relationship with Lila as a brief departure from his usual self-interested pursuit of women who could be useful to him. When her own relationship with Nino ended, Elena began to think of him as above all a "cultivator of useful relationships," making choices that were always in line with his ambitions. Beyond every one of Nino's career advances, Elena saw the mediation of a woman. Elena herself was one of those useful relationships, a well-connected woman with ties to a major publishing house. She helped Nino, whose writing skills were inferior to hers, to rewrite his essays; prevailed upon her publisher to bring out a collection of his essays; and acted as his publicist, persuading the influential people she knew to review his book. For the first time Elena realized that only for Lila had Nino (for a time) risked his personal ambitions. During that summer on Ischia, and for a year afterwards, Nino surrendered to a romance that would have done nothing to advance his career and would surely have become a burden, "an anomaly in the journey of his life" (SLC, 402). Throughout her relationship with Nino, Elena feared that his love for Lila had never quite been extinguished: "If our season of love was already darkening, the season of Ischia would always remain radiant for him" (SLC, 235–36).

For Lila, the experience of abandonment by a man she had loved so deeply left its permanent scars. Although she developed a mutually supportive relationship with Enzo, a kind man who loved her very much, there were no more passionate love affairs for Lila. Lila's attitudes towards sexuality were formed during her first marriage, characterized by violence and marital rape. Even with Nino, whom she passionately loved, sexual intercourse gave her no pleasure—"the bother of fucking," as she put it (TWL, 176). When asked by an interviewer from the *Guardian* about Lila's and Elena's very different attitudes towards sexuality, Ferrante replied: "The ways Elena and Lila behave are just two different aspects of the same arduous and almost always unhappy adjustment to men and their sexuality."[4]

Elena's attitudes towards sexuality are more complicated than Lila's, and her behavior goes beyond merely adjusting to male sexuality. Elena had embarked on an unsuccessful quest for sexual satisfaction. Her first sexual experience was a sexual assault by Donato Sarratore, the father of the young man she loved. Fifteen-year-old Elena did not resist Donato and the experience was a mixture of repulsion and the stirring of sexual desire. Confused and ashamed, she told no one about the experience. Elena tells the reader that the narrative she is writing about her long friendship with Lila is the first time she has tried to put into words her tangled emotions about that deeply disturbing experience.

Ferrante has brilliantly described the frustrations of adolescent sexuality in a sexually repressed culture. Elena felt strong sexual stirrings with her first boyfriend, Antonio. Her reasons for getting involved with him had more to do with her desire to keep up with Lila than for any emotional connection she had for Antonio. Elena had asked Antonio to accompany her to Lila's wedding, an invitation he interpreted as evidence of Elena's serious interest in him; he went into debt to buy a new suit for the wedding—an expenditure he could ill afford. Elena appeared oblivious to Antonio's feelings and humiliated him by ignoring him at the wedding reception and instead spending time with the young man she really loved—Nino Sarratore. Although Ferrante's Neapolitan Quartet is generally thought to be about men's mistreatment of women, the roles are sometimes reversed, with Elena callously using Antonio. Despite Elena's obvious interest in Nino, Antonio believed Elena's protestations and managed to convince himself that she really did care for him. Eager for the sexual experiences she imagined the just married Lila was enjoying, Elena tried to get Antonio to have sexual intercourse with her, but at the last minute he literally pulled out, telling her that he wanted to make love with her the way it's done with a wife. Elena is left frustrated and unsatisfied.

Elena's desire for sexual experience, both for its own sake and as a way of keeping up with Lila, led her to tolerate a second sexual advance by Nino's predatory father. In this second encounter, Elena was not simply a victim; she wrote that the entire time, she didn't once regret having accepted Donato's advances. At the time, she was proud of herself for losing her virginity, seeing herself as using Donato for her own ends. When Donato asked her where they could meet the next day, Elena told him that he must never look for her again and that if he should try to contact her, she would have Michele Solara beat him up. Elena thought her sexual relationship with Donato had no emotional significance; intercourse with Donato was simply a way to lose the burden of virginity. Years later, Elena saw the experience differently; she viewed it as "degrading," and was ashamed of it. She incorporated the incident into her first novel and found that writing about the incident calmed her, "as if the shame had passed from [her] into the notebook" (SNN, 433).

After losing her virginity with Donato, Elena continued her quest for sexual satisfaction at the University of Pisa. Her lover in her first year at the university introduced her to new intellectual worlds, but showed little interest in satisfying her sexually. Before the feminist movement emerged in Italy, Elena was developing a feminist consciousness and she explored male sexual selfishness in her first novel. She described male irritation, "the boredom of one who has already had his orgasm and now would like to go to sleep," a sexual honesty which resonated with many of her female readers (TWL, 176). Of all the many scenes of bad sex in Ferrante's novels, Elena's descriptions of her sexual relations with her husband Pietro are among the worst, leaving her "hurting and unsatisfied" (TWL, 231). It wasn't until her extra-marital affair with Nino, that Elena experienced real sexual pleasure.

Elena had married Pietro because she saw Nino as hopelessly out of reach and because of the social advantages which came from marrying into the well-connected Airota family, connections she hoped would further her career as a writer. But marriage and two small children made it difficult to pursue a career, and her husband did not encourage her literary ambitions. Pietro never asked her about her writing projects and seemed relieved when she no longer mentioned writing. In a particularly riveting scene, Elena in a state of exhaustion asked her husband to watch the baby for a few hours so she could get some sleep. Awakened by the baby's screams, Elena discovered that Pietro had put the baby's crib into his study and was immersed in his work, taking notes as if he were deaf to his daughter's cries. When an enraged Elena shouted that he didn't give a damn about his daughter, Pietro coldly asked her to leave the room and take the crib with her, calmly stating that he had an important deadline to meet.

Elena's unhappiness in her marriage reached the breaking point when Nino, now a professor, re-entered her life. Part of Elena's attraction to Nino was his encouragement of her literary efforts. Nino respected Elena's intellectual ability and he was not sexually selfish. He did care about satisfying his partner, but in every other respect he was self-absorbed. Ferrante allows the reader to see aspects of Nino's character that Elena does not permit herself to see. Always quick to find excuses for Nino's bad behavior, when she learned that he had an affair with a student and fathered a child with her, Elena tried to rationalize his predatory, irresponsible

7. Love, Sex, Betrayal

behavior as part of the sexual revolution of the 1960s and 1970s: "Girls wanted him, he took them, there was no abuse of power, there was no guilt, only the rights of desire" (TWL, 88). At that point in her life, Elena decided there was nothing wrong with what Nino had done and that he knew how to enjoy life with those who shared his sexual exuberance and zest for life. She was not disturbed by Nino's frequently callous behavior such as his cruelty towards Pietro whom he had befriended because he saw a relationship with the Airota family as a career advantage. Elena's largely suppressed class resentments emerged in her admiration and elation in seeing a cultured, extremely well-educated Airota losing ground, appearing disoriented, and responding "feebly to the swift, brilliant, even cruel aggressions of Nino Sarratore, my schoolmate, my friend, born in the neighborhood like me" (TWL, 378).

The dissolution of Elena's marriage and her decision to abandon Pietro for Nino is every bit as harrowing as the marital breakdown described in *The Days of Abandonment*. However, here it is the husband suffering the torments of abandonment, and like Olga in *The Days of Abandonment*, Pietro was in a state of total denial. Elena reflected that perhaps when facing abandonment, we are all alike, and that "not even a very orderly mind can endure the discovery of not being loved" (TWL, 412). Elena thought of herself as someone who had always repressed her desires if they did not conform to social expectations. She had always managed to sublimate every forbidden desire, but now the good girl had had enough, saying to herself, "let it all explode," herself most of all (TWL, 399). Believing that something momentous was happening that would "dissolve the old way of living entirely and [that she was] part of that dissolution," she saw the break-up of her marriage as part of much larger rebellion against outmoded traditions (TWL, 418). She was part of a wave of new women, inspired by the feminist movement and benefitting from expanding opportunities, women who left unhappy marriages in the quest for personal fulfillment.

Her optimism would be sorely tested. Nino seemed oblivious to the difficulties his affair with Elena would cause Elena and her family. He insisted that she leave her husband for him, but although he promised to also leave his wife, he soon returned to her, and for some time lied to Elena about his reluctance to end his economically advantageous marriage. Elena continued to find excuses for his behavior. When Nino confessed that in a fit of envy, he had thrown in the trash an article a teenage Elena expected him to help her publish, at first she was disoriented and didn't know how to reconcile that contemptible act with the high regard in which she had held him ever since she was a girl. But Elena quickly decided that his confession of something he had no need to reveal reflected well on him and concluded from that moment that she could always believe him.

It took a great deal for Elena to finally lose faith in Nino. She continued to believe that he had left his wife until finally Lila told her the truth—that Nino had never left her, and that he had been appointed director of a research institute funded by his wife's wealthy father. Elena confronted Nino and as usual he tried to defend his despicable behavior; however, Elena could not bring herself to put a definitive end to the relationship. She acknowledged that although she wrote about and gave lectures on women's autonomy, she didn't know how to live without "his voice, his body, his intelligence" (SLC, 99). Elena struggled to rationalize her relationship with Nino, trying to convince herself that they were among a new wave of men and women, discovering new forms of living together. This is a familiar tale, the strong feminist in an unequal relationship she cannot give up, but told with an intensity that makes it new. Elena was tormented both by Nino's infidelity and by what she saw as her own hypocrisy in tolerating it. She wondered if she was lying to herself and to her readers when she portrayed herself as an independent woman, free and self-sufficient, when in reality her emotional life and her desires were no different from those of more traditional women.

When Nino told Elena that his wife Eleonora was seven months pregnant and that he could not leave her, Elena decided that even this evidence of continued connection with Eleonora was not enough to end her increasingly conflict ridden relationship with Nino. Elena, from time to time, reminds us that we are reading the recollections of a woman in her mid-sixties, struggling to understand her younger self. She now thinks her reaction to the news of Eleonora's pregnancy was excessive; however, at the time she saw the pregnancy as the most unbearable wrong Nino could do to her. She told Nino that she had to get accustomed to doing without him, but that for now it wasn't possible. She needed time. However, despite her realization that she would have to eventually sever ties to Nino, Elena had a child with him, thus tightening the bond between her and Nino. Again she finds herself acting like many traditional women, getting pregnant in the hope that having a child will strengthen a relationship in danger of falling apart.

7. Love, Sex, Betrayal

But the long, slow process of separating from Nino had begun—one of the most powerful descriptions of falling out of love I have ever read. In various ways Elena began to see him more clearly. Nino is a type recognizable to many women; intellectually he is a feminist, but in his personal behavior he is anything but. Elena exposes Nino as a hypocrite in front of a group of friends, telling them that in the early stages of their relationship he helped with the housework, clearing the table and washing the dishes, but that now he doesn't even pick up the clothes he drops carelessly on the floor. Elena accused him of wanting to "liberate the women of others but not his" (SLC, 233). Nino replied, that her liberation should not automatically mean the loss of his freedom. Elena wondered why such behavior had made her so angry with Pietro, but she was generally willing to tolerate it with Nino. She also noted that other men were beginning to change, including Lila's partner Enzo and Roberto, the husband of her childhood friend Carmen, whereas Nino, despite all his reading in feminist theory, was stuck in the patriarchal past.

The breaking point came when Elena discovered Nino having sexual intercourse with her housekeeper Silvana, described as an enormous woman of around fifty. Elena was stunned that Nino would be having sex with a heavy-set woman, worn-out by the struggle to survive, the polar opposite of the cultured, well-dressed women he brought to dinner at her apartment. In a state of rage and grief, Elena wrote that she hated Nino more than she had ever hated anyone. She turned to Lila, who is horrified that even after this, Elena was not yet ready to leave Nino and was searching for an excuse to forgive him. In order to convince Elena that she must leave him, Lila finally told Elena that Nino had repeatedly asked her to come back to him, both before his relationship with Elena and after. Lila also sent Elena's old boyfriend Antonio to tell Elena the results of his detective work. In the manner of someone accustomed to giving detailed reports, Antonio read a list Nino's many lovers. Some were women he had brought to Elena's house, including the gynecologist who had delivered her daughter Imma. Ferrante may have had had the famous catalogue aria from Mozart's *Don Giovanni* in mind with Antonio as Leporello and Elena as Donna Elvira, gradually taking in the horror of this 20th-century Don Juan. (Nino's given name is Giovanni Sarratore.)

> My dear lady, this is a list
> of the beauties my master has loved...
> In Italy, six hundred and forty;

> in Germany, two hundred and thirty-one;
> a hundred in France; in Turkey ninety-one.
> In Spain already one thousand and three.
> Among these are peasant girls,
> maidservants, city girls,
> countesses, baronesses ... women of every rank,
> every shape, every age...
> In winter he likes fat ones,
> in summer he likes thin ones.
> He calls the tall ones majestic.
> The little ones are always charming.
> He seduces the old ones
> for the pleasure of adding to the list...
> It doesn't matter if she's rich,
> ugly or beautiful;
> If she wears a petticoat,
> you know what he does.[5]

Elena did not doubt the truth of what Lila and Antonio told her, but nonetheless she found it hard to separate from Nino. She recalled that it took months and that it tormented her both to see him and to refuse to see him.

At first Nino denied everything, even telling her that what she had seen with Silvana was simply a misperception, the result of fatigue and jealousy. When that didn't work, he embarked on a lengthy erudite monologue, which he hoped would convince Elena that his infidelity wasn't his fault, but rather something over which he had no control. The dissolution of their relationship was ugly. Elena told Nino that she had had sexual relationships with other men and to hurt him said they had been far better lovers. Elena realized that what upset Nino was not that he had lost her love, but that she had other lovers. One morning he burst into her apartment demanding that she denigrate her recent lovers and profess that her "only desire was to be penetrated by him. He wanted, in other words, to reassert his primacy." In a scene reminiscent of Olga's realization in *The Days of Abandonment* that she no longer loves her unfaithful husband, Elena realized that she no longer had any feelings for Nino: "The long time that I loved him dissolved conclusively that morning" (SLC, 257–58).

After Nino, Elena does not marry or establish a meaningful relationship with a man. She allowed herself to be courted and entered into several relationships, but none lasted. She suspected that some of the men wanted her because of her success as a writer. They wanted to give her their manuscripts to read or in some cases to borrow money, which they failed to repay. As she grew older, she found that men no longer noticed her; the important relationships in her life were with Lila and with her daughters and grandchildren. The enormous changes in gender roles that occurred in the 1960s and 1970s allowed Elena to build a career and divorce her husband, have an affair with a married man and a child outside of wedlock without experiencing the social ostracism that would have been the fate of previous generations of women; but those changes also led to a world in which relationships are less stable and much easier to dissolve.

The retreat from marriage and life-long, intimate partnerships is a trend observed throughout the developed world. Rebecca Traister in *All the Single Ladies: Unmarried Women and the Rise of an Independent Nation* traces the phenomenon in the United States and also includes comparative statistics from Europe and Japan. Traister notes that in Italy the number of marriages per 1,000 inhabitants fell from 7.7 in 1960 to just over 3 in 2013.[6] The rate of decline varies from country to country but in every case the direction is downward. Elena's life exemplifies the trajectory of many women's lives in the 21st century—education as the path to upward mobility and financial independence, with the single life as an alternative to unfulfilling or abusive relationships. At the conclusion of the Neapolitan novels, Elena has more or less made her peace with this new state of affairs.

8

The Neapolitan Novels: Violence and Masculinity

> *"We had grown up thinking that a stranger must not even touch us, but that our father, our boyfriend, and our husband could hit us when they liked, out of love, to educate us, to reeducate us."*—Elena Ferrante, *The Story of a New Name*

In the opening pages of the first section of *My Brilliant Friend* Elena describes the world in which she and Lila grew up, stating that she had "no nostalgia for our childhood: it was full of violence" (BF, 37). The catalogue of catastrophes she lists includes many incidents that recall the extent to which Naples was a casualty of World War II. Entire families died in the bombardment, desperately clinging to each other, crying out in terror; some had died inhaling gas; others died of typhus; children died because they stumbled across bombs that had not been exploded. Then there is the internecine violence—fathers beating children, husbands beating wives, gangs of young men endlessly fighting. When at the age of thirty-eight, Elena decided to move back to the neighborhood where she grew up, she found that violence was still all-pervasive: She could hear the cries of men, women, children in the apartments, especially at night—"the feuds between families, the hostilities between neighbors, the ease with which things came to blows, the wars between gangs of boys" (SLC, 261).

The pattern of violence traced in the Neapolitan novels is very much gender-based violence, with the frequency of such incidents normalizing violence against women. Elena and the other young women of the neighborhood had seen their fathers beat their mothers ever since they were children: "We had grown up thinking that a stranger must not even touch us, but that our father, our boyfriend, and our husband could hit us when they liked, out of love, to educate us, to reeducate us" (SNN, 52). The community's acceptance of such violence is deeply disturbing; when Lila's father threw her out the window, seriously injuring her, no one in the neighborhood reacted. Especially unnerving, is female tolerance of male violence. In an interview with the *Sydney Morning Herald* Ferrante noted that women have experienced a millennia of mistreatment by men: "Sometimes fear, sometimes even love, makes us think of it as an inevitable part of relationships, something that is accepted, taking into account that on the whole things work and that, if he were to leave, things could get even worse."[1] The women of the neighborhood accepted abuse as an unavoidable fact of life. When Lila's husband, Stefano, tried to beat her into submission, most of the women thought she deserved the beatings. There was no outrage, and sympathy for Stefano actually increased; he was seen as "someone who knew how to be a man" (SNN, 45).

Ferrante in an interview with the *Financial Times* claimed that this brutal world was her background and that she grew up in a world where it was normal for men to beat their wives, their daughters, sisters, and girlfriends and to assume they had the unquestioned right to hit them in order to "correct" them, to teach them how a woman should behave, all ostensibly for their own good. Ferrante notes, "Luckily today much has changed but I still think the men who can really be trusted are a minority. Maybe this is because the milieu that shaped me was backward. Or maybe … it's because male power, whether violently or delicately imposed, is still bent on subordinating us … in the real world, too many are punished, even with death, for their insubordination."[2] We now know that Ferrante is not the voice of a woman who grew up in an impoverished working class neighborhood in Naples but rather the fictional creation of the author (or authors). Is this something experienced by Anita Raja, despite her middle class background? Or does the depiction of male violence against women draw on the background of Domenico Starnone, who has described his father as a violent, abusive man? I have tried to avoid reading the Neapolitan novels this way, but find it difficult to resist speculation about the possible connection between the author(s)' biography and the powerful depiction of Neapolitan working class life.

Although the Neapolitan Quartet is primarily a tale of male violence against women, the women of the neighborhood (including Lila) are also capable of violence. Elena thinks that in some ways the women were more prone to violence, fighting among themselves more frequently than the men. Also, although the men were quicker to anger, their rage and violent behavior usually subsided, whereas when the women usually, silent and submissive, did become angry, they "flew into a rage that had no end" (BF, 38). When Marcello Solara, the Camorrist Lila loathed, grabbed Elena by the wrist, Lila whipped out a knife and put it against his throat, threatening to kill him if he touched Elena again. Elena was absolutely certain that Lila was capable of slitting Marcello's throat. The most horrific example of female violence occurs in *The Days of Abandonment*, when Olga, the betrayed wife, violently attacked her husband, knocking him down in the street, tearing his shirt, and threatening to tear his lover's earrings from her earlobes.

The culture of violence is a trap for both men and women, a culture both have accepted—part of the air they breathe. Ferrante's sympathies extend to the young men who are trapped in the sexist script written for them from time immemorial. Before their marriage, Stefano had promised Lila that his values were different from those of the neighborhood and that he wanted to break the cycle of violence and revenge. He had demonstrated his willingness to change when he decided to make peace with the wife and children of Alfredo Peluso, the man accused of murdering his father, by inviting them to his New Year's party, thus demonstrating to the entire neighborhood that he was not his father, Don Achille Caracci and that Guiseppina Peluso and her children were not Alfredo Peluso. A consensus emerged in the neighborhood that life was difficult enough and reducing tensions would be in everyone's interest, so on New Year's Eve the old enemies gathered at the house of the Caracci family to celebrate the New Year together, with Stefano being especially kind to Signora Peluso, first filling his mother's glass with spumante and then the glass of Signora Peluso.

When Lila asked him if he was really different, Stefano replied, that was his intention, but well aware of the difficulty of breaking with the mores of the neighborhood, he admitted that he didn't know if he could keep his promise. When Marcello Solara, furious that Lila had chosen Stefano over him, spread obscene rumors about Lila, Stefano and Lila decided to reject revenge and rise above the values of the neighborhood; they would act as if the Solaras did not exist. Stefano did not defend the honor of his fiancée, Lila ignored the slander, and the Solaras continued to spread lies. Elena did not understand what was happening. She found the Solaras' behavior more comprehensible, more consistent with the world in which they had grown up than Stefano and Lila's refusal to seek revenge.

Although Stefano was able to rise above the revenge culture of the neighborhood, he was unable to transcend the deeply sexist mores of his world. When Lila refused to have sexual relations with him on their wedding night, Stefano resorted to violence. Ferrante suggests that after a marriage occurs, the pressure to conform to traditional gender roles becomes overwhelming. Stefano appeared to be assimilating "an order that was coming to him from very far away, perhaps even before he was born. The order was: be a man, Ste'; either you'll subdue her now or you'll never subdue her" (SNN, 41). Everything in his culture reinforced the idea that a wife had to accept that she has a duty to obey her husband. Elena recalled her conversation with Stefano, who was both driven by and disturbed by the role he had been conditioned to play. He resorted to the familiar defense of the male perpetrator ringing across cultures—"She made me do it," telling Elena he had no choice but to beat Lila on their wedding night, that every day she provoked him on purpose to humiliate him, forcing him again and again to beat her and to act in a way that he never wanted, and that made him deeply ashamed.

While some men in the neighborhood were beginning to reject traditional gender roles, Stefano as he grew older, found himself increasingly trapped in the traditional male role. Although his marriage to Lila had fallen apart and he was involved with his childhood friend Ada, a sick form of jealousy took possession of him. Acting more like a jealous husband than ever, Stefano kept his estranged wife a prisoner in the house, forcing her to do all her shopping by telephone, watching her every move, as if he thought his affair with Ada had given Lila permission to be unfaithful. He was obsessed with the fear of becoming a laughing stock by any infidelity on Lila's part. In contrast, Pasquale was beginning to move beyond the traditional male code of honor that demanded that a man betrayed by his wife or lover avenge the insult. When Pasquale, who was engaged to Ada, learned of her affair with Stefano, his first impulse would have been to murder them both, but he was restrained by his role in the Communist Party. Thanks to his education as a Communist, he made an effort to see men and women as equals. "Caught therefore between rage and broad-mindedness," Pasquale confronted Ada, but instead of harming her, confined himself to punching holes in the wall (SNN, 394).

Although some men were beginning to change, male violence was woven into the fabric of Elena's and Lila's lives, as was the omnipresent sexual harassment they endured on the streets of Naples. Elena and the other girls from the neighborhood simply accepted this abuse as their lot in life—except for Lila. Elena noticed that on the streets of Naples the men harassed all the girls, whether they were attractive, not so attractive, or ugly. She and the other girls had learned to pretend not to hear the obscenities hurled at them, to instinctively lower their eyes, and keep walking. Everyone behaved this way except for Lila. If someone stared at her, she stared back. If a man said something to her, she stopped walking and stared threateningly at him as if she couldn't believe he was talking to her. Elena found going out with Lila to be a nerve-wracking experience and she made no attempt to follow Lila's example. It was not until Elena had published a successful, critically acclaimed novel that she finally gained the self-confidence to resist. Now when men harassed her on the streets or groped her on public transport, Elena no longer pretended not to notice—the usual survival strategy most women employed and which she had relied on all her life. Now whenever on a crowded bus or train, she felt men's hands on her body, she gave herself "the sacrosanct right to fury and reacted with cries of contempt" (SNN, 456).

As Elena moved into an upper middle class world, she learned that sexual harassment was not confined to the uneducated men and boys of the neighborhood. Her publisher had arranged for Elena to be accompanied to a book signing by an elderly professor, Tarratano. After dinner at the hotel restaurant, when they were in the hotel elevator, to Elena's surprise and disgust Tarratano tried to kiss her. She managed to extricate herself from his embrace, but he wouldn't give up. At that stage in her life, it would not have occurred to her that a respectable elderly man would behave in such a way. The next day Elena felt "the stain of the physical contact" as well as a disturbing continuity with the kind of vulgar behavior she associated with the neighborhood (TWL, 67).

For women from the neighborhood, low socio-economic status often led to acceptance of abuse. For men with few economic resources, the feelings of powerlessness resulting from poverty were more likely to lead to violence. For women, poverty may have severely limited their options but did not diminish their sense of themselves as women; for men, poverty threatened their very identity as men. Lila's brother Rino was humiliated by his lack of money and desperate to become economically successful. Consumed by envy of the Solaras, lords of the neighborhood who disre-

8. Violence and Masculinity

spected him, Rino became obsessed with the idea of becoming rich by opening a factory to make the shoes that Lila had designed. When his father rejected the idea, Rino went on a rampage, frightening his mother, other family members and the neighbors. He overturned furniture, broke plates, and swore he would kill himself rather than work (in his father's shoe shop) for a pittance. Rino's response to dashed dreams of upward mobility and to class-based insult was to resort to physical violence.

Ferrante portrays male violence as endemic to the neighborhood, but also something that well-educated, privileged men like Elena's husband Pietro are capable of. The difference is their shame when they succumb to the temptation of physical abuse. During an argument in which Elena taunted her husband, telling him that everything he has he owes to his parents, he slapped her. According to Elena, who had endured many blows in the course of her life, she took it far better than Pietro did. She was certain that Pietro had never done this before; family violence was not part of his world.

Elena feared that the cycle of male violence would continue to be passed down from one generation to the next. Her fears were confirmed when she overheard her daughter Dede and a little boy Mirko pretending to be a mother and father having a fight, with Dede telling Mirko that he had to hit her. Yet there were signs that the old pattern the children were mimicking might be starting to break down. Although men across the socio-economic spectrum were capable of violence against women, Ferrante presents two characters who are not—Nino and Alfonso. Nino, despite the havoc he creates with sexual infidelity, does not exhibit a trace of that disposition to violence that characterizes most of the male characters. He represents another model of masculinity—not violent and not bound by the honor code that demands that male relatives avenge the smallest slight to their female relatives' "honor."

Both men and women experienced the burden of the honor code. When the Solara brothers invited Elena for a ride in their car she refused because she knew that if her father had found out, he would have beaten her to death and that her little brothers would feel obligated now and in the future to murder the Solara brothers. When the Solaras dragged Ada into their car, her brother Antonio felt honor-bound to confront the Solaras despite knowing the inevitable consequence would be a savage beating. Nino, on the other hand, did not feel any such need to defend the honor of his female relatives. When Elena, Nino, and his sister Marisa went out for a walk in Ischia, Elena was astonished that when the young and not so young men looked at her and Marisa with a leering glance, Nino showed no trace of that inclination to violence that Pasquale, Rino, Antonio, and Enzo displayed when someone looked at Elena and her friends with sexual intent. As Elena remarked ironically, as an "intimidating guardian of our bodies, [Nino] had little value" (BF, 218). Nino had respect for women's intelligence and was not particularly macho except in one key respect—his sense of sexual entitlement, his inability to be faithful to any of his many sexual partners.

Alfonso, the close childhood friend of both Elena and Lila, quietly challenged gender norms—not because he chose to be a rebel, but because of his sexual identity. From an early age both Alfonso and his family sensed that he was different. Ferrante provides the clues for the reader starting with the loss of Elena and Lila's dolls. When they accused Alfonso's father Don Achille of having stolen their dolls, Don Achille asked his children if they had taken the dolls. His daughter replied no; we are told Alfonso's response was (probably nervous) laughter. Elena felt that Don Achille "was unexpectedly pained, as if he were receiving confirmation of something he already knew" (BF, 67).

As an adolescent, Alfonso quietly distanced himself from traditional male behavior. Ferrante described a New Year's Eve party in which the young men of the neighborhood engaged in a dangerous war of setting off firecrackers. While the other young men became increasingly energized by the frenzy, Alfonso withdrew from the group. When one of the older women of the neighborhood was terrified by the exploding firecrackers, Alfonso seized the opportunity and offered to take her home, escaping from the increasingly dangerous scene. Elena found Alfonso reassuring, the kind of young man, unusual in the neighborhood from whom "you needn't expect any cruelty," and she became very close to him during their high school years (BF, 254). When Elena asked him if he would ever beat his future wife as his brother Stefano had done to Lila, Alfonso assured her that he would not, because he knew her, because they had long conversations and went to school together. Elena was moved by Alfonso's acknowledgment of her influence on him and thankful to him for that tangled message.

Both Elena and Lila noticed dramatic changes in Alfonso on the day of the opening of the new shoe store, a partnership between his brother Stefano and the Solara brothers, located in a fashionable part of town.

8. Violence and Masculinity

Elena noted Alfonso's cheerfulness and elegance; something once silent in Alfonso appeared to have awakened. Lila too was surprised and perplexed by the transformation; when Elena asked her what had happened to Alfonso, all Lila could say was that she didn't know. Elena thought Alfonso seemed so much more at home in this affluent part of the city, and that "he concealed inside himself another person" that was beginning to emerge (SNN, 127). When years later Alfonso realized that Elena didn't know the truth about his sexuality, he asked her in bewilderment if Lila had never said anything to her. Alfonso had turned to Lila when he needed to unburden himself and tell someone his secret. He now realized that she had kept his secret—that if she had never told Elena, she hadn't told anyone. Elena's reaction was dismay that Alfonso had confided in Lila not to her, his long time friend. Elena was still haunted by the possibility that teachers, friends, lovers—everyone preferred Lila to her. Alfonso then told Elena that he was sure she knew; however, Elena's self-absorption was such it had never occurred to her.

Alfonso's relationship with Lila deepened and he became a trusted employee at the computer company she founded. He gradually became open about his sexuality. When Lila and Elena went shopping for maternity clothes Alfonso took them to a dress shop run by his friend. Lila picked out a dress and then, and as if there were no mirror in the shop, asked her former brother-in-law to show her how the dress looked on her. Alfonso disappeared into a dressing room and when he emerged, Elena was stunned; Alfonso was a replica of Lila. Elena thought perhaps at that moment he was more beautiful than Lila, both male and female, the type she had written about in her last book. Alfonso described himself as something other, something that has no name, something that is "hidden in the veins ... and waits" (SLC 211).

Alfonso had become sexually involved with Michele Solara, who after years of obsessively pursuing Lila was now, as Lila characterized it, running after the shadow of her shadow. Both Elena and Lila viewed Michele as a despicable character with no redeeming qualities. However, Alfonso suggested Michele had another dimension, telling Elena that she and Lila were wrong about Michele and didn't know what he was really like. Despite her dislike for Michele, Elena acknowledged that unlike the fickle Nino, Michele "was capable of an absolute passion," his unrequited love for Lila (TWL, 213). When Elena encountered Michele and Alfonso, she found that they were uncomfortable in her presence. She was annoyed that they were hiding their relationship from her, as if she couldn't understand, she, who had traveled in circles far more advanced that those of the neighborhood, who had written a widely-praised book on the fluidity of sexual identities. Elena was familiar with the academic literature on the instability of gender and saw herself as an expert on sexual identity, although ironically it took her a long while to recognize the truth about her old friend Alfonso. Her ability to theorize exceeded her ability to see what was before her eyes.

Elena's old bond with Alfonso had endured. She had not understood how his difference from other boys was rooted in his sexuality, but she was fond of him because of this difference, especially because of his alienation from the typical male behavior of the neighborhood. Despite his rejection of traditional gender roles, Alfonso was drawn towards Michele whose cruel, aggressive masculinity represented the worst of the neighborhood, but whose involvement with Alfonso broke with traditional masculine values. Something goes terribly wrong with Alfonso. His tragic end is told solely from Elena's perspective and the reader is left to fill in the gaps. Alfonso had become indispensable to the operation of Lila's business, but was becoming unreliable. He missed appointments and when he did show up was heavily made up and frequently showed signs of beatings. There is the suggestion of drug addiction, at that time rampant in the neighborhood, leaving him vulnerable to attacks. He was beaten to death, and his body thrown into the sea. The person most affected by his death was Lila; Elena witnessed Lila collapsing on the floor, overcome with grief. From that moment Elena thought that Lila had loved Alfonso more than she had, had helped him more than anyone else, had understood him and helped him to understand himself.

Alfonso's mother and siblings did not come to his funeral—indicating the depth of homophobia in the society. Michele and Marcello Solara were among the few mourners at the sparsely attended funeral with Michele clearly deeply disturbed, continually looking around with the "eyes of a madman" and Marcello, not so obviously upset as his brother but appearing remorseful (SLC, 306). Lila accosted Michele, demanding to know why he had come and if he felt any remorse. Because the Solaras were responsible for bringing drugs into the neighborhood, Lila saw them as implicated in Alfonso's tragic end. The cycle of violence would continue with the Solaras themselves gunned down in broad daylight very soon afterwards.

8. Violence and Masculinity

Male violence is all-pervasive in the Neapolitan novels and is a recurrent theme throughout Ferrante's work, even in the *Beach at Night*, Ferrante's children's book, thought by some reviewers to be too frightening for children. *The Beach at Night* is narrated by Celina, a doll who has been abandoned by Mati, the little girl who owns her, and left to spend the night on the beach. Celina endured a night of horrors including an attack by a vicious beach attendant, carrying a large rake with which he threatened to open up her chest. The evil beach attendant sang to the terrified Celina, "Your heart I'll shred/Until it's dead."[3] I realize that Grimm's fairy tales are filled with similar horrors, but I would think twice before giving *The Beach at Night* to a young child.

Yet along with male violence recurring throughout Ferrante's work, including even her children's book, there is nonetheless a sense of changing conceptions of masculinity, with different models of manhood emerging. Some men share domestic responsibilities; to Elena's surprise, Roberto, the husband of her old friend Carmen, set the table and cleared and washed the dishes. Until that moment Elena had never seen a couple of her generation share everyday chores so easily so well, so obviously happy to be together. Lila's partner Enzo also represents a new model of masculinity helping with household chores and caring for Lila's son Gennaro. He and Lila have forged an equal partnership and Elena is struck by the contrast between Enzo's appreciation of Lila's intellect and Pietro's disparagement of her own abilities.

However, we see Pietro grow in sensitivity and awareness over the course of the Neapolitan Quartet. Despite his left wing politics, Pietro's expectations of marriage were very traditional and he didn't appreciate the extent to which marriage had become a cage for Elena. Although an atheist who refused to get married in a church, Pietro was nonetheless at least in one way culturally Catholic—in his opposition to contraception and divorce. Although Elena grew increasingly antagonistic towards and contemptuous of her husband, Ferrante allows us to see him from the perspective of other characters, who appreciate his basic decency. Elena's mother told her daughter that she was fortunate to be with Pietro and that she did not deserve him. When Elena told Lila she was leaving Pietro for Nino, Lila told her that she was crazy to leave him, that Pietro was an "extraordinary man, good, extremely intelligent"; she cautioned Elena to think of the harm she was inflicting on her daughters (TWL, 416).

Many years after their divorce, Elena began to appreciate the good side of Pietro, who had learned from the mistakes he made during their marriage. Elena needed help when she was a single mother with three children and Pietro provided it. As a husband Pietro had hardly ever exerted himself to make things easier for his wife, but now that he and Elena were separated, he didn't want to leave her alone with three children, one of whom was a newborn child. After Elena gave birth to the child she had with Nino, Pietro offered to stay for a few days, but Elena could not accept his help as Nino harassed her, demanding that Pietro leave. When Pietro left, Nino, true to form, was too busy with his own job to offer Elena any help. As the years wore on, the pattern intensified—Pietro becoming more responsible, Nino descending deeper into selfishness. Elena observed that since Pietro no longer had to be a father every day, he had become a very good father. She thinks that perhaps with men, "things can't go otherwise: live with them for a while, have children and then they're gone" (SLC, 393).

Although many readers have seen the Neapolitan Quartet as a "searing portrait of male cruelty,"[4] in reality Ferrante's portrayal of gender roles is far more nuanced, with some of her male characters taking tentative steps towards gender equality. In many ways, some significant such as his support for his ex-wife Elena who was struggling to care for three young children, and some relatively minor such as his break from gender norms by marrying a woman six years older, Pietro subverts traditional expectations of male behavior. In late middle age, Elena also departs from norms governing respective ages of heterosexual couples by becoming involved with a man eight years younger than she. In ways large and small, both men and women are beginning to depart from traditional expectations.

One area in which gender patterns persist is in female vs. male friendships. In addition to her powerful exploration of the complexities of female friendship, Ferrante also includes a tale of male friendship—albeit a minor thematic strand and one to my knowledge not noted in any of the many book reviews and essays on Ferrante's work. Like Lila and Elena, Pasquale and Enzo maintain a relationship over a lifetime, although their friendship is considerably much less fraught with tension than is Lila's and Elena's. They bond over shared values—their commitment to social justice and loyalty to family, friends and neighborhood. Loyalty is paramount. When Pasquale and Antonio were enraged by the arrogance of the Solara brothers and wanted to confront them, Enzo tried to convince them to avoid a fight. When they refused, Enzo replied that if they stayed, he would stay as well. The unquestioned loyalty extended throughout Enzo and Pasquale's long friendship.

Pasquale and Enzo also shared a deep love for Lila. When Pasquale made an impassioned declaration of love for Lila and asked her to become his fiancé, she replied that she loved him, but not as a fiancé, and further that she would never become anyone's girlfriend. Although Pasquale accepted her answer and did not continue to pursue her, his feelings for her remained. Enzo had, in some ways, a similar relationship with Lila; when he rescued her after she was abandoned by Nino, he accepted that at that point in their relationship she did not want a sexual relationship with him. He stayed with her on her terms, supporting her emotionally and financially and helping to care for her son Gennaro. Enzo did not question Lila's decisions and was always ready to defend her. Although Pasquale also supported Lila, he did at times raise questions about her choices, at one time implying that Lila's fiancé Stefano had bought her with the money his father had made in the black market. Enzo challenged Pasquale about what he meant by "bought" and the two were about to come to blows when their friends intervened and separated them. They got over their anger in a few days; there was no lingering ill-will and simmering tensions, unlike the friendship between Lila and Elena, with its resentments, often not directly expressed but remaining below the surface, emerging sometimes when least expected, never truly resolved.

After Enzo rescued Lila from the horror of her marriage to Stefano, everyone from the neighborhood, including Lila's family, ostracized Lila and Enzo. Pasquale alone continued to see them, bonding once again with Enzo over their shared political passion, with Pasquale drawing both Enzo land Lila further into his political crusades. At one point, to protect Enzo, Lila asked Pasquale not to tell Enzo about her struggles with sexual harassment at the factory where she worked, but Pasquale could not withhold the information from Enzo. Elena reflected that "friendship between men had its own inviolable pacts, not like that between women" (TWL, 160). Over the course of their friendship, Elena and Lila withheld a good deal from each other; Enzo and Pasquale did not.

As Pasquale became more deeply involved with the radical left, Enzo became more focused on building a career and providing economic support for himself and for Lila. But the close connection between the two men persisted. When Pasquale joined the armed struggle, Enzo did not abandon him, despite disagreeing with his choice. There are frequent references to Enzo visiting relatives in Avellino; when the police finally captured Pasquale, he was found in Avellino, in a farmhouse rented by Enzo's relatives. Ferrante creates the impression that Enzo had been helping Pasquale evade capture, although there's no indication that Elena has made that connection. Elena noted that despite the different roads they chose, she thought both Enzo and Pasquale continued to think in the political categories of their youth, concepts they had learned in the 1960s and 1970s. Their political commitment continued to be the basis of their friendship, as did loyalty to the family, the neighborhood and their shared love for Lila.

Just as we don't know for certain if Lila's gesture with the lost dolls is the final act in the long saga of Lila and Elena's friendship, Ferrante does not tell us whether or not Enzo and Pasquale maintain contact while Pasquale is serving a term of life in prison. Both friendships have lasted a very long time from childhood to old age, although the basis for the friendships are in many ways very different, shaped by different rules and expectations. Ferrante portrays a world in which men also develop deep emotional bonds, a world in which gender roles are changing, with at least some of her male characters a part of that change.

9

The Neapolitan Novels: The Climb Up the Class Ladder

"Class origins cannot be erased, regardless of whether we climb up or down the sociocultural ladder."—Elena Ferrante, *Frantumaglia: A Writer's Journey*

Upward mobility is very much part of the story of post–World War II Italy, with the boom years of the 1960's bringing increased prosperity and educational opportunities. Elena and Lila's story is bound up with these larger social forces; however, upward mobility in Europe and North America has not been not as great as is generally thought. Thomas Piketty's ground-breaking study, *Capital in the Twenty First Century*, demonstrated that those who moved up the class ladder usually moved up merely a notch and that such movement tended to occur when socio-economic forces enabled large groups of people to advance.[1] For example, in the United States the post-war boom coupled with social measures such as the GI Bill enabled returning veterans to acquire a college education, thus allowing many working class people to enter the middle class.

Although in post–World War II Italy access to higher education had become increasingly available, many university graduates did not find the careers they had hoped for. In an interview in *The New Yorker*, Ferrante has described the dashed hopes of those for whom education did not provide a path to upward mobility: "In post–Second World War Italy, education cemented old hierarchies, but it also allowed for a modest assimilation of the deserving, so that to some extent those who remained at the bottom could say to themselves, 'I ended up here because I didn't want to study' ... [but] some characters study and still they stumble."[2] Ferrante sees the unemployed graduates as dramatic evidence that educational opportunity cannot be used to legitimize social hierarchy; education does not inevitably lead to upward mobility.

Elena Greco was among those included in that "modest assimilation of the deserving" and Ferrante has written the best account I have ever read of the struggle to climb the class ladder—in Elena's case, making several leaps from deep poverty to the intellectual elite of Italian society. Elena's rise was a steep climb and she moved into the world that she and Lila had dreamed of when, in their childhood, they fantasized about writing a book together. Their lives diverged when Elena was allowed to continue her education and Lila was denied that opportunity and forced to leave school after the fifth grade. The education that for middle class girls of their generation would have been a birthright was available only to those working class girls fortunate enough to have some combination of talent, luck, and sheer grit. In 1962, the Italian government instituted compulsory education up to the age of fourteen, about seven years too late for Lila.[3]

Many of Ferrante's American readers such as Roxana Robinson have tended to de-emphasize the class dimension of the Neapolitan novels. From a report of a session on Ferrante's work at PEN World Voices Festival: "The Ferrante novels are ultimately about 'what happens to women' and the ways that they are trapped by their gender, Robinson said. Brilliance, she argued, could not be enough when Lila was prevented by her father from continuing her education and married at 16. 'Her choices are really taken away from her by the presence of her body—her female body—and that is what is the cage,' she says."[4] However, in the Neapolitan novels, the class and gender themes are tightly interwoven, and Lila is trapped as much by class as by gender.

Although we see the diverging paths of Elena and Lila primarily from Elena's perspective, through the inclusion of Lila's notebooks and through Elena's recollections of Lila's words, Ferrante provides a powerful account of Lila's experience of the injuries of class. Lila's despair at not being able to continue her education is heartbreaking; she took Latin books out of the library and continued to study on her own, enabling her to tutor Elena who was struggling with Latin grammar and syntax. For Elena, education was mostly a means to an end; she rarely appeared to take joy in learning. Lila, on the other hand, had a passion for learning in itself; being deprived of the opportunity to continue her education was devastating. Both class

9. The Climb Up the Class Ladder

and gender combined to limit Lila's future possibilities. Lila's father could not entertain the idea that his daughter should continue her education; it was just not part of his view of the world, and furthermore, he did not see it as economically possible.

However, Elena's father could consider the possibility of his daughter continuing her education in part because his family was not as economically burdened as Lila's, whose large extended family was supported by her father's work as a shoe repairman. Ferrante signals this difference in the economic status of the two families in the description of the girls' dolls in opening pages of *My Brilliant Friend*. Elena recalled that her doll was beautiful and newer than Lila's doll; hers had a plastic face and plastic hair and eyes and wore a blue dress that her mother "had made for her in a rare moment of happiness" (BF, 30). She recalled that Lila's doll was dirty and ugly and had an old-fashioned cloth body filled with sawdust. The difference in resources between the two families was not great, but apparently just enough to foreclose the option of further schooling for Lila.

Elena, as she advanced from elementary to middle school to high school, saw her future prospects expanding. When her father took her on a tour of Naples to introduce her to the route she would take to high school, she experienced a sense of possibility beyond the neighborhood. Her father took her to the sea holding tightly to her hand as if fearing she would slip away. Elena did in fact wish to leave him, "pretending I was alone in the newness of the city, new myself with all life ahead" (BF, 138). Elena realized that her dream of escaping the neighborhood meant distancing herself from old friends. One of the first indications that Elena would do whatever was necessary to get ahead occurred when her former elementary school teacher Maestra Oliviero saw her chatting with Pasquale Peluso, and warned her not to waste time with him. Maestra Oliviero noted that Pasquale was a construction worker, unlikely to ever go farther than that, and that his father was a communist. Elena indicated her assent and quickly left without saying good-bye to Pasquale.

Although Maestra Oliviero encouraged Elena academically and imagined a future for her that Elena's own mother could not see, the teacher also communicated her class snobbery, both to Elena and Elena's parents. Maestra Oliviero reported to Elena's father that she had seen Elena alone with Pasquale Peluso, a young man completely unsuitable for a girl with Elena's potential and aspirations. Her father readily agreed with the teacher, telling Elena never to speak to Pasquale again. When out of Maestra Oliviero's sight, Elena continued a friendly relationship with Pasquale, while believing it would soon come to an inevitable end. Despite having a good deal of affection for her old friends, Elena was focused on moving into another world and at that point in her life was willing to leave them far behind.

At Lila's wedding, Elena became acutely aware of her sense of alienation from the boys of the neighborhood. She had grown up with them, was accustomed to their violent behavior and rough language, but as she advanced from middle school to high school, she had been following every day a path completely unknown to them. Elena's mother, who had assimilated Maestra Oliviero's message, agreed that Elena should keep her distance from these young men. At Lila's wedding reception, Elena's mother insisted that she stay away from Antonio, a neighborhood boy who had fallen in love with her, telling her daughter that her parents were not paying for her education in order to have her fall in love with a mere auto mechanic.

The wedding reception filled Elena with horror. She recalled when Maestra Oliviero asked her if she knew what "the plebs" were and she now understood what she hadn't fully grasped years ago: "The plebs were us. The plebs were that fight for food and wine, that quarrel over who should be served first and better, that dirty floor on which the waiters clattered back and forth, those increasingly vulgar toasts. The plebs were my mother, who had drunk wine and now was leaning against my father's shoulder, while he, serious, laughed, his mouth gaping, at the sexual allusions of the metal dealer" (BF, 329). Elena had internalized much of Maestra Oliviero's class prejudice and now saw her family and friends through Maestra Oliviero's eyes, even at one point referring disparagingly to Nino as merely the son of a railway worker.

When Maestra Oliviero went to see Elena's mother to tell her that she had arranged a vacation in Ischia for Elena, who was worn-out from studying, Elena observed that her teacher spoke to her as if she were her mother and as if her real mother were "only a disposable living being … not to be taken into consideration" (BF, 208). Elena had absorbed Maestra Oliviero's values on a deeper level, valuing above all the pursuit of individual advancement over solidarity. Angry with Lila's family for refusing to let Lila continue her education, Maestra Oliviero told Elena she should forget Lila and think only of herself. For the most part Elena did just that,

9. The Climb Up the Class Ladder

but her feelings for Lila and her old ties to family, the neighborhood and the powerful pull of the ethic of solidarity were never entirely erased.

The classism that characterized a teenage Elena's reaction to Lila's wedding is evident decades later in Elena's reaction to her sister Elisa's wedding to the Camorrist she loathed, Marcello Solara. Thanks to Elisa, Elena could now count the Solaras among her in-laws. Elena noted that she was struck by how the very provincial "vulgarity" in evidence at Lila's wedding had been "modernized," and had become a "metropolitan vulgarity," reflecting the wealth and increasing influence of the Solaras in Naples. Lila herself was a part of it, in her habits and in her clothing. Elena noted that at Elisa's wedding nothing clashed, except for her and her daughters who with their "sobriety were completely out of place in that triumph of excessive colors, excessive laughter, excessive luxuries" (SLC, 275). Elena had clearly on one level assimilated the values of her northern Italian mother-in-law; class status was a matter of taste and education as much as it was of wealth.

Ferrante traces both Elena's growing determination to climb the class ladder and her awareness that class privilege is far deeper than a matter of money. Elena first realized this when she, Lila and their friends took a walk in a fashionable part of town. For Elena, it was like crossing a border; she saw the women as totally different from the women of the neighborhood: "They seemed to have breathed another air, to have eaten other food, to have dressed on some other planet, to have learned to walk on wisps of wind." These women passed by without seeing Elena and her friends—they were not "perceptible" (BF, 192). Claiming a Neapolitan background like Elena Greco's, Ferrante told journalist Gudmund Skjeldal, "often between the poor areas and the rich areas there are distances that can't be crossed. For my friends and me to leave the rough streets we had known since birth and go to unknown places, with handsome buildings and the avenue along the sea and a beautiful view over the bay, was a dangerous adventure."[5]

Among the wealthy young people Elena found so intimidating was a girl dressed all in green with a green bowler hat. Lila's brother Rino made insulting remarks about her, resulting in a brawl with Rino badly beaten and the Solara brothers coming to his rescue. Years later, when the store featuring shoes designed by Lila and her brother was about to open in the part of town where the brawl had taken place, Lila asked Elena if she remembered the girl in green. Sensing that Lila was in some way looking for reassurance that she belonged in that fashionable part of town, Elena replied that the difference between her and that girl was just a matter of money, the world was changing, and that anyway Lila was more beautiful than the girl in green. But Elena's reassurance was insincere. She admitted to herself that she was lying to Lila; it was more than just money. She understood there was "something malevolent in the inequality" digging deeper than money and now realized "the cash of the two grocery stores, and even of the shoe factory and the shoe store, was not sufficient to hide our origin" (SNN, 125).

Elena's growing awareness of the complexities of class, that it was a matter of cultural capital as well as money, resulted in a changing dynamic in her relationship with Lila. When Elena's mentor, Professor Galiani, invited her to a party at her home in the upscale Vomero district and suggested she bring a friend, Lila unexpectedly offered to go with her. Elena feared that Lila would embarrass her among the upper middle class people in Professor Galiani's world, but simultaneously feared that Lila would upstage her. She worried that Lila would dress inappropriately, that she would speak in dialect, that she might make a vulgar remark, thus making it all too obvious that her education had not gone beyond elementary school. But at the same time Elena was afraid that when Lila spoke everyone including Professor Galiani herself would be mesmerized by her intelligence.

Elena had nothing to fear; she was the queen of the party while Lila retreated into the shadows. Hurt and humiliated, Lila turned on Elena, accusing her of wanting to be "a puppet from the neighborhood" who performs for the wealthy people of the Vomero so she can be invited to their homes and gain access to their world (SNN, 163). The bitter feelings from that night led to the first major break in their relationship and to a long painful separation. Elena turned to her new friends—Nino and Professor Galiani's children Armando and Nadia, young people she thought knew how to appreciate her. Elena believed they saw in her what Lila, who had "only the gaze of the neighborhood," was unable to see (SNN, 169). Lila was well aware that Elena saw her as potential source of embarrassment. When Lila accompanied Elena to say good-bye to professor Galiani before she moved to Florence, the Professor asked Lila if she would attend Elena's wedding. Lila replied that Elena had not invited her, that she was ashamed of her. Elena, who had planned a small wedding limited to immediate family, said that Lila was speaking nonsense, but both she and Lila knew that Lila was speaking an uncomfortable truth.

Although Elena's self-confidence increased dramatically, the hidden

9. The Climb Up the Class Ladder

injuries of class were never far from the surface. She realized that she would never achieve the self-assurance of those who were born into privilege: "Suddenly I was aware of that *almost*. Had I made it? Almost. Had I torn myself away from Naples, the neighborhood? Almost...." Elena was intimidated by those who had that cultural capital without the *almost*, with a self-assurance she lacked. She became aware that the knowledge most of her fellow students possessed included an understanding of how to build a career, familiarity with the university hierarchies and the names of the people who mattered. Elena realized that she didn't know "the map of prestige" (SNN, 402–03).

Despite her academic success and her later success as a writer, Elena continued to feel that she was an impostor. At a book signing for her first well-received, autobiographical novel, she was easily intimidated by a critical comment from a man in the audience, becoming once "again the poor little girl from Naples, the daughter of the porter with the dialect cadence of the South, amazed at having ended up playing the part of the cultured young writer" (TWL, 30). For Elena, the class prejudice she experienced was compounded by northern Italian prejudice against southerners. Her husband's family shared the northern Italian bias against Naples and her mother-in-law told her she would never let her grandchildren grow up in Naples.

When Elena was a student at the University of Pisa, a girl from Rome mocked her Neapolitan accent, and the other students laughed. Although she was hurt by the ridicule, Elena laughed too, and even emphasized her accent as if to demonstrate that she was not at all bothered by the mockery. The same girl from Rome who had mocked Elena's Neapolitan accent accused her of stealing money that was missing from her purse. She had no reason for assuming that Elena was the culprit, other than the stereotype of Southern Italians as prone to crime. Eventually, she found the missing money and apologized to Elena. Elena did not dwell on such slights; she accepted the girl's apology, kept her eyes on the prize and moved on. However, despite her desperate attempts to fit in, Elena, at this stage in her life, could not get rid of the imprint of her background. Even after her years in Florence, she feared that she might fall back into the habits of her old world. When she returned to Naples for the first time in many years, she realized that she was using words from Neapolitan dialect, that her voice was assuming the cadence of the dialect, that she was indeed reverting to the language of the neighborhood.

Elena's desire to escape the neighborhood and move into another world led her to marry a man she didn't love. She despaired of ever marrying Nino Sarratore, the man she had loved from childhood, so she turned to Pietro Airota, the son of an elite northern Italian family. She did not love him but saw him as a way out of the world she was eager to escape. She appeared not to be concerned that she was being dishonest with Pietro, forcing herself to repress all thoughts of Nino, telling Pietro that she wanted to marry him as soon as possible. Elena was obviously taking advantage of Pietro; however, from another perspective, she was making a choice completely understandable, if not justifiable, given her impoverished background.

Elena was well aware that she was not the person Pietro's parents would have chosen for their son; her class background, her Neapolitan accent and general lack of sophistication must certainly have put their liberal views to a hard test. For the most part Elena, who had spent her whole life trying to please those who had the power to help her advance, repressed any hostility she might feel about the Airotas' sense of class superiority. It surfaced briefly when she read an article written by Pietro's father in which he described the expectations of female university students from poor families. Elena saw this as a reference, possibly unconscious, to her and wondered if she were a "jewel in the crown of the Airotas' broad-mindedness" (TWL, 54). However, despite any reservations they might have had, the Airotas accepted her and consented to the marriage. Elena saw herself as entering a family that would support and protect her, a "sort of well-fortified castle" (TWL, 183). As an Airota, she began to benefit from the privileges of class; her mother-in-law Adele's support for her writing and her connections at a major publishing firm were instrumental in the publication of Elena's first novel.

Elena also realized that she was in a position to use her relationship with the Airotas to help Lila. As she put it, thanks to the Airotas, she was "no longer a small match seller down to the last match"; she was now in possession of a large stock of matches (TWL, 184). Her mother-in-law Adele secured appointments with medical specialists to diagnose and treat a seriously run-down Lila; her sister-in-law secured a lawyer who would help Lila regain the back wages she was owed from the owner of a sausage factory; Elena's husband Pietro used his connections to help Lila's partner Enzo secure employment in the emerging information technology sector. Although Elena saw herself as motivated solely by a desire to help Lila,

9. The Climb Up the Class Ladder

Ferrante allows the reader to see what Elena herself does not fully recognize—her pride in her newly acquired connections and her pleasure in displaying them. She was stunned when Pasquale bitterly mocked her attempt to find individual solutions to the exploitation of the working class. He attacked her for trying to get a little money for Lila and demanded to know if she had any understanding what the class struggle was about. To Elena's consternation, Lila agreed with Pasquale.

Elena's connections with powerful, influential people were contingent on being a member of the Airota family. When Elena decided to end her marriage, her mother-in-law Adele threatened that she would take away everything she had given her. Adele's class biases, which she had suppressed in her interactions with Elena, now rose to the surface. Adele asked Elena why she had treated her son dishonestly, marrying him although she loved someone else. Elena struggled to answer and at the end of their heated exchange told Adele, that she was Elena Greco, not Elena Airota, that her daughters were her daughters, not Adele's daughters and that she didn't give a damn about the Airotas. Adele replied with an insulting reference to Elena's background: "It's obvious you are Elena Greco, it's now far too obvious" (SLC, 75).

When Elena had her final break with Adele, they attacked each other in class-laden language. Elena contrasted her honesty in leaving Pietro with Adele's concealed affairs, calling her, a "hypocritical little bourgeois who hides her dirt under the carpet." Adele returned the insult, telling Elena that behind a pleasing façade, she hid an "extremely vulgar craving to grab everything, which neither studying nor books could ever tame" (SLC, 98). After Elena left their son for Nino Sarratore, the Airotas also made disparaging remarks about Nino's class background. Pietro's father Guido referred to Nino, whom he had once liked and respected, as "intelligence without traditions," "a man who would rather gain the approval of those in power than fight for a principle" (SLC, 74). When Elena questioned what he meant by "intelligence without traditions," Adele replied that Nino is a "nobody," and for a person from his background, the most important thing is to be recognized as a person of consequence. Ambition comes first, thus he is an unreliable political ally. Despite their left wing allegiances, both Airotas saw the world through the lens of their class privilege; from that vantage point both Elena and Nino were vulgar arrivistes.

As Elena achieved success as a writer, her confidence increased and she became less vulnerable both to the injuries of class and to the indignity of sexual harassment. When male passengers on a bus put their hands on her, instead of meekly trying to get out of their way, she fought back. She eventually became confident enough to make use of her class background as a source of literary material. No longer did she see herself as a victim of her origins; rather she could now analyze and interpret her history, taking control of the story of her life. She moved back to the neighborhood in order to finish her book on the world of her childhood; the world that had been dragging her down was now the vehicle for climbing higher.

Despite her success and increased confidence, however, Elena's fear of falling down the class ladder never completely disappeared. Elena worried about her daughter Dede's infatuation with Lila's son Rino, who was not educated and very much enmeshed in the world of the neighborhood. Her own anxiety about her daughter's making a choice which would foreclose possibilities for a life in the upper-middle class led her to "understand and excuse" Nino when he abandoned Lila and "understand and excuse" Adele's reservations about her son's marriage to a woman from a very different socio-economic background (SLC, 405). The high value Elena placed on upward mobility led her to suggest a moral equivalence between Adele's class prejudices and Nino's cruel abandonment of a destitute, pregnant Lila.

Ferrante further explores the ways in which upward mobility is a gendered path, with Nino's rise up the class ladder contrasted with Elena's. The hidden (and not so hidden) injuries of class are more of an obstacle for Elena than they appear to be for Nino, who seems to be able to brush them off. Of course we do not get Nino's account and we see his climb up the class ladder primarily through Elena's eyes. When Elena discovered that Nino was working in England and learning to speak English, she asked Lila to imagine what it would be like if they could travel to England, questioning why Nino had the freedom to travel and they did not. In Elena and Lila's world, women and girls had to stay under the protection of male relatives, and such freedom of movement was unthinkable.

Distancing oneself from one's family of origin was much more difficult for women. Elena saw herself and Nino as similar in their refusal to lead their lives according to their families' values and she described herself as struggling most of her life to get away from her mother. However, Elena, despite her frequently antagonistic relationship with her mother, was much more closely connected to her family and friends than was Nino. The strength of this connection became apparent when Elena, despite her heroic struggle to free herself from Naples and the neighborhood, returned to Naples to be with her then lover Nino. They lived in an apartment in the Via Tasso, in an affluent section of Naples; for Elena, the old neighborhood was "urban debris" and she was determined that it would not recapture her. However, she began to resume relationships with her family and her old friends, especially with Lila. Her mother was still enraged that Elena had left her husband, and Elena found her old friends from the neighborhood far more welcoming than her family, noting that her old friends were not critical of her choices, were clearly happy that she had returned to Naples, and eager to once again have her as part of their lives. When Elena's relationship with Nino finally ended, despite her fear that a return to the neighborhood would be proof that she "had touched bottom," Elena left the affluent Via Tasso, and moved back to the old neighborhood. The neighborhood, and especially Lila, provided her with the support system she needed if she were ever to rebuild her career as a writer.

Nino had a much less complicated relationship with his family and their world, and with without much inner turmoil, had broken with his father. Unlike Elena, he maintained no ties with the neighborhood; the friends that Elena still saw and valued were all strangers to Nino. He was free to concentrate on the new relationships he was cultivating, friends and lovers who could advance his career. The competing value systems of individualism and solidarity are intertwined with the theme of class mobility with Nino as the extreme individualist who left the world of his childhood and never looked back. Elena's life is dominated by the struggle for individual advancement, but she still maintains some degree of loyalty and emotional attachment to her old friends from the neighborhood. Solidarity matters to Lila and Enzo and above all to Pasquale who cautioned Elena "remember who you are and which side you are on" (SNN, 328). Pasquale's old friends remained loyal to him, even if he had committed the violent acts the newspapers attributed to him; even if they disapproved of the political choices he had made, they would never reject him.

Nino shared none of their loyalty to old friends, had no sense of solidarity with family or any one else from his class background. He benefited from having cut ties to his background and also from his society's acceptance of behavior in men that would never be tolerated in women. Elena realized that no woman could have multiple, simultaneous extramarital affairs with men and maintain her reputation as a respected intellectual.

Nor could a woman abandon her children to concentrate on advancing her career and still maintain a position in society as Nino had done. Nino abandoned a pregnant Lila, who he thought was carrying his child; then he had an affair with a student Silvia, had a child with her, and soon abandoned her and the child, without any consequences for his career. When Elena learned about his relationship with Silvia, her first reaction was disgust and she saw him as an animal that left behind, like the "residue of a careless pleasure, living material, conceived, nourished, shaped within female bellies" (TWL, 88). However Elena, desperate to rationalize his behavior, struggled to see him in the context of the sexually liberated 1960s and 1970s.

Elena resented Nino's freedom to escape the consequences of his sexual behavior; she saw her career derailed by children and bitterly compared her situation with his. Every time she came upon an article by Nino, she was depressed and resentful, noting they were born in the same environment and that both had managed to escape. She questioned why she was the one falling into despair. Was it because of marriage, because of motherhood, because she was a woman, burdened with caring for house and family, forced to spend her days, continually cleaning up and changing diapers? Elena paid for her class ascent in ways Nino did not. She had to work much harder to build a career and felt that as a consequence, she missed many of the pleasures of youth. As she put it because of her self-discipline, she "missed the joy of letting go" (TWL, 255). Of course the "joy of letting go" could have serious consequences for a young woman. In a world in which traditional values still held sway, the climb up the class ladder was much steeper, much more fraught with danger for a woman.

When a middle-aged Elena met with Nino, then a member of Parliament, to ask him to get information about charges brought against Pasquale, Nino remarked that he and Elena had both climbed very high. Elena read in his gaze that he did not see them as having risen to equal heights and that he saw himself as far more successful than she. However, the wheel of fortune would turn a few more times for Nino. He would be charged with corruption, lose his seat in parliament, but would eventually be cleared of charges and, by shifting to the right, would manage to regain his seat, thus proving the point Adele had made years before that for Nino ambition trumped principle.

While Nino and Elena pursued upward mobility, Lila, trapped in a disastrous marriage, devoted herself to educating her son, hoping to give

9. The Climb Up the Class Ladder

him the intellectual advantages he would need to enter the world beyond the neighborhood. Having read that the first years of life were critically important for a child's intellectual development, Lila immersed herself in books on early childhood education, played games with her son designed to stimulate his intellect, and spoke to him only in standard Italian. She included her nephew Dino in her educational project and told her skeptical sister-in-law that she would like to involve all the children in the neighborhood. For Lila, imbued with the ethic of solidarity, upward mobility was not just an individual pursuit but also a collective endeavor. She soon discovered there were limits to what she could do to counter the influence of the neighborhood. At the home of Professor Galiani, Lila learned a bitter lesson about the difficulty of escaping class background; despite all Lila's efforts, Professor Galiani's three-and-a-half-year-old grandson Marco could read more fluently than her five-year-old son Gennaro. In no way could Lila compensate for the head start in life little Marco enjoyed by virtue of his class advantages.

Ferrante has argued that "class origins cannot be erased, regardless of whether we climb up or down the sociocultural ladder."[6] There is a strand of political pessimism in the Neapolitan novels, with frequent references to the characters carrying their ancestors in their bodies. Sometimes the pessimism appears to be rooted in biological determinism as when Stefano's monstrous father appeared to be emerging from his body: "The father was cracking his skin, changing his gaze, exploding out of his body" (SNN, 41). Other times the pessimism seems culturally determined as when Lila realized that all her attempts to develop her son's intelligence would be undermined by the brutal world in which he was growing up. However, the trajectory of Elena's and Nino's lives undermines this pessimistic strand. Both managed to carve out a path very different from what might have been expected given their origins. Yes, there were scars, particularly in Elena's case, but with time and success "the enduring weight of class origins" had certainly diminished.

Elena had successfully climbed the class ladder and brought her daughters along with her. At the end of the fourth volume of the Quartet, Elena congratulates herself that her three daughters were securely ensconced in the upper middle class. At the age of fifty-eight, Elena was surrounded by her daughters and their partners who had come to visit her over the Christmas holidays. She reflected that ultimately nothing had defeated her, nothing had her pulled her down, nor derailed the lives of her daughters: "We're safe, I brought them all to safety" (SLC, 457). She acknowledged that her daughters belong to other places, and other languages, but what mattered was that her very intelligent daughters had not experienced any of the difficulties she had faced.

Yet Elena was far from triumphant in late middle age. She feared that her image as a successful writer who had risen from an impoverished background would be forgotten, that her works would not endure, and that "her entire life would be reduced to a petty battle to change [her] social class" (SLC, 459). Despite having written a brilliant depiction of the injuries of class and the struggle to transcend one's class background, Ferrante surprisingly told the *Paris Review* that she "had always rejected out of a personal distaste, giving space to social ascent, to the weight of class origins, a weight that not only doesn't disappear but doesn't even really diminish."[7] It is difficult to believe that someone could write so powerfully about an experience she never wanted to explore. I cannot help but speculate that this strand of the Neapolitan Quartet is Starnone's story.

10
Italy in the Years of Lead: Ferrante as Political Analyst

> *"The dream of unlimited progress is in reality a nightmare of savagery and death."*—Elena Ferrante, *Story of the Lost Child*

The Neapolitan novels cover a time when traditional class relations were being challenged by a post-war prosperity that brought more and more working class people within reach of the middle class. Expanded educational opportunity in the 1960s and 1970s led to a resurgent student left which questioned the justice and inevitability of a class-based society and made common cause with an increasingly militant workers' movement. Ferrante's readers and reviewers have largely ignored the powerful political dimension of the Neapolitan novels. This may be the case because those interested in political struggle may not be likely to read novels marketed as books about female friendship. Also, those drawn to books about women's intimate lives may not be all that interested in political struggles—particularly in what many of Ferrante's readers would no doubt view as long-ago struggles about outmoded ideas.

Apparently the original manuscript of the Neapolitan Quartet contained additional material about Italy's political unrest in the late 1960s through the mid–1980s—the so-called *"Anni di piombo"* or "Years of Lead." The only significant edit Ferrante's publisher, Sandro Ferri, recalled was cutting sections from the third volume of the Neapolitan Quartet, dealing with the political struggles of those years. According to Ferri: "When you talk about terrorism, the extreme left, the fascists ... it is still very hot in Italy." He noted that books that probed too deeply into this history had failed. "Of course, [Ferrante] is very good so she knew that. There were parts where [Ferri's wife] Sandra said, 'Maybe this is too political.' And [Ferrante] can immediately throw away pages."[1] I would give a lot to see those discarded pages.

Ferrante has said: "I don't have any special passion for politics, it being a never-ending merry-go-round of bosses big and small, all generally mediocre. I actually find it boring. I confuse names, minor events, their political positions. But I have always paid careful attention to social and economic conflicts, to the dialectic—if we can call it that—between high and low."[2] Although Ferrante, the fictional character shielding the identity of the author(s), may find politics boring, I am convinced that one of the probable authors, Domenico Starnone, a longtime culture editor at the Communist paper *Il Manifesto*,[3] was very interested in politics and was closely involved either as an observer and possibly as a participant in the political life of the 1960s and 1970s Italian Left. Furthermore, Starnone (born in February 1943) like Elena and Lila in the Neapolitan novels (both born in August 1944) is much more likely to have been influenced by the political turmoil of the late 1960s and 1970s than was Anita Raja (born in 1953). I had direct experience of those years (albeit in the United States rather than in Italy) and when reading the sections in the Neapolitan novels describing the divisions and arguments then current among the radical left, I was convinced the author was writing from direct experience. It was pitch perfect. Furthermore, Starnone's novel *First Execution* explores similar terrain with characters struggling with the question of whether political violence can ever be justified.

At some point in the mid–1970s, the euphoria of the Italian left in the late 1960s and early 1970s gave way to a deepening sense of despair. The late 1960s and early 1970s were marked by violent clashes but many on the left were convinced that a better world would emerge from the turmoil. Most Americans are unaware of the extent of social unrest and political violence in Italy during the so-called "Years of Lead." According to historian Alessandro Orsini, from 1968 to 1973 Italy had the highest level of political turmoil in Europe. Battles, such as those at the sausage factory where Lila worked and organized, were commonplace throughout Italy. Orsini reported that in 1969 alone, 145 bomb attacks occurred, 96 of which were traced to the extreme right.[4] Lila described attacks by fascist gangs as a black cloud hanging over the neighborhood and all of Naples, as the fascists marched throughout the city attacking their political opponents with iron bars and knives. Violence was perpetrated by both ends of the political spectrum, with the political unrest viewed by many as a continuation of the civil unrest that had raged in Italy at the end of World War II.[5] Elena described the "fascists who knifed and killed, the comrades who did no less" (TWL, 348).

Like a growing number of Italians in the 1970s, Elena found that the political violence now touched people close to her, including her former boyfriend Franco Mari, who had been brutally beaten by fascist gangs and who had lost an eye. Also, her childhood friend Gino, who had joined the fascists, was murdered in broad daylight presumably by leftist gangs, possibly by Pasquale, another childhood friend now a member of the radical left. Then a "commando group" consisting of two men and a woman broke into Bruno Soccavo's sausage factory where Lila had worked and killed him. When Elena told Lila about Bruno's murder, Lila replied that Elena was giving her very bad news; since it is unlikely Lila would consider the murder of a man she detested as bad news, her comment suggests she thought Pasquale might have been involved. Irrational fear got the better of Elena and for a brief period she thought that Lila might have joined Pasquale in the armed struggle and that she would suddenly reappear triumphant, as a leader of the revolution. Elena was nonplussed when she learned that instead Lila was working for one of Michele Solara's enterprises, and that she had become a successful businesswoman who now referred scornfully to the "revolution, the workers, the new world, and that other bullshit" (TWL, 317).

As the 1970s wore on, disillusionment on the left was growing. Elena's former boyfriend Franco Mari, once a committed revolutionary, now spoke sarcastically of the approaching end of a period that had been *"objectively* revolutionary" but that was now succumbing to the forces of reaction (TWL, 78). His sarcastic tone suggests that he thought he and his former comrades had been deluded about the extent to which Italy was ripe for revolution. Mari fell into a deep depression, in part as a consequence of serious injuries from a brutal beating by a fascist gang and in part due to his growing realization that the political climate was changing. While some like Mari were losing hope in the possibility of revolutionary change, others on the left turned increasingly to political violence, culminating in the Red Brigades' 1978 kidnapping of Aldo Moro, former Prime Minister and chair of the center-right Christian Democratic Party. Many on the left justified the kidnapping and some justified the subsequent execution of Moro. Elena, ever the opportunist, tried to straddle the divide on the Italian left over the killing of Moro, but at a book signing she let slip a description of his kidnappers as murderers. She noted that she frequently had difficulty finding the right words to describe a political situation; her audience demanded that she "calibrate them according to the current usage of the radical left," and she was very careful to oblige (SLC, 87). Elena was attacked by the audience, who insisted that the fascists, not the Red Brigades, were the real murderers. Elena wondered why someone who commits murder should not be called a murderer; however, she did not challenge the audience and instead remained silent about Moro's killers.

Leonardo Sciascia's *The Moro Affair*, which analyzed the documents related to the kidnapping, makes for painful reading.[6] Sciascia includes Moro's own letters, in which Moro argued for negotiating with the Red Brigades in order to save his life; however, the Italian government refused to negotiate with the terrorists, reflecting the changing political climate in Italy. In the middle 1960s acceptance of "revolutionary violence" had begun to gain ground among the Italian left. When Elena was invited to a party at the home of Professor Galiani, the professor's son Armando responded to Nino's support for non-violent means of social change by arguing that planning would not change the world: "It will take blood. It will take violence" (SNN, 159). Armando was a familiar type in the world of the 1960s left—a son of privilege who casually advocated violence from the safety of his comfortable upper middle class life. Political scientist Roberto Batali has analyzed the extent of support for political violence among the Italian middle and upper middle classes and described "a network of help and support, a sort of sea in which the armed party was able to swim with ease for more than ten years."[7] Although some on the left continued to refuse to describe the terrorists as murderers, by the late 1970s, in part as a consequence of Moro's murder, the glorification of "revolutionary violence" was fading.

The Neapolitan novels contain a political drama that reviewers generally have not commented on, a dimension that has also been missing from recent dramatizations of the novels. Susannah Clap, in her generally favorable review of the London's Rose Theater adaptation of the Neapolitan Quartet, notes: "The only substantial loss is in the treatment of political engagement." The actor who plays Nino "turns him into a chump who makes all political theory sound merely academic and absurd, comic relief rather than something with the power to stir."[8] However, in the Neapolitan novels political ideas are treated seriously. Ferrante has intertwined the political and personal strands so effectively that the political debate never feels intrusive. Characters take political positions that emerge organically from their circumstances and personalities, and that do not in any way detract from the personal drama.

Nino Sarratore is the reform-minded technocrat, an upwardly mobile careerist, looking for feasible solutions to social problems. He is fascinated by the mechanisms of government and how they can be harnessed for progressive change. He is never seduced by the idea of revolution, no doubt realizing that in Italian society there was not much opportunity for career advancement through advocating violent revolution. Elena's father-in-law Guido Airota, a member of the affluent academic elite and a leader in the Socialist Party, described Nino as a reformer committed to making the "gears of neocapitalism function" rather than joining those demanding profound transformations in society (SLC, 73). He saw Nino as essentially an opportunist, concerned above all with career advancement, a tendency that became more pronounced as Nino grew older. Elena, who had tended to look at Nino through rose-colored glasses and was ever ready to rationalize his less desirable characteristics, began to see him as overly sensitive to the approval of those in power.

If Nino represents the reformer eager to work within the current system, Elena is the fellow traveller who sympathizes with the left wing project of social redistribution but who is not particularly interested in the mechanisms for achieving that goal. Uninterested in everyday politics, Elena found herself attracted to extreme positions, hoping that "something great" was about to emerge. She was drawn to the drama of the political movements of the 1970s; as she put it, "I was attracted by that fever heat" (TWL, 253). Feeling trapped within marriage and motherhood, she longed for the sexually liberated world of the student left; she wanted to break all the rules, as the whole world appeared to be breaking the rules.

At the same time, Elena was unnerved by what she saw as the left-wing challenge to the life she had tried to build. Noting the rough language and sexually free behavior of affluent young women who were part of the student left, she feared that the correct language she had struggled so hard acquire was no longer valued. Elena observed that her sister in-law Mariarosa used language more vulgar than what she and Lila had used in the neighborhood, never using a noun "that wasn't preceded by 'fucking'" (TWL, 255). Elena began to wonder why she had worked so hard to transcend the language of the neighborhood, which had now become fashionable.

She had been learning one set of rules about political attitudes and social mores, which combined radical politics with an educated vocabulary and elite social status. Now she was confronted with something altogether different, with highly educated men pretending to be lower class. For Elena, political knowledge was primarily something she acquired to be able to say the right things in the circles in which she traveled. She did not feel that political issues were deeply connected to her personal life; rather, political knowledge had been information to display, part of her own individual battle to climb the class ladder. But now what counted as political knowledge was changing; the language of the streets, along with new freewheeling attitudes towards sex and drugs, had become fashionable among the left wing intelligentsia. Elena felt left behind.

While Elena was attracted to the drama of the student left, her husband Pietro was appalled by the excesses. He believed in the redistributionist project of the left, but was disgusted by what he saw as the bad behavior and disrespect for cultural tradition that characterized the student left. He was harassed by his students for holding them to high academic standards, and by many of his colleagues for not being more understanding towards students involved in political protests. I can personally attest to scenes like this playing out on American university campuses during the height of the Vietnam War. Unmoved by the pleas of students who failed to complete the requirements for his courses, Pietro failed a politically active student from a prominent family. When the student aimed a loaded gun at him, Pietro told him that either he'd better be serious and shoot, or that he'd better get rid of his weapon because Pietro intended to report him to the police. The student fled; Pietro reported him to the police and the student was arrested. The young man's family appealed to Pietro's father to persuade his son to withdraw the charges, but despite considerable pressure from his father, Pietro refused to give in. Elena did not see her husband as taking a courageous, principled stand, but instead berated him for not being more understanding.

Ferrante allows the reader to see a side of Pietro that Elena does not. When the police tried to get him to identify suspected terrorists, Pietro again took a principled stand. Elena's old friend Pasquale Peluso and his girlfriend (and apparently partner in crime) Nadia Galiani had left Naples to avoid arrest and arrived uninvited at Elena's house. They were the guests from hell, brazenly making themselves at home, carelessly leaving their things everywhere and insulting their host. Pasquale told Pietro that he was dead, but didn't know it, that everything is dead, "the way you live is dead, the way you speak, your conviction that you're very intelligent, and democratic, and on the left" (TWL, 287). Pietro later told Elena that the police had shown him photographs of terrorists and that Pasquale and Nadia were among them. He had not told the police that Nadia and Pasquale were in their house, not because he wanted to protect Elena, but because he was concerned that the authorities were now criminalizing dissent. Elena, at the time consumed by her love affair with Nino and no longer interested in politics, didn't immediately understand what her husband was talking about and replied only with a nod.

Pietro is the principled, culturally conservative left wing academic; Elena is the political dilettante, attracted by the "fever heat" of student protests, but bored by theoretical debate and the nuts and bolts of politics; and Nino is the technocratic reformer trying to learn how to use the mechanism of government to effect social change. Lila is something altogether different. Unlike Elena, she was intensely interested in political questions. As an adolescent, Lila turned to their friend Pasquale, a member of the Communist Party, for an explanation of their world and then to the history books to provide a deeper explanation of the socio-economic history of Naples—the rule of the fascists, then World War II, the near destruction of Naples in the Allied bombing, the post-war black market in their neighborhood controlled by loan shark Don Achille, and the growing influence of the Camorra crime syndicate. Although Lila agreed with Pasquale's analysis, she rejected the Communist Party's project to improve the lives of workers. For Lila, the remedy was the end of dehumanizing work, which she saw as a terrible condition that should not be improved, but rather should be totally eliminated. Although the word *Autonomia* was not used in the Neapolitan novels, Italian readers familiar with the history of the left would have recognized Lila as in some ways the voice of *Autonomia*, a movement which began as a workers' movement, but quickly moved beyond the demand for better wages and working conditions to question the very idea of work itself. *Autonomia* was essentially an anarchist movement described by Professor of Italian Studies, David Moss as "an archipelago of heterogeneous collectives, united by active antagonism to all institutions."[9]

In his 1971 novel *We Want Everything* Nanni Balestrini, one of the "leaders" of *Autonomia*, provided a compelling portrait of this decentralized, non-hierarchical movement. The narrator is a man who has emigrated from southern Italy to find work, is hired at the Fiat plant, and takes part in the legendary strike against Fiat in 1969. He has come to see work as a fraud and doesn't understand why work should be celebrated: "People in prison are freer than us, chained to these disgusting machines."[10] "*Vogliamo tutto*" (We Want Everything) became the mantra of the striking Fiat workers. In his 2013 afterword to the English translation of *We Want Everything* Balestrini argued that *Autonomia's* refusal of work was prescient: "More and more the automation of production ... requires a laughably small quantity of human labour power ... a new era is waiting for humanity, when it will be freed from ... the suffering of a forced labour that is already unnecessary."[11] Lila's belief that work should be eliminated, once a wildly utopian idea, is now at least theoretically possible.

In many ways similar to the Occupy movement that erupted in the United States in 2011, *Autonomia* operated outside the established political system as an amorphous movement without a hierarchal leadership structure. It has been described in terms which could easily be applied to Occupy: "An indefinable mixture of groups and varied tendencies, a veritable mosaic of different fragments, a gallery of overlapping images, of circles and collectives without any central organization."[12] Although there was apparently some overlapping membership between the decentralized collectives that comprised *Autonomia* and groups engaged in political violence, for the most part *Autonomia* was not involved in the armed struggle and was committed to revolutionary social change through non-violent means. However, as the 1970s wore on, hope for change through non-violent means began to diminish.

During Lila's brief career as a union organizer, she became convinced that incremental improvement was useless and that the system should be torn down. However, she became increasingly pessimistic about the possibility of change and, worn down by her struggle to change conditions in the factory where she worked, she eventually gave up. Her friend Pasquale did not see withdrawal from political activism as an option; for him, it was "blasphemy" for a member of the working class to declare that she had her own problems and wanted to tend to her own business (TWL, 144). As Pasquale saw it, each person must do whatever she could in the struggle for social justice. On some level, Lila shared Pasquale's ethic of solidarity, but not his belief in the possibility of revolutionary change. She was sharply critical of what she saw as the naiveté and arrogance of the radical students who had little understanding of the working class people they hoped to organize and to whom they were handing out a "densely written leaflet for people who had difficulty reading" (TWL, 131). Given the students' lack of understanding of the realities of working class life, Lila had little faith in their ability to forge a worker student/alliance. Increasingly, she came to think that Pasquale had misread the political climate and wondered if there really existed all that revolutionary fervor in the world or if Pasquale and Nadia were just imagining it.

While Lila, her body weakened by the strain of factory work and the stress of union organizing, withdrew from the struggle, Pasquale and Nadia, frustrated with the slow pace of change and unglamorous day-to-day work of union organizing, disappeared into the underground world of political violence. The brief explosive period in the mid–1970s when students and workers joined forces to transform Italian society came to a bloody end. As a participant/observer of such worker/student alliances in the United States, I find that Lila's criticisms of student radicals ring true. There were, however, dramatic differences between Italy and the United States; working class participation in the social movements of the 1960s and 1970s in Italy was significantly greater than in the United States. Also, the class divide was much greater in Italy than in the United States, where the major fault line was race. American workers had just experienced a period of increased prosperity. As a consequence of a booming economy, capitalists were willing to share some of their rising profits and were not automatically, implacably hostile to unions, with the result that American workers, for the most part, were not attracted to radical politics. In Italy, especially in Southern Italy, the working class was less prosperous, much more likely to identify with socialism or communism, and the pro-capitalist forces more determined to crush the workers' movement than was the case in the United States in the 1960s and 1970s.

Pasquale Peluso's response to right wing repression was to fight harder and to escalate the struggle. The left's growing disillusionment with the possibility of effecting change through the democratic process was greatly influenced by an event mentioned only in passing in the Neapolitan novels—the violent overthrow of the democratically elected government of Salvador Allende in 1973. Elena noted that right after the coup in Chile, her daughter Dede would not let her father watch the television news. Perhaps an indication of how important it was for Pietro to watch that news report, he spanked his daughter much too hard. The Allende government had been the great left-wing hope for a non-violent transition to socialism; its overthrow strengthened the hand of those arguing that such a peaceful transition was not possible and that revolutionary change could only come about through armed struggle.

Pasquale exemplifies those elements on the left who despaired of change through non-violent means. He had quit the Communist Party because of too many ugly internal conflicts, too many cowardly compromises; he could no longer endure the dreariness of the party bureaucracy. He then joined a radical collective where he met Nadia Galiani, a young girl from a privileged background whose parents, like Pasquale's, were communists. She also found the politics she had grown up with to be hopelessly compromised and was seduced by the possibility of revolution. Her relationship with Pasquale was an affirmation of her commitment to the revolutionary struggle. In a sense they personified the worker/student alliance—its strengths (the idealism, the eagerness to break down class boundaries) and its weaknesses (underestimating the difficulty of making revolutionary change, the turn to violence, and persistent, unacknowledged class biases). Demonstrating Ferrante's oft-expressed belief that one's background is never far from the surface, Nadia turns to class-based insult in an angry exchange with Elena. She refers to Elena and Lila as "two pieces of shit and nothing can change you, two examples of underclass filth" (TWL, 287).

Tensions were rising among those who identified with the left contributing to the fracturing of organizations and coalitions. While the relatively small radical left in the United States was winding down in the early 1970s, in Italy the radical left was a force, albeit a dwindling force, through the mid–1980s. Elena's political beliefs began to change in response to the political violence on the left, the state's determination to crush the radical left, and the increasingly conservative political climate in the late 1970s and early 80s. At the time of the publication of her first book in the late 1960s, Elena had ended book-signing events with references to revolution, as that seemed to resonate with her audience. In the late 1970s she avoided the term revolution, acknowledging that the capitalist system was likely to last much longer than she had expected. Elena was increasingly afraid of the threatening slogans of the left-wing demonstrators and the violence of the right-wing gangs, the "revolutionary hatred of everything" (SLC, 85).

In the early 1980s, when the social movements of the left had receded, Elena gave up the effort of acquiring political knowledge. She lost interest in what she now saw as "petty politics." Unlike Nino, she no longer wanted to follow the byzantine intrigues of the five governing parties and their never-ending struggles with the Communists, but she nonetheless continued to pay close attention to the "corrupt and violent drift of the country" (SLC, 222). Elena didn't appear to see the connection between the workings of government and the pervasive corruption and political violence engulfing the country; nor did she appear to see a connection between government and the major advances in her lifetime—for example, the expansion of compulsory education, the legalization of divorce, the reform of family law resulting in increased rights for women and for children born out of wedlock. She told Nino that politics as he thinks about it bored her.

As the political climate changed, to Elena's dismay, Nino opportunistically began to shift evermore rightward, becoming increasingly sensitive to those in authority, ready to argue that the fascists were not always wrong, that wages had to be frozen to save the Italian economy, that it was time to "end the childish aversion to power," and join those on the inside where decisions are made. He began to mock Elena as a sensitive soul, ignorant of how the real world functioned. In the 1980's, the tide of public opinion turned dramatically against the left: "Anarchist, Marxist, Gramscian, Communist, Leninist, Trotskyite, Maoist, worker were quickly becoming obsolete labels, or, worse, a mark of brutality" (SLC, 424). The pursuit of maximum profit formerly considered an evil was now seen as the foundation of freedom and democracy.

The Italian state stepped up its efforts to arrest the dwindling band of violent revolutionaries still at large and many people, guilty and innocent alike, were swept up in the police dragnet. According to historian Tom Behan, the repression was fierce. In the late 1970s the Italian government enacted a series of draconian laws that "brought fear and demoralization to much of the far left," including a law giving the State the authority to hold anyone suspected of terrorism in custody for up to eleven years, without any requirement to produce evidence.[13] In the mid–1980s Elena learned that Nadia Galiani had been arrested, or as Lila noted, more likely turned herself in to bargain for a lenient sentence. Soon after Pasquale was arrested; Elena and Lila were in a situation similar to that of many other Italians, confronting the crimes committed by their friends and relatives to advance a cause they believed was just. Pasquale's sister Carmen reconciled her love for Pasquale with horror at his crimes by defending him in terms of the ideals, which had motivated his actions. She continued to see her brother as a basically good person, even contending that she, Lila, and Elena were in a sense more wicked than Pasquale. They were focused on attending only to their personal affairs but Pasquale had never disavowed the commitment to social justice their father had taught them. On some level, Carmen shared Pasquale's belief that putting individual needs and desires ahead of solidarity with the working class was "blasphemy": however, she devoted herself to her family rather than to the class struggle.

Elena who had dedicated her life to the pursuit of individual advancement certainly did not share Pasquale's commitment to solidarity above all else and could not justify what Pasquale had done, but she couldn't distance herself from him, either. Elena turned to Nino, now a member of Parliament for information about Pasquale's situation. Nino agreed to help, saying he was in Parliament to insure that everyone's rights were protected, but that he would tell Pasquale that the families of the people he murdered have rights as well. Nino learned that Nadia's detailed confession blamed Pasquale for a long list of violent crimes and that she was implicating many others, ruining people who thought they were safe. Elena was torn between her bond with Pasquale and her "horror of so much blood stupidly shed" (SLC, 403).

Armando Galiani's casual defense of revolutionary violence made almost two decades earlier at a party in his mother's upscale apartment had largely disappeared from the discourse of the Italian left. The Italian government in the 1980s was determined to put an end to political terrorism and the mass arrests continued. Anyone thought to have any connection to terrorist activity was swept up in the dragnet. Lila's partner Enzo was one of those arrested, apparently among the many named by Nadia as co-conspirators. He was detained for two years and was eventually released, but like many others who were acquitted, his life was shattered by the experience. His business fell apart and his relationship with Lila, which had been unraveling before his arrest, finally ended. Given the suffering of many Italian families, both those of terrorists and those falsely accused of terrorism, one can understand the fears of Ferrante's publishers that Italian readers might not want to relive those years. The wounds still fester. As historian Tom Behan has noted, despite the fact that that there were a far greater number of right wing attacks during the Years of Lead, "nearly all these attacks have remained unpunished, whereas virtually all left wing terrorists have been captured and brought to trial, constitut[ing] a running sore for Italian democracy."[14]

One of those captured terrorists, Pasquale Peluso, is the only character in the Neapolitan novels who maintained his political commitment over a lifetime, although the vehicle changed from the Communist Party, with its focus on electoral politics and union organizing, to the branch of the radical left engaged in armed struggle. Pasquale's story raises the question of what could motivate a basically decent human being to become a terrorist. Pasquale's impassioned commitment to social change was fueled by a burning sense of injustice at the situation of Southern Italian workers and, on a personal level, by the injustices suffered by his father Alfredo, whose carpenter shop and tools had been appropriated by the loan shark Don Achille. When Don Achille was murdered, Alfredo was accused of the crime; he vehemently denied his guilt, but was convicted and sentenced to life in prison. Pasquale at one point stated that his father was right to kill Don Achille, who had been a spy for the fascists and made his money preying on poor people; however, it's not clear that Pasquale really believed his father was guilty. Lila is one of the few who believed Alfredo was innocent; she asked who controlled the money-lending market Don Achille had once dominated and thus had really benefited from the death of Don Achille. Lila concluded that the evidence pointed to Manuela, the mother of the Solara brothers, who herself was later murdered, apparently by a rival criminal gang. Whether or not Alfredo was paying for a crime actually committed by the Solaras, Pasquale harbored a deep and abiding hatred for the Solara family and all they represented.

Of course not every victim of injustice like Pasquale Peluso turned to revolutionary violence; however, the social turmoil of the late 1960s and early 1970s and the widely held belief that revolutionary change was possible, certainly played a part in pushing Pasquale over the edge. His transformation is easier to understand than that of his comrade in arms, Nadia Galiani, the daughter of Elena's teacher, Professor Galiani. Nadia's willingness to abandon her life of upper middle class privilege for the path of revolutionary violence is less plausible than Pasquale's decision, but it was a road taken by other idealistic young women from relatively privileged backgrounds, such as Ulrike Meinhardt in Germany. Nadia eventually repudiated the radical left, turned herself into the police and began to implicate many others in return for a lighter sentence. Pasquale never talked to the police and consequently received a sentence of life in prison. For Pasquale, solidarity trumped individual concerns. When, at the end of the Neapolitan Quartet, Elena in her sixties visited Pasquale in Poggioreale

Prison, she noted that Pasquale's political commitment and values were unchanged: "He hadn't moved a hairbreadth out of the space of generous ideas in which his father had enclosed him as a boy" (SLC, 470).

As the Neapolitan Quartet comes to a close, Ferrante depicts a growing malaise, a sense of disintegration both in the larger society and in Elena and Lila's world. The radical left had collapsed and the center left political parties were weakened by corruption scandals and tarnished by what were considered unsavory compromises. Unlike the United States, where the left was marginalized, Italy had left-wing parties that were part of the government—the Socialist Party and the Italian Communist Party. The tensions between these two parties are woven into the stories of the characters, although this strand was probably not of much interest to Ferrante's readers and, to my knowledge, never alluded to by Anglophone reviewers. When Guido Airota, a member of the Socialist Party, argued with his children Pietro and Mariarosa about the Communist Party's decision to work with the center right Christian Democrats—the so-called "Historic Compromise"—I suspect most readers glossed over the specifics of the political debate.

The Neapolitan novels are very much political novels with the characters' lives and values shaped by the political turmoil of the 1960s, and 1970s. Excitement about a world where the old order was questioned and fundamental change in social relations seemed possible gave way to deep pessimism about the future. Elena now saw the "dream of unlimited progress ... in reality a nightmare of savagery and death" (SLC, 337). Elena's pessimism is in tune with comments made by Ferrante in various recent interviews. Italian writer Nicola Lagioia in an interview originally published in *La Republica* described the Neapolitan Quartet as a "sorrowful hymn to the illusions of the second half of the twentieth century." Probably referring to Thomas Piketty, Lagioia cites historians who view "the forty years from 1950 to 1990 (the period in which inequalities diminished, social mobility became a reality and the masses were often protagonists) as a small moment of discontinuity in a larger picture where vast inequalities are the rule." Lagioia asked Ferrante if she thinks the second half of the 20th century was an aberration. Ferrante replied that the 21st century began with widening inequality: "The new fact is that the poor no longer have any horizons in life besides the capitalist system, or any horizons for redemption besides religion."[15]

As always with these interviews, we do not know if this is Ferrante the fictional character speaking or if this represents the view of the author[s]. However, the political pessimism Ferrante has expressed in this and other interviews is countered by the life story of Elena Greco. Although the socialist goal of economic redistribution is no longer ascendant, if the left wing project is defined more broadly to include those who have been historically excluded, progress has been made. The Neapolitan Quartet is deeply political in that the characters' personal histories are intertwined with larger social forces, their beliefs and values shaped by their social world, but there is no easily extractable political philosophy.

11
Ferrante as Feminist Theorist

> *"The solitude of women's minds is regrettable, I said to myself, it's a waste to be separated from each other, without procedures, without tradition."*—Elena Ferrante, *Those Who Leave, Those Who Stay*

The Neapolitan Quartet has been seen as a feminist bildungsroman, tracing the growth of Elena Greco's feminist consciousness and her relationship to the feminist movement of the late 1960s and 1970s. My initial reaction to the Neapolitan novels was in some ways very similar to my response to Simone de Beauvoir's *The Second Sex*. Almost all the major themes of feminist thought are contained in *The Second Sex*—Beauvoir had mapped the terrain. Ferrante did in the form of a novel what Beauvoir had done in a theoretical treatise. Both challenged the notion of the male as the human norm: the idea that "there is an absolute human type, the masculine.... He is the subject, he is the Absolute—she is the Other."[1] Both explored the range of themes that have formed the core of feminist literature—the tension-filled relationships between mothers and daughters; ambivalence towards children, especially when a woman tries to balance professional success with care for children: the omnipresence of gender-based violence, the ongoing struggle to get men to assume domestic responsibilities. Feminist theory has evolved since Beauvoir's *The Second Sex*, and is now focused on how gender is experienced differently by women of different races, classes, and sexualities. Ferrante comes much closer than Beauvoir to what we would call an intersectional feminism through her exploration of how gender is experienced by women of different classes and regional backgrounds and through her depiction of the fluidity of gender identity.

Despite theoretical divisions in "second wave" feminist thought (essentialists vs. social constructionists; equality feminists vs. difference feminists), all have taken as their starting point Beauvoir's challenge to the notion of the male as the human norm—a previously unexamined assumption in all academic disciplines. Like Beauvoir, they reject the normalcy of men and the corresponding abnormality of women and call for an expansion of our vision of the human norm to include those qualities historically associated with women. Sometimes the emphasis has been on the special and unique qualities women possess; at other times the emphasis has been on the extent to which men and women both contain within themselves qualities wrongly considered as uniquely male or uniquely female. The major theoretical divide in feminist thought is often considered to be the division between those who focus on gender difference and those who stress sameness/equality. As feminist theorist Ann Snitow has put it: "A common divide keeps forming in both feminist thought and action between the need to build and identify 'woman' and give it solid political meaning [the maximizers] and the need to tear down the very category 'woman' and dismantle its all too solid history [minimizers]."[2]

Although Beauvoir and Ferrante explore the same issues, they do so from a very different perspective. Beauvoir is clearly a minimizer whereas Ferrante has identified herself as a difference feminist or a maximizer, to use Snitow's terms. Unlike Beauvoir, Ferrante sees women's distinct qualities as attributes worthy of celebration. Yet she is also aware of the danger inherent in arguments that emphasize male/female difference: celebration of women's special attributes and values comes dangerously close to the stereotypes which have been used to justify the subordination of women. Unlike Beauvoir, who often reveals a dislike for women and qualities associated primarily with women, Ferrante likes women and embraces much that is traditionally feminine. As Joan Acocella put it: "Yet there is no repudiation of the trappings of femininity: the dolls, the bracelets, the buttons and bows. The book fairly teems with women's things, women's bodies, which, furthermore, are imagined as being in a state of constant flow, as if they were part of some piece of French *écriture féminine*."[3]

In her answer to a question about the extent of feminist influence on her writing, Ferrante replied: "I've read a fair amount of feminist writing, and passionately, yet I have no militant experience. I have a lot of sympathy for the thinking of difference feminism."[4] Both Lila and Elena are in some sense "difference feminists." Having grown up in society where gender boundaries were clearly marked and where transgressing those boundaries was fraught with danger, both see women's experiences as radically different from men's. Elena's feminism is based largely on her intellectual exploration of feminist theory; Lila's feminism is derived primarily from her experience, but both see men and women as radically different. A teenage Elena observed that she knew nothing about "dark depths that men could have, none of us did" (SNN, 366).

Lila responded to her old childhood friend Alfonso, who confessed his desire to be a woman by telling him to stop thinking that he could ever be a woman like her. He could only manage to be what a woman is as men have imagined her; although he could try to imitate her, even create a convincing facsimile, she insisted that "my shit will always remain mine, and yours will always be yours" (TWL, 345). Although she wouldn't have used these terms, Lila is clearly an essentialist or difference feminist. Alfonso is what we would now call a transwoman, something Lila would almost certainly have considered impossible. The Neapolitan novels are infused with this sense of female experience as fundamentally different from male experience, a difference rooted as much in biology as in culture. At a time when many feminist theorists no longer see conceptions of male and female as anchored in biology or rigidly determined by culture but rather understand gender as fluid, the Neapolitan novels portray deep and abiding gender difference.

The feminist movement of the late 1960s and 1970s had a major impact on Elena's life; as a university graduate and wife of a professor, she was very much influenced by the university-based feminist movement. This strand of feminism arose as a reaction to an educational curriculum that devalued women's experience and also to the sexism of the student left. Elena observed that there were few women involved in the university-based left wing organizations and they were mostly the girlfriends of male activists. She recalled that no women stood out in the chaos of the student left and that the young heroes had names like "Rudi Dutschke, Daniel Cohn-Bendit, and as in war films where there are only men, it was hard to feel part of it" (TWL, 63). The absence of women was no doubt a consequence of the outright hostility towards feminism on the part of some members of the male left, who saw feminism as a petit bourgeois deviation, a distraction from the class struggle. When her husband Pietro noticed that Elena was reading feminist theory, he warned her she should not allow herself to be influenced by feminism. He considered it nonsense and made every effort to point out what he considered the logical flaws in feminist literature.

Ironically Nino, whose serial infidelity caused Elena so much heartbreak, was an enthusiastic proponent of feminism. Elena grew to believe that Nino's veneration of female intelligence, his belief that the "waste of women's intellectual resources is the greatest waste of all" had its origins in his relationship with Lila, whose extraordinary intellectual gifts he was quick to recognize (SLC, 235). Nino's beliefs were all the more remarkable given the pervasive hostility to feminism on the part of the left. It was not just men who criticized the nascent feminist movement from a left-wing perspective; Pietro's mother Adele also did not think feminist issues could be dealt with independently of the class struggle.

Ferrante accurately describes Italian leftists' hostility to feminism; it was not just a matter of verbal derision. During the first congress of the Women's Liberation Movement held at the University of Rome in 1971, the female delegates decided to meet separately from the male delegates. The men forced open the doors of the women's meeting room and violently assaulted the women. According to anthropologist Amalia Signorelli, the incident sparked an intense debate among the Italian left and contributed to the growth of a separatist strand among Italian feminists.[5] The hostility towards separatism on the part of the male left continued through the 1970s and Elena refers to an incident when the radical left group *Lotta Continua* attacked a separatist women's demonstration. Violent reactions to feminism on the part of the male left were not just an Italian phenomenon. In one infamous incident that occurred at an anti–Vietnam War demonstration in Washington, D.C., in 1969, male activists shouted down a feminist speaker with cries of "Take her off the stage and fuck her!" and "Fuck her down a dark alley!"[6] The violent reaction to the demand for gender equality convinced many American women, like their Italian counterparts, that they had to break with the male left and form a separate movement.

Feminists were separating not just from their male comrades on the left but also from an entire male-dominated cultural tradition. In Italy the ground-breaking feminist thinker was art historian Carla Lonzi whose 1970 feminist pamphlet, *Let's Spit on Hegel*, attacked Hegel as a philosopher who epitomized the male modes of thinking which had legitimized gender inequality. Lonzi's work had a profound impact on Elena; every sentence resonated for her, especially the urgent need for women to free themselves from masculine intellectual traditions and resist the waste of female intelligence. She called on women to "spit on Hegel" and on Marx, on Engels, on Lenin, on Stalin, urging women to free themselves from male dominated political movements such as communism and socialism, to reject terrorism and left wing dogmas such as the dictatorship of the proletariat and the class struggle. Lonzi called for a rejection of Freudian psychoanalysis and a refusal to participate in institutions such as marriage and the family, which served to perpetuate patriarchal culture. Finally she rejected the "trap of equality," placing her firmly in the tradition of "difference feminism" (TWL, 280).

Although an attack on patriarchal thinking may seem like a commonplace in the 21st century, it is difficult to overstate what a shock it was for many women and men to read such sweeping denunciations of patriarchal culture from thinkers like Lonzi. Elena saw her own work as derivative, not engaged in radical questioning like Lonzi's. She believed that if Lila had been able to continue her education she would know how to think like Lonzi. When Elena contacted Lila, hoping to engage her in a conversation about the feminist books she was reading, Lila laughed derisively at the titles like *The Clitoral Woman and the Vaginal Woman*, and mocked Elena's interest in feminist literature: "What the fuck are you talking about, Lenù, pleasure, pussy, we've got plenty of problems here already" (TWL, 282).

Elena was not able to draw Lila into her explorations of feminist thought, so she continued her education through reading feminist writers like Lonzi and briefly joining what Americans would call a consciousness raising group and Italian feminists called *autocoscienza*, the method of starting from oneself. Sandra Kemp and Paolo Bono have described "the distinctively Italian character" of *autocoscienza*, noting that women have always met to talk about their lives particularly in Mediterranean cultures, taking part in what has usually been called gossip. Bono and Kemp note that *autocoscienza* "involved transforming an age old debased practice (gossip) into the self-determined and self-aware process of achieving a new confidence or awareness."[7] Elena soon decided that participating in these groups was not for her. She was convinced she understood well enough what it meant to be born a woman, and had no desire to engage in the work of consciousness-raising with the women in these groups; furthermore she had no interest in speaking in public about her relationship with her husband or with any other man (TWL, 281).

Elena's comments about *autocoscienza* are reminiscent of Korean-

American feminist Shirley Geok-lin Lim's analysis of her experience with such groups, which although generally seen as "safe spaces," also served to re-enforce race/class divisions. Lim noted that these "safe spaces" are problematic because of "who gets defined out-side these spaces" and that "women of color, immigrant women, blue collar women whose class and familial positions did not permit them the time to participate, women who did not easily share the cultural values that enabled them to openly discuss 'the intimate details of their lives' were much less likely to be invited to participate in consciousness raising groups."[8] Elena's upbringing may have made it difficult for her to talk publicly about her sexuality and to reveal intimate details about her life with Pietro. Despite her determination to remake herself in the image of a sophisticated upper middle class intellectual, vestiges of class background could not be totally erased.

Although Elena was not interested in consciousness-raising groups, she was interested in the individual's practice of *autocoscienza* and wanted to explore her own experiences, particularly her relationship with Lila, to probe what they had been unable to talk about. At times Ferrante refers to her narrators' probing of their motivations, their deepest fears and desires as *sorveglianza* (surveillance). In a letter to her publisher, Sandra Ozzolo, Ferrante states that Olga in *The Days of Abandonment* and Delia in *Troubling Love* both practice a "conscious surveillance of themselves." While women of previous generations were closely watched over by their families and communities, they did not examine themselves except "in imitation of their watchers, like jailers of themselves."[9] Delia and Olga were practicing a new kind of surveillance, motivated by their desire to expand their lives.

Unable to interest Lila in the project of conscious surveillance of their lives, Elena turned to research into representations of women in literature and once again found her voice as a writer. She discovered everywhere "female automatons created by men. There was nothing of ourselves" (TWL, 354). She repudiated her former attempts to give herself "male capacities," asking herself if she really cared about politics or if she was just trying to make a good impression on men, striving to be at their level. She deplored the time she spent in memorizing "fashionable jargon," realizing that "after the hard work of learning," now she must unlearn (TWL, 282). Fortunately for Elena, she was trying to build a career as a writer when there was tremendous demand for books exploring female experience from a feminist perspective.

The sections on Elena's development as writer incorporate Ferrante's interest in feminist thought. Ferrante told Elissa Schapell in an interview for *Vanity Fair*: "Today I read everything that emerges out of so-called post-feminist thought. It helps me look critically at the world, at us, our bodies, our subjectivity. But it also fires my imagination, it pushes me to reflect on the use of literature. I'll name some women to whom I owe a great deal: Firestone, Lonzi, Irigaray, Muraro, Caverero, Gagliasso, Haraway, Butler, Braidotti."[10] Luisa Muraro, who, along with other feminist writers in 1975 founded the Milan Women's Bookstore Collective, is credited with developing the concept of *affidamento* or "entrustment," which some literary critics have seen as a useful conceptual framework for understanding Ferrante's work—in particular, *The Lost Daughter*. According to Dayna Tortorici, "The Milan Women's Bookstore Collective encouraged women to seek out symbolic mothers and symbolic daughters." Tortorici cites Luisa Muraro's definition of entrustment as tying "yourself to a person who can help you achieve something which you think you are capable of but which you have not yet achieved." Tortorici also cites Teresa de Lauretis, who described entrustment as a relationship "in which one woman gives her trust or entrusts herself symbolically to another woman, who thus becomes her guide, mentor, or point of reference—in short, the figure of symbolic mediation between her and the world."[11]

Without an adequate reading knowledge of Italian, it is difficult to develop a sense of the extent to which Ferrante was influenced by Italian feminism, as much of the theoretical and literary work has not been translated. Also, Italian feminists were certainly not alone in their search for female role models. Adrienne Rich in her influential and widely read *Of Women Born* wrote: "Many women have been caught—have split themselves—between two mothers: one usually the biological mother who represents the culture of domesticity, of male centeredness, of conventional expectations, and another, perhaps a woman artist or teacher who becomes the countervailing figure. Often this 'counter-mother' is ... an unmarried woman professor, alive with ideas who represents the choice of a vigorous work life, of living alone and liking it."[12] This quest for the "counter-mother" or "symbolic mother" characterized many strands of feminist thought in the 1970s and 1980s. Perhaps Ferrante was influenced by Muraro's and de Lauretis' emphasis on the guidance of symbolic mothers, and perhaps their theory of "entrustment" shaped both *The Lost Daughter* and the Neapolitan novels. However, such inspiration could be found in the writings of a wide range of feminist thinkers, not to mention the life experiences of many women seeking feminist role models.

Many feminist thinkers in the 1970s and 1980s turned their attention to motherhood, whether biological or symbolic. Carla Lonzi, whose text "Let's Spit on Hegel" had such a profound influence on Elena, saw motherhood as "an essential female experience."[13] Lonzi's distinction between motherhood as experienced by individual women and motherhood as an oppressive social institution is very similar to Adrienne Rich's approach in *Of Women Born*. For western feminists, the 1970s and 1980s were marked by intense debate and considerable conflict over the meaning of motherhood. According to Laura Benedetti, while some Italian feminists shared Lonzi's perspective and "sought to reconcile militancy and motherhood, [others] saw women's liberation and motherhood as essentially antithetical."[14]

Elena's eventual reconciliation with her mother is reminiscent of 20th-century African American feminists' appreciation of their mothers, who, despite the crushing burdens and limited options available to them, nonetheless managed to nurture and inspire their daughters. A racial divide on the issue complicated the feminist debate on motherhood in the United States, with many African American feminists such as Alice Walker and Patricia Hill Collins celebrating their mothers' contributions, and many white feminists eager to distance themselves from their mothers. The largely white 1970s second wave feminist movement has frequently been characterized as a "daughters movement," young women often antagonistic to their mothers. African American feminist scholar Patricia Hill Collins in her groundbreaking study *Black Feminist Thought* argued that Black feminists must "honor our mothers' sacrifice by developing an Afrocentric analysis of Black motherhood." Collins contended that motherhood for many African American women has often brought power and recognition, but although "black motherhood can be rewarding it can also extract high personal costs."[15] Novelist Alice Walker in her influential essay "In Search of our Mothers' Gardens" also calls for honoring African American mothers and grandmothers both for their sacrifices and for handing on the "creative spark, the seed of the flower they themselves had never hoped to see."[16] It took Elena many years to develop an appreciation of her mother's strengths. Eventually she rejected her symbolic mother—her cultured, well-educated mother-in-law Adele—asserting that her own mother, despite her lack of formal education, was the better mother. She no longer wore the expensive jewelry she once did in imitation of Adele, preferring instead her mother's old silver bracelet. If the theory of entrustment has indeed influenced the Neapolitan Quartet, Ferrante has complicated the theory with a rejection of the symbolic mother and embrace of the biological mother.

African American feminists have also explored the concept of the symbolic mother, albeit with different terminology, "othermothers" rather than "symbolic mothers." Patricia Hill Collins, for example, has written extensively about the role of "othermothers" in African American communities, women who nurture children who are not their biological offspring. She also examined the "mothering the mind relationships ... between Black women teachers and their Black women students," noting that unlike traditional mentoring "this relationship goes far beyond providing students with technical skills or a network of academic and professional contacts."[17]

Elena and Lila's elementary school teacher Maestra Oliviera is a very different representation of the teacher as symbolic mother or "othermother" than that described by Hill Collins. When she lost her star pupil Lila, Maestra Oliviera focused all her attention on Elena, acting as a surrogate mother, imagining a path for Elena her own mother could not. However, her support was intermingled with class bias, with Maestra Oliviera treating Elena's own mother contemptuously, acting as if she were her real mother, and insisting that Elena not socialize with uneducated boys from the neighborhood. Although a source of support and encouragement to Elena, Maestra Oliviera was also capable of callousness and scorn for those she called the "plebs." Her disappointment that Lila's family would not allow her to continue school led Maestra Oliviera to treat Lila with cruelty, rudely refusing Lila's invitation to her wedding, later telling her she had been destined for greatness and berating her for wasting her intellectual gifts. Yet despite this treatment, Lila challenged Elena and Nino when they belittled Maestra Oliviera, stating that the teacher had meant a great deal to her. However, with her savage treatment of students who disappointed her and contempt for her students' families, Maestra Oliviera was a far cry from the othermothers envisioned by African American feminists, teachers who nurtured the minds and hearts of their students and saw themselves in solidarity with their students' families and communities.

From the late 1970s through the early 1990s some of the very same constructs, such as the role of the non-biological, symbolic mother, seem to have sprung up simultaneously and apparently independently in parts of the world as different as Northern Italy and the African American communities of the United States. It is unlikely that Ferrante is familiar with African American feminist thought. Although a major influence on feminism in the United States, references to African American feminists are largely absent from European feminist texts and are not among the many feminist texts Ferrante cites.

Although Ferrante's reading in feminist philosophical and literary traditions may not have included African American writers, she certainly has read widely in feminist theoretical and literary texts. In her many interviews, she cites a range of literary influences including Jane Austen, Clarice Lispector, Elsa Morante, Alice Munro, and Virginia Woolf.[18] Ferrante told an interviewer for *Vanity Fair*: "The novel that is fundamental for me is Elsa Morante's *House of Liars*."[19] When asked by an interviewer for the *Sydney Herald* if there is one writer "whose vision and truth" she tries to live up to, Ferrante replied, "Yes, the Italian writer Elsa Morante."[20] Both Ferrante and Morante are storytellers. As Ferrante noted in a *New York Times* interview: "I'm a storyteller. I've always been more interested in storytelling than in writing. Even today, Italy has a weak narrative tradition. Beautiful, magnificent, very carefully crafted pages abound, but not the flow of storytelling that despite its density manages to sweep you away. A bewitching example is Elsa Morante. I try to learn from her books, but I find them unsurpassable."[21]

There are some similarities between the Neapolitan Quartet and *House of Liars*; both are long novels spanning many years, with a large cast of characters, in many ways reminiscent of 19th-century fiction. Both books explore the struggle to move up in a class bound society. However, the *House of Liars* was set in early 20th-century Sicily, a semi-feudal society without much of a middle class and where the option to change status through education was much more limited. Both books explore troubled mother/daughter relationships; both explore gender fluidity and gender ambiguity. Despite the thematic and structural similarities, there are striking differences in the quality of the writing. Ferrante's prose dazzles on the sentence level; Morante's does not, no doubt in part due to what is generally considered a poor English translation. Morante disavowed the 1951 translation by Adrienne Foulke and found the novel "unrecognizable."[22] I found myself at times skimming sections of *House of Liars* and struggled to finish the book. With Ferrante, I was never tempted to skim passages; I devoured every word. If I had read *House of Liars* and the Neapolitan Quartet without any knowledge of Ferrante's claim that Morante had influenced her, I'm not sure I would have seen a connection between these books. Perhaps the connection is not so much similarities in the text as in the inspiration Morante provided. According to Ferrante, in *House of Liars* "I discovered what literature can be. That novel multiplied my ambitions, but it also weighed on me, paralyzing me."[23]

In addition to expanding her literary horizons, Morante's life may have contributed to the Neapolitan Quartet in another way; her life story may have been one of the sources for the character of Lila. According to her biographer Lily Tuck, Morante, like Lila, was a child prodigy who taught herself to read and write at a very early age. Of course the trajectory of their lives was very different. Although she experienced periods of economic hardship, Morante—unlike Lila—had an educated mother who encouraged her ambitions. Yet biographer Lily Tuck's description of Morante could very well be a description of the adult Lila: "EM was not amiable, she was not genial, she was not sweet or always nice.... A truth teller, she intended to say hurtful things. She was immensely talented, passionate, often impossible, courageous, quarrelsome, witty, ambitious, generous.... She detested any sort of posturing, falsehood, she detested the abuse of power."[24] Given her intense interest in Morante, it's likely that Ferrante had some knowledge of Morante's life story and it's possible that she read Tuck's book.

Interestingly, Ferrante doesn't refer to Simone de Beauvoir when she cites feminist writers who have influenced her. She was clearly familiar with Beauvoir's work and *The Days of Abandonment* has been read by literary critics Lisa Mullenneaux and Stefania Lucamente as Ferrante's response to Beauvoir's *The Woman Destroyed*.[25] Olga, the narrator of *The Days of Abandonment*, as a teenager was profoundly affected by *The Woman Destroyed*; Monique, the narrator of Beauvoir's novel, represented everything Olga rejected. Given that one of Ferrante's works was in some ways a response to Beauvoir's *The Woman Destroyed* and given Beauvoir's enormous influence on feminist thought, particularly European feminist thought, I find it surprising that Beauvoir is not included among the many writers Ferrante sees as her feminist forebears. Perhaps this can be explained by Ferrante's declared interest in "difference feminism," a strand of feminist thought very different from Beauvoir's, but the omission of Beauvoir is nonetheless surprising.

German novelist Christa Wolf is another notable omission among those Ferrante identifies as feminist foremothers, no doubt because it would provide a clue as to Ferrante's identity. Not until Claudio Gatti provided evidence that Anita Raja (probably in collaboration with her husband Domenico Starnone) was the author of the Neapolitan Quartet did I learn that Raja had translated Wolf's novels into Italian. Gatti quotes Raja's recollection, published in the Italian newspaper *Il Manifesto* in March 2015: "I met Christa in 1984, and with time our relationship turned into friendship.... It was very formative for me." Gatti notes that in a statement published in 2011 on the website of the Goethe Institute, Raja wrote that Wolf's "way of verbalizing has affected my own poorer and more unrefined relationship with my language. It's given it new power, pushing me in directions I would never have thought of going." Gatti cites Rebecca Falkoff, professor of Italian studies at New York University, who is convinced that Ferrante's novels show the influence of Wolf. Gatti further cites a March 2009 article in which Raja and Starnone acknowledge the influence of Wolf and also discuss their own collaborative efforts: "Every book by Christa that [Raja] translated into Italian led to months of intense discussions between the two of us, an opportunity to reflect, to learn."[26]

After reading this, I re-read Wolf's *The Quest for Christa T.*, which I had read sometime in the late 1980s. Wolf is a writer I had wanted to like, tried to like, but she did not speak to me. Her spare, restrained style seemed to have little in common with the Neapolitan Quartet, with its impassioned prose, its large cast of characters, teeming with life. Although I never would have connected the two authors without Gatti's prompt, I can see traces of Wolf in Ferrante's novels. There are some similarities between the narrative framework of the Neapolitan Quartet and that of *The Quest for Christa T.* with the unnamed narrator standing in for Elena and the talented, unorthodox Christa T. for Lila. In *The Quest for Christa T.*, the narrator traces her friendship with a childhood friend until the friend's untimely death in her mid-thirties. The narrator is fascinated by Christa T.'s daring, unorthodox behavior. While walking with a group of her classmates, Christa T. suddenly transforms a newspaper into a makeshift trumpet and blows it with her shout Hooohaahooo. From that moment on, the narrator longed to follow that shout: "I wanted to share in a life that produced such shouts as her *Hooohaahooo*."[27] Similarly Elena, fascinated by Lila, longed to keep pace with "that terrible dazzling girl." She decided that she had to model herself on Lila, "never let her out of my sight, even if she got annoyed and chased me away" (BF, 46).

Christa T., like Elena and Lila, wanted to become a writer and from the age of ten kept a small notebook bound in blue flowered silk which passed into the hands of the narrator after Christa T.'s death. The narrator, through Christa T.'s writings and through her own recollections of their relationship, wanted to create a text that would finally capture her elusive friend. Similarly Elena sought to create a text that would capture Lila, despite Lila's desire to erase all traces of her existence. In both stories, there is the sense of lost opportunity, wasted talent, but in Christa T.'s case the loss is the consequence of illness and early death, while in Lila's case the lost opportunity is the result of poverty. Elena says of Lila: "What she would have made of my luck" (SNN, 337). The narrator says of Christa: "[If she had lived], she would have done it, all of it."[28] Despite these similarities between the narrative framework of the Neapolitan Quartet and that of *The Quest for Christa T.* there are major differences. In *The Quest for Christa T.* we learn very little about the narrator; the focus is all on Christa T., and the dense social world of the Neapolitan novels is absent. In the Neapolitan Quartet, on the other hand, the stories of the two women and their complicated relationship are fully developed and placed within a vivid portrait of Italy in the second half of the 20th century.

Wolf's use of classical mythology may be another influence on Ferrante's novels. Stefania Lucamante notes that among the many versions of the Medea story in western literary tradition from Euripides and Ovid to Corneille, Christa Wolf's is the first version in which we see "Medea's torment suddenly appearing in the garb of an everyday life experience."[29] Ferrante's *The Days of Abandonment*, frequently seen as a recreation of Euripides' Medea, depicts a Medea-like figure, who emerges from ordinary everyday life. Also, in the Neapolitan Quartet, Elena Greco exhibits Medea-like qualities when she responds to verbal attacks from her lover Nino's wife Eleonora. Unlike Medea and Olga in *The Days of Abandonment*, who did actual harm to the woman who replaced them in their husband's affections, Elena with "evil in her heart" only fantasized about savagely attacking her rival. She vowed that if Nino's wife Eleonora should show up at her door as she had threatened, Elena would spit on her, throw her down the staircase, "drag her out to street by the hair, shatter that head full of shit on the sidewalk" (TWL, 407). Both Medea, the woman betrayed who seeks vengeance, and Virgil's Dido, the woman betrayed who, maddened with grief, kills herself, are powerful presences in Ferrante's work. As Olga is in some sense enhanced by the implicit analogy to Medea, Ferrante's suggestion of a connection between Lila's and Nino's passionate love affair and the tragic tale of Dido and Aeneas lends a larger dimension to Lila and Nino's sad story of love and betrayal.

As with Wolf's work, classical allusions abound in the novellas and throughout the Neapolitan quartet. Elena observed that Marcello Solara looked like the portrait of Hector in her school copy of the *Iliad*, underscoring her fascination with the Solara brothers' good looks and status in the neighborhood. While watching the young men of the neighborhood get ready for their New Year's Eve battle, armed with firecrackers and explosives, Elena thought that if a civil war should occur "like the one between Romulus and Remus, between Marius and Sulla, between Caesar and Pompey, they will have these same faces, these same looks, these same poses" (BF, 174). The classical allusion conveys Elena's growing awareness of and attraction to young men while also suggesting the age-old historical drama of male violence. Such allusions to the classical tradition recur throughout the Neapolitan novels suggesting that Ferrante, like her narrator Elena Greco, had a background in the classics.

Finally, there may be echoes of Wolf's observations on the suppression of women's voices in Ferrante's description of Elena's development as a writer. Wolf describes women "wearing themselves out trying to integrate themselves into the prevailing [male] delusional systems."[30] Similarly, Elena castigates herself for her former attempts to develop "male capacities," asking herself, why had she tried so hard to master male-dominated cultural traditions. Of course, rejection of the sexism embedded in the literary canon pervaded much of the feminist literature that Ferrante tells us she has read; she need not have been influenced directly by Wolf.

Given how much time a translator spends with an author's work, it is not at all surprising that something of Christa Wolf should have seeped into the Neapolitan Quartet—or perhaps more accurately into Anita Raja's contribution to the Neapolitan Quartet. The author(s) of the works attributed to the fictional character Elena Ferrante, have clearly read widely in world literature, feminist literature and feminist literary theory. As Ferrante told the *Paris Review*, "There is no work of literature that is not the fruit of tradition, of many skills, of a sort of collective intelligence. We wrongfully diminish this collective intelligence when we insist on there being a single protagonist behind every work of art."[31] And as literary critic Dayna Tortorici noted pointing to the tradition from which Ferrante drew: "The name Elena Ferrante is not a credit but an homage—to Elsa Morante, to the feminist collectives, to the literary tradition before her, to her mothers. There's more truth in this name than any other she could give."[32]

Ferrante's feminism (like Elena's) is best developed, most passionate, when she explores its impact on her writing. As a young woman she was convinced that the greatest narrators were men; if she wanted to become a writer, she had to learn to write like them. She did not want to write in the style of "Madame de La Fayette or Jane Austen or the Brontes ... but like Defoe or Fielding or Flaubert or Tolstoy or Dostoyevsky or even Hugo."[33] Her introduction to women writers like Elsa Morante opened a whole new world: "I wouldn't recognize myself without women's struggles, women's nonfiction, women's literature—they made me an adult.... We have to show that we can construct worlds that are not only as wide and powerful and rich as those constructed by men but more so. We have to be well equipped, we have to dig deep into our difference, using advanced tools."[34] Elena is determined to resurrect and expand women's literary traditions. Echoing the laments of such feminist thinkers as Christine de Pizan in the 15th century and Mary Wollstonecraft in the 18th, she deplored "the solitude of women's minds ... it's a waste to be separated from each other, without procedures, without tradition" (TWL, 354).

Gerda Lerner in her ground-breaking study, *The Creation of Feminist Consciousness* has noted that Christine de Pizan's "most important feminist insights found no echo among women for centuries to come." In the absence of communities of women who could have built on her insights, de Pizan's "ideas, new and revolutionary for their time, fell like seeds on rocky ground."[35] Mary Wollstonecraft developed her theories in the 18th century without having access to the long-forgotten work of de Pizan. Lerner has documented the "cruel repetitiousness" by which individual women, lacking knowledge of the work of their predecessors, unknowingly repeated the efforts made by other women in previous centuries. Feminist thinkers like Elena Greco (or her creator Elena Ferrante) need not fear a fate similar to that of Christine de Pizan. Feminist writers reached a critical mass in the second half of the 20th century; the insights of these writers will not so easily be erased.

Elena's feminism is very much a literary, intellectual strand of feminism, questioning the centrality of the male tradition in literature, and in all academic disciplines. There is little of the feminist activism which expanded opportunities for women in public life, changed institutions and laws, granting women the freedom to divorce and to control if and when they would have children. In her comments made in her many interviews, Ferrante suggests that her feminism was very much like Elena's. She told an interviewer for *Vanity Fair* that although she was "a passionate reader of feminist thought," she did not consider herself a militant and believed that she was "incapable of militancy."[36] The social activism of the 1960s and 1970s is very much a part of the Neapolitan novels, but it is the activism of the class struggle, very much part of Pasquale's story and, to a lesser extent, Enzo's story, and for a brief period during her time as a union organizer, Lila's story, but not part of Elena's story.

Surprisingly, in a series of novels in which feminist thought plays such an important role in the life of the narrator, there is no mention of the movement for abortion rights, and despite not wanting to have a second child, Elena never considered abortion. Elena feared having an abortion—"the very word made [her] stomach hurt" (SLC, 258). When her mother-in-law Adele brought up the subject, Elena avoided it, telling Adele that it would be better for her daughter Dede to have a sibling. It was then 1973 and abortion would not be legal until 1977; however, affluent well-connected women could always arrange abortions and Elena's mother-in-law would certainly have known how to do so.

Although abortion is something neither Elena nor Lila ever considered, the fear of unwanted pregnancy is very much a part of Elena and Lila's story. Prior to the ready availability of birth control pills, contraception required the cooperation of the male partner, and as Elena discovered, even well educated, politically progressive men like her husband Pietro were sometimes opposed to contraception. While the reader of the Neapolitan novels would never know there was a powerful movement for abortion rights in Italy in the 1970s, there is a reference to the movement to make contraceptives widely available. When Lila, having just learned about the existence of birth control pills, asked a doctor for a prescription, he referred her to a feminist doctor who refused to accept payment, saying that she and her friends had a mission to provide access to a safe, reliable form contraception. Such access made a tremendous difference in Lila's life and the lives of many women of her generation.

The enormous change in the lives of women in the period covered by the Neapolitan Quartet is the optimistic strand in the novels. Ferrante both in her novels and in her interviews is deeply pessimistic about the left wing project of the redistribution of wealth and power. The class gaps have widened, but within the capitalist system at every rung of the ladder, relations between men and women have changed. Yes, the women who have benefited the most are those, by virtue of their social class, best positioned to take advantage of new opportunities. In Europe and North America women with educational/economic advantages have made enormous progress; as we see feminist ideas spreading around the globe, the same pattern obtains with women from elite backgrounds registering the greatest gains.

However, the change in expectations is pervasive among women from a broad range of socio-economic backgrounds. Amalia Signorelli, during the course of a research project completed in 2000, interviewed many young women from Southern Italy. They did not have a university education, were married and had children; most were unemployed not by choice but because of the high unemployment rate in Southern Italy and they shouldered the entire burden of domestic work and childcare. Signorelli and the other members of her research team "were surprised by the conviction and pride with which most of them declared that they attended a gym, a swimming pool or a beauty parlor at least once a week and that they would allow nothing to stop them doing so. They did this not to become more attractive or to please their husbands ... [but because they] feel entitled as women. They feel they have a right to do something for themselves. This is what has changed."[37] This is an attitude inconceivable in a previous generation of Southern Italian women; Lila's and Elena's mothers would never have insisted on their personal space, on pleasure just for themselves.

However, Ferrante sees these gains as fragile: "Even if we're continually tempted to lower our guard—for love or weariness, for sympathy or kindness—we women shouldn't do it. We can lose from one moment to the next everything that we've achieved."[38] The idea that the conflict is far from over and that the gains women have made could be lost recurs throughout her many interviews: "regression is always possible. The problem is that real change takes a long time."[39] Ferrante does not see the danger of regression as stemming solely from male reaction to women's gains; rather the greatest danger now is female nostalgia for "the 'real men' of bygone days.... The crowd of women who adore the sensibility and sexual energy of the worst male characters in *My Brilliant Friend* illustrate this temptation."[40]

At the end of Neapolitan Quartet, Elena reflected on the lives of her daughters, now adults living in the United States and in France: She noted that their lives were very different from hers, that the world has changed dramatically during her lifetime, belonging less to her and more to her daughters, that her daughters have desires and a sense of entitlement that even at this point in her life she would not permit herself. Elena thinks her daughters attribute their success to their father but that she now believes that she was the source of their privileges. Ferrante would also surely credit the feminist movement, which fought so hard for the changes that made Elena's daughters' lives possible.

12
Naples and the Camorra

> *"A permanent stream of splendors and miseries, a cyclical Naples where everything was marvelous and everything became gray and irrational and everything sparkled again...."*—Elena Ferrante, *The Story of the Lost Child*

My interest in Naples, often referred to as a major character in the Neapolitan Quartet, preceded my love for Ferrante. My husband and I were in Naples in 1999 and fell in love with the city; my love for Ferrante's books inspired a return trip in 2016. Apparently many other Ferrante fans have descended on Naples, a city that until recently has been neglected by tourists. Neapolitan tour guide Francesca Siniscalchi has complained bitterly about the Italian government's failure to invest resources in tourism to Naples with the result that tourists would "go to Capri, Pompeii, or the Amalfi coast skipping the city. It seems that the national government is deliberately excluding the city, and this appears quite clearly from the project of a direct fast train connecting Rome to Pompeii. The target is a quick and hit and run kind of tourism from which Naples is completely excluded."[1] Siniscalchi noted that for many years the only information about Naples was "its dirt and danger"; she credits the Internet with changing the image of Naples, allowing tourists to share their impressions and counter the negative perceptions of the city. Those perceptions are well entrenched. According to a 2015 survey conducted by national newspaper *Il Sole 24 Ore*, Naples was rated as the Italian city with the worst quality of life, largely due to organized crime's involvement in waste disposal, leading to concerns over possible contamination of food and water supplies.[2]

However, despite the long-standing negative images of the city, "Ferrante Fever" appears to be changing perceptions of Naples and is apparently responsible for a recent uptick in tourism. I had originally intended to go on one of the widely advertised Ferrante tours and visit the places mentioned in the Neapolitan Novels. Then came Claudio Gatti's revelations. Pre-Gatti, I had assumed Naples was the place where the mysterious author of the novels had grown up. Ferrante certainly reinforced this belief in numerous interviews, telling an interviewer for *Vanity Fair*: "Naples is a space containing all my primary, childhood, adolescent, and early adult experiences. Many of my stories about people I know and whom I have loved come both from that city and in its language."[3] Since Ferrante has turned out to be a fictional character, camouflage for the identity of the presumed real author (who grew up in Rome), I lost my enthusiasm for trying to track down the impoverished neighborhood where the main characters grew up.

I decided to forego the incredibly expensive Ferrante tours advertised on various travel sites and instead do what I love best when visiting European cities—wandering around, taking in the open-air architectural museum. Getting to know Naples' neighborhoods deepened my love for Ferrante's Neapolitan novels. Yes, there are many run-down sections, but some of them, particularly in the old quarter, are incredibly picturesque. Naples is a very vertical city, with the desirable residential neighborhoods in the hills—such as the Vomero, where Professor Galiani lived and Posillipo, where Michele Solara lived. Naples appears much more prosperous than it did in 1999, with many more expensive shops around the Via Mille and The Piazza Martiri, the place for high-end shopping in the 1960s when the Solara brothers opened their shoe store there. It continues to be the place to go for luxury goods.

Apparently quite a few Ferrante-inspired tourists have tried to track down the sites mentioned in the Neapolitan novels. The "Rione Luzzatti" in the eastern outskirts of Naples has been identified by various Ferrante tours as the neighborhood in which the book is set. One Ferrante tourist posted a detailed account of her visit to places mentioned in the Neapolitan Quartet: the Church of the district; the little square with its gardens; the public library where Elena and Lila borrowed books; and the tunnel that leads to the sea. She reported "the same drop of water mentioned by Elena, and experienced the same feeling on leaving the tunnel, when we are literally dazzled by the light of the great avenue that leads to the sea and the building sites of the port."[4]

Anglophones living in Naples have reported increasing requests from friends who want to visit them. According to writer Katherine Wilson, ever since she moved to Naples twenty years ago she has encouraged her Anglo-American friends who were planning a trip to Italy to come to Naples. The response was always: "No, thanks. We've heard that it's dirty and dangerous. Gritty, rough, corrupt." But thanks to Elena Ferrante's novels, Wilson's friends now want to visit Naples. Wilson herself is a Ferrante fan who values the way Ferrante "captures the contradictions that are at the heart of Naples and Neapolitan culture. She/he/it recreates the gritty, the dangerous, and the lurid and sets it against the sensory paradise that is Napoli." Wilson rightly notes that Naples has been a tourist destination for three thousand years, with rich Romans vacationing along the coastline of Posillipo; furthermore, in the 18th century and early 19th century, Naples drew famous tourists such as Jean-Jacques Rousseau who said, "If you want to know if you have a spark within you, run—no fly!—to Naples...."[5]

Naples most famous booster was Wolfgang von Goethe, who saw Naples as "a school for easy, happy living,"[6] and wrote in his journals: "As they say here, '*Vedi Napoli e poi muori!*—See Naples and die!' One can't blame the Neapolitans for never wanting to leave this city, nor its poets for singing its praises in lofty hyperboles."[7] Naples continues to be a source of inspiration for writers, particularly Anglophone writers such as novelist Francine Prose, who see beyond the filth, crime and danger to discover "brilliant colors, the energy, the wildness, the sheer sensory overload of Naples [that] make Palermo—until now my personal gold standard for the most attractive example of chaotic urban vitality—seem, by comparison, as orderly and restrained as Zurich."[8]

Book-length explorations of contemporary Neapolitan life which complement Ferrante's novels include Dan Hofstadter's *Falling Palace: A Romance of Naples*,[9] part travelogue, part love story which interweaves a vivid portrait of Naples street life, the architectural treasures of the city and the author's love affair with an enigmatic Neapolitan woman; Shirley Hazzard and Francis Steegmuller's *The Ancient Shore: Dispatches from Naples*,[10] a collection of essays about their love affair with Italy, their life together in Capri, and their reflections on the history and cultural legacy of Naples; and Benjamin Taylor's *Naples Declared: A Walk Around the Bay*,[11] a walking tour of Naples which incorporates his deep knowledge of 3,000 years of Neapolitan history into his reflections on the present-day city. All these books are written from the perspective of tourists who do not have to cope with the day-to-day struggles of life in Naples or expatriates with the economic resources to insulate themselves from these difficulties.

Ferrante describes a real city as it is experienced by Neapolitans without economic resources. Although the poverty of Elena and Lila's childhood no doubt strikes many readers as extreme poverty, Rutgers University History Professor Paola Gambarota notes that there were many Neapolitan families in far worse circumstances. According to Gamborata, many children, like Lila, dropped out of school at an early age to earn money for their families; however, as the daughter of a shoemaker, Lila would not have been among the most impoverished: "Poverty there [in the 1950s] meant you lived seven people to one room, and that there was nothing to eat. People with no shoes.... It's not the poverty that we know here."[12]

The city described in the first volume of the Neapolitan Quartet, *My Brilliant Friend*, was struggling to recover from the devastation of World War II. According to historian Tom Behan, Naples experienced much greater damage than major northern Italian cities; over one hundred Allied bombing raids left 200,000 Neapolitans homeless and seriously damaged the area around the port.[13] During the postwar reconstruction of Naples, organized crime became an ever more powerful force in the city. In Elena and Lila's world, the growing influence of the Camorra crime syndicate was personified by the Solara family, which gained control over the increasingly prosperous neighborhood economy. The late 1950s and 1960s was the time of the so-called "economic miracle," an economic expansion fueled by cheaper energy and American aid through the Marshall plan. Historian Tommaso Astarito considers the most remarkable change to have been in food consumption, noting that "after decades of shortages and poor diet, and severe hunger during and soon after the war, by the 1960s Italians began to have access to plentiful and varied food."[14]

Ferrante seamlessly integrates the socio-economic history of Naples in the 1950s and 1960s into Elena and Lila's story. Elena described the many changes the neighborhood underwent during her middle school years, the period of the so-called economic miracle. Elena described the expansion of Solaras' bar which had become a well-stocked pastry shop, and supporting Astarito's point about changes in food consumption, she noted that the neighborhood grocery store was stocked with all sorts of good food overflowing onto the sidewalk. As she passed by, she "caught a whiff of spices, of olives, of salami, of fresh bread, of pork fat and cracklings that made you hungry." Elena observed enterprises flourishing throughout the neighborhood. New businesses were emerging and existing ones were expanding—a dry goods store expanded to become a ladies' clothing shop; an auto repair shop was now getting into motorcycles. Elena described a neighborhood in the throes of change where everything was in motion, "arching upward," striving to transcend the ugliness, the ancient quarrels and hatreds and instead "to show a new face" (BF, 108–09).

As a teenager, Lila struggled to understand the history of the neighborhood and the power relations of her world. She turned to Pasquale Peluso, whose world view was shaped by his involvement in the Communist Party, to help her make sense of the recent history of Naples, and then turned to the poorly stocked neighborhood library to go beyond Pasquale's small store of knowledge. Armed with these new ideas, Lila ascribed concrete motives, and ordinary faces to the atmosphere of ill-defined fears and vague anxieties that pervaded the neighborhood, part of the air she and Elena breathed. The impact of Fascism, Nazism, World War II on the neighborhood had not disappeared, with neighborhood villains such as Don Achille and the Camorrist grandfather of the Solaras, and even her own father, "all—in her eyes stained to the marrow with shadowy crimes, all hardened criminals or acquiescent accomplices … all bought for practically nothing" (BF, 154–55).

Unlike Lila, Elena was not particularly interested in understanding her city's recent history, but rather on her single-minded struggle to escape Naples. According to historian Paola Gambarota, the longing to escape was especially common among women: "In order to evade that daily violence, that daily force that you were subjected to—and there are some small things but really very difficult things—you just have to go away.… And this has happened to so many of us. You just have to get away. You just have, at a certain point, a feeling that there is nothing that you can change."[15] Elena longed to escape Naples and eventually did; Lila was enmeshed in the life of the city and did not leave until her mid–60s, when she mysteriously disappeared. Elena and Lila are in a sense defined by their relationship to Naples—Elena by her desire to escape, Lila by her reluctance not only to leave Naples but her reluctance to leave the neighborhood. This tendency was there from the very beginning of their friendship. Shortly before the end of their final year in elementary school, Lila convinced Elena to skip school and explore the world beyond the neighborhood; their goal was to reach the sea. When it became apparent that a thunderstorm was on the horizon, Lila became agitated and insisted

12. Naples and the Camorra

they turn back. Elena realized that a "mysterious inversion of attitudes" had taken place; she found herself "joyfully open to the unknown" and wanted to continue whereas Lila always the fearless, adventurous one, wanted to rerun to the confines of the neighborhood (BF, 75–78). Elena had a similar response to her first trip to Ischia, the first vacation she had ever taken; she described a sensation that recurred throughout her life, what she called "the joy of the new" (BF, 211).

Elena exulted in immersing herself in other cultures, discovering the provisional nature of what she had once considered universal. Increasingly contemptuous of Lila's provincialism, as an adult Elena at one time entertained the cruel thought that Lila would spend the rest of her life "looking out on the trucks passing on the Stradone" (SLC, 26). However, Lila was far from provincial. She may not have left Naples before her disappearance at the age of sixty-six, but her mind roamed far and wide. In old age, Lila welcomed the influx of Asian and African immigrants in Naples. Delighting in the aroma of foreign cuisines, she told Elena, that she may not have traveled around the world, but the world had come to her.

For many years after she had escaped, Elena had a horror of being dawn back into Naples. When she returned to Naples for the first time after years of living in Florence, she felt trapped by the city, once again subjected to its unwritten laws. She found the noise intolerable, the incessant honking of horns, the scurrilous insults the drivers shouted at [her then husband] Pietro, who unused to the chaotic streets of Naples, wavered and slowed down. The day-to-day difficulty of life in Naples is a recurrent theme in the Neapolitan novels. When Elena returned to live in Naples to be with Nino, she gave up driving because she was always stuck in traffic; she realized how much she struggled with the endless demands of daily life, so much more than was ever the case in Florence or Milan. Then there are the countless references to the intolerable heat, the torments of a Neapolitan summer before air-conditioning.

Yet despite their day-to-day difficulties, Ferrante's characters, to varying degrees, do appreciate the beauty of the city. When Elena was about to leave the confines of the neighborhood to go to high school, her father took her on a tour of the city, to "Piazza Carlo III, the Albergo dei Poveri, the Botanical Garden, Via Forio, the museum." At the end of the tour, he brought her to the water's edge to see Vesuvius close up. For Elena it was a moment she would never forget: Vesuvius was a graceful, pale violet shape, the sea was loud and turbulent, with waves crashing onto the street.

Her father held tightly to her hand as if he feared she would be swept away. At that moment she did want to leave him. Transfixed by the powerful gusts of wind, the waves and the brilliant sunlight, Elena recalled that at that moment, she pretended she "was alone in the newness of the city, new myself with all life ahead" (BF, 137–38). Her mother's interest in the history of Naples was awakened by Elena's husband Pietro, when he came to Naples to meet Elena's family. Her father was acting as tour guide; then Pietro, a classics professor, began to talk about the history of Naples, its art and its monuments. Elena and her mother were impressed by his wealth of knowledge, but realizing that her father felt upstaged, Elena signaled to Pietro to stop. To Elena's surprise, her mother with one of her unpredictable twists, hung on his arm and asked Pietro to continue, saying that she liked listening to Pietro's stories, that no one had ever told her any of this.

Before leaving Naples to live with her husband in Florence, Elena visited a childhood friend now living in an apartment high in the hills of the Posillipo district; she was awestruck by the view of the bay, finding herself mesmerized by the beauty of Naples. The night before Elena left for Florence she took a pre-dawn walk through Naples to the sea. She wondered what conception she might have had about herself and about her city if she had grown up in one of the wealthy neighborhoods by the sea rather than in her impoverished neighborhood. She fantasized about a Naples inhabited by citizens who were not deformed by poverty and who could delight in the beauty of the landscape. But far more than any momentary nostalgia for Naples, Elena was driven by the desire to escape.

Lila, in late middle age, developed an intense interest in Neapolitan history and culture, spending days in the Biblioteca Nazionale, learning everything she could about Naples. She introduced Elena's daughter Imma to the wonders of Naples—"to a permanent stream of splendors and miseries, a cyclical Naples where everything was marvelous and everything became gray and irrational and everything sparkled again" (SLC, 440). While Lila was immersing herself in the history of the city, Elena was putting Naples behind her. She left Naples once and for all in 1995, a time when the city was supposedly reviving. Elena no longer believed in resurrections; she saw the revival as only cosmetic, a "powder of modernity applied randomly, and boastfully, to the corrupt face of the city" (SLC, 335). However, when Lila began to speak about the city as if it had made visible only to her a secret sparkle, Elena began to see Naples as a city rich in meaning, and regretted that she had never made an effort to know it. Lila had retained her ability to make Elena share her enthusiasms.

Although both the splendors and miseries of Naples are interwoven into the Neapolitan Quartet, Ferrante's readers are unlikely to come away from the novels with the splendors of the city foremost in their minds. Particularly in the final volume, *Story of the Lost Child*, the twin themes of crime and corruption dominate. Ferrante has skillfully interwoven the history of the corruption scandals of the early 1990s with the lives of her characters, such as Nino Sarratore and Guido Aiorta, who were among the many politicians caught up in the *Tangentopoli* scandal (some times translated as Bribesville) which erupted in Milan in 1992. Journalist John Hooper described *Tangentopoli* as a deeply ingrained system of bribery in which "the price of everything supplied to the public—from airports to paper napkins in an old people's home had been inflated."[16] The difference between a fair price and the inflated price actually paid was channeled to the politicians and the political parties with the power to award the contracts. Sometimes the cash was used to pay the expenses of the political parties and some of it went into the pockets of individual politicians.

According to historian Paul Ginsborg, political corruption increased throughout Europe in the 1980s and early 1990s, in some cases as a consequence of increasing deregulation and privatization. In the case of Italy, the corruption was not merely a consequence of the political and economic developments of the 1980s, but was deeply rooted in the political culture of the country. Ginsborg has argued that "the 1980s witnessed a new and organized rapacity on the part of politicians, a spoils system which extended throughout the peninsula." The system of kickbacks came to be seen as normal procedure, the "cost of politics."[17] The Socialist Party was particularly compromised and its members openly defended their corrupt practices. They denigrated "old style moralists ... cretins who still don't understand how the world goes round."[18] Ginsborg sees them as latter day Machiavellians: "The group of Socialists who clustered around their charismatic leader [Bettino Craxi], for the most part intelligent and able men, seemed at times to have learned by heart Machiavelli's famous line from the fifteenth chapter of *The Prince*: 'How we live is so far removed from how we ought to live, that he who abandons what is done for what ought to be done, will rather learn to bring about his own ruin than his preservation.'"[19]

Like the socialists described by Ginsborg, in the 1980s Nino Sarratore began to argue that corruption was just the price of doing politics. Elena thought Nino went too far, ridiculing what he saw as Elena's naiveté, claiming that there are "too many sensitive souls around ... a [political] party can't be anything other than a distribution of favors in exchange for support, ideals are part of the furniture." He maintained that if you wanted to change society, you had to get your hands dirty. Elena was slowly growing estranged from Nino on a political as well as a personal level, finding that he no longer convinced her the way he once did. She saw the contradictions in his thinking, the facile rationalizations of ethically dubious positions. When Nino said that laws were necessary for the world to function, Elena reminded him that he had also said that the judiciary should not be independent, "that judges should be controlled" (SLC, 227–29). Nino's aversion to an independent judiciary took a personal twist when he was swept up in the anti-corruption dragnet of the *Tangentopoli* scandals. Nino, with his usual readiness to rationalize his bad behavior, blamed his arrest on a left that he no longer considered a left, but was actually much worse than the Fascists. Ever the opportunist, he shifted further to the right and eventually regained his seat in parliament.

The *Tangentopoli* scandals involved all sectors of Italy's political, professional and economic elites. John Hooper reported that "more than 5,000 people were placed under investigation, of whom 2,735 were indicted in Milan alone. Another 1,785 cases were sent to other jurisdictions." According to Hooper, only the disposition of the Milan cases has been examined in detail. The wheels of justice in Italy apparently turn very slowly; a decade after the launch of the first investigation, more than one sixth of the cases was still awaiting a verdict, with another one sixth ending in acquittal. Of the remaining two thirds, almost none of the defendants received a prison sentence, either because of a plea bargain or because charges had to be dropped due to a statute of limitations.[20]

Ferrante depicts a society in which citizens have little faith that the legal system will bring lawbreakers to justice—whether they are corrupt politicians or common criminals. When one of Lila's accountants stole millions from her company, she and Enzo fired him and filed charges, but nothing happened. Lila said she was fed up with waiting for the law to respond and she called Antonio, who served as an enforcer for the Solaras and for Lila. The money was quickly returned, "without a trial, without lawyers, and without judges" (SLC, 274). When Lila's daughter Tina disappeared, no one in the neighborhood expected the police to find Tina. Instead all Lila's friends and relatives mobilized to search for her, but to no avail. Criminal gangs acted with relative impunity shielded by corrupt politicians, many of whom, like Nino, managed to avoid a conviction when he was charged in the *Tangentopoli* corruption scandals.

The prosecutors in the *Tangentopoli* scandals emphasized the link between the struggle against organized crime and the struggle against corruption in public life. Roberto Saviano has explored this connection in *Gomorrah*, a powerful expose of the Camorra crime syndicate, which dominated Naples just as the Mafia dominated Sicily. According to Saviano, "Camorra is a non-existent word, a term of contempt used by narcs and judges, journalists and scriptwriters.... The word clan members use is *System*—'I belong to the *Secondigliano* System'—an eloquent term, a mechanism rather than a structure."[21] With a history longer than the Mafia's, the Camorra, according to historian Paul Ginsburg, was a mass organization comprising more than a hundred bands, likely to be structured horizontally by a group of brothers (like the Solaras) and more willing than the Mafia to involve adolescents in the drug trade.[22] The Camorra syndicate or "the System" is a presence in the Neapolitan novels from the beginning. The Camorra of the 1950s and 1960s, represented by the Solara brothers, was largely involved in activities such as money laundering and loansharking, while in the late 1970s and 1980s, it became increasingly involved in the drug trade. After the 1980 earthquake, the syndicate was heavily involved in reconstruction, with the battle for lucrative contracts leading to the Camorra wars of the 1980s, a cycle of violence that claimed the lives of the Solara brothers.

Ferrante has skillfully integrated the major events in recent Neapolitan history with the lives of her characters, with the earthquake that struck Southern Italy in 1980 becoming a test of the characters' ability to handle crises. Lila's psychological vulnerability led to her near breakdown during the earthquake. Elena reported that for the first time Lila used the term "dissolving boundaries" to describe the terrifying hallucinations she was experiencing. Elena realized the mental fragility underlying Lila's intelligence and competence. Lila no longer resembled the woman who just a few minutes before the earthquake Elena had envied for her verbal skills; her composure shattered, Lila's beautiful features were now disfigured by anguish. Unlike Lila, Elena despite her fear remained calm and in control. When the quake subsided, those who had fled returned to the devastated city. Lila's partner Enzo and her son Gennaro returned to the neighborhood "exhausted, overwhelmed, looking like survivors of a horrendous war, with a single concern: How was Lila" (SLC, 182). In sharp contrast, Nino came back many days later, looking like he had returned from a vacation, telling Elena that he took his children and fled to his in-laws' country villa. He apparently forgot all about Elena and about their child that she was carrying.

Historian Tom Behan reported that according to government figures, the earthquake was responsible for 2,735 deaths, 8,848 injuries and left 300,000 people homeless.[23] The money that poured into Naples for reconstruction in the aftermath of the earthquake was largely commandeered by the Camorra and, along with the lucrative drug trade, greatly increased the wealth and power of the syndicate. When Lila told Elena that the neighborhood Camorrist Marcello Solara had brought drugs into the neighborhood, at first Elena did not understand the implications. Drugs were part of the world of the bohemian left she met at her sister-in-law Mariarosa's house, people for whom drugs were a form of relaxation, a means of expanding consciousness. After learning about a neighborhood boy's death from a heroin overdose, Elena soon understood that in the neighborhood drugs were not a relatively harmless form of recreation, but had become a "viper, a poison that spread through the blood of my brothers, of Rino, perhaps of Gennaro" (SLC, 169). The drug epidemic touched Lila's and Elena's lives directly. Elena's younger brothers were working in the drug trade; Lila's brother Rino had become a heroin addict and she discovered needle marks on the arms of her son.

Alfonso, probably because of the strains of dealing with a society that did not accept his sexuality, began to show signs of addiction—missing important appointments, becoming increasingly unreliable, increasingly careless about his safety. As a consequence, he was beaten to death, his body thrown into the sea and eventually found washed up on the beach. Lila was devastated by the death of Alfonso and her lifelong hatred of the Camorrists reached the boiling point. She convinced Elena to collaborate with her on a newspaper article that would expose the dealings of the Solaras, drawing on material she had gathered while working for Michele Solara. Elena enjoyed the work, as it was a long time since she and Lila had undertaken anything together. Elena sent the completed text to her editor asking him to check with the lawyers at the publishing house if the material was enough to send the Solaras to jail. His response was that it wasn't enough for even one day in jail. The Solaras had the money to buy political support and Elena and Lila's text was not enough to ruin them; however, the editor insisted that Elena publish it to expose the level of corruption in Italy. Elena equivocated as the Solaras had threatened her with a lawsuit, but Lila sent the text to the newspaper telling Elena that since she could not make up her mind, Lila would do it for her. To Lila's great disappointment, the editor turned out to be correct—nothing happened to the Solaras, although the publicity at least caused them to lower their profile and drop their lawsuit against Elena. It wasn't until the next decade that the Italian judicial system took on organized crime syndicates and the political corruption that enabled them.

As public construction contracts became a major source of income for the Camorra, the organization strengthened its ties to the political establishment. Politicians doled out contracts to the Camorra and in return the Camorrists delivered votes. Tom Behan noted, that given the covert nature of the Camorra, it is impossible to quantify its general political influence and the extent to which it could control voting behavior. However, Behan considered it beyond doubt that the Camorra's influence was highly significant as the votes it delivered could make the difference between electoral defeat or victory.[24] The Camorra's political and economic power depended on its ability to deliver votes; hence the Solara brothers' unremitting hostility towards Lila, when she organized a get out the vote operation for the Communists. The Solaras were furious because, despite the Camorrists' decades long control of voting behavior in the neighborhood, Lila had managed to shift a significant number of votes to the Communists.

Tensions in the neighborhood were further exacerbated when in the early 1980s a deadly gang war broke out as various Camorra factions fought for control of the drug trade and the earthquake reconstruction contracts. The Camorra wars of the 1980s had a direct impact on the neighborhood when the Solaras joined the many other members of organized crime syndicates among the list of the murdered. Ferrante complicates the portrayal of the Solaras who despite their criminality were still sons of the neighborhood. Although Lila had no sympathy for the murdered Solaras, Elena had some feeling for them and remembered the time the Solaras came to the defense of Elena and her friends when they were attacked by young men from the wealthy neighborhoods of Naples. She recalled that the Solaras had always seemed so handsome to the girls of the neighborhood, as they drove around the neighborhood in their Fiat 1100 "like ancient warriors in their chariots" (SLC, 375).

Although Marcello Solara is portrayed as an ordinary man who despite his criminal activities exhibits an occasional flash of decency, Michele is highly intelligent, capable of extreme brutality, but also of an "absolute passion." Michele appreciated Lila's extraordinary qualities and had loved her for years, ever since she was a child. Like Dante's love for Beatrice, which also began when she was a child, Michele's unrequited love for Lila was not primarily sexual; rather he desired her imagination and "subtlety of her mind" (SLC 208). It might seem far-fetched to draw comparisons between Michele and Dante, but the *Divine Comedy* like the *Aeneid* is a presence in the Neapolitan novels. When Elena observes that some patron saint in Paradise is necessary to make one's way in the underworld, there is an echo of Dante enlisting Virgil as his guide to the Inferno. In search of information about Pasquale and Enzo, now in police custody, Elena enlists Nino as her Virgil to help her navigate the underworld of the Italian criminal justice system. Elena again echoes Dante's *Inferno* when she describes Nino and Lila as adulterous lovers, condemned "to the infernal whirlwind" recalling the punishment meted out to Francesca da Rimini and Paolo Malatesta, the doomed lovers in the second circle of hell in the *Inferno* (SNN, 237).

Thanks to Ferrante's incandescent prose, these allusions to Dante or to the Greek and Roman classics are subtly interwoven with the narrative and never feel forced or inappropriate, even when the classical allusions apply to the likes of Michele and Marcello Solara. Not only does Ferrante use literary allusions to give Michele and Marcello Solara a larger than life dimension, likening them to "ancient warriors in their chariots," but she also portrays them, as very much a part of the fabric of life in the neighborhood. Historian Paul Ginsborg has noted the extent to which the Camorra was deeply embedded in Italian society, and thus the difficulty of estimating the impact of organized crime on the economy. He noted that in 1986 it was thought that 12.5 percent of Italian GDP was the product of organized crime, of which nearly half was from the drug trade.[25]

Not only was the Camorra integrated into the Italian economy, the syndicate also to a large extent controlled access to public officials and to essential services. When Elena's mother was hospitalized with a terminal illness, her family turned to Marcello Solara to get her out of the hospital and into a far more comfortable, Camorra-controlled clinic. The doctors in the clinic lacked the skills of those in the hospital, but Marcello managed to bring one of the specialists who had been treating Elena's mother in the hospital to the clinic. Elena noted that the specialist who had been "curt" when treating patients in the hospital was "extremely cordial' when in the Camorra-controlled clinic. Nino, disgusted by Marcello's machinations and the Greco family's willingness to rely on him, complained bitterly that in Italy even for a "bed in a hospital you have to be a member of a lodge or rely on the Camorra" (SLC, 219).

Elena described how the entire neighborhood was one way or another complicit in the activities of the Solaras. Some were employed by the Solaras in the drug trade; others in the Solaras' legitimate businesses. Many had been part of the celebrations which marked the opening of their businesses, had bought pastries at their bar, had been present at their marriages, had bought their shoes and been guests in their houses, had taken their money, had tolerated their violence, pretending it was nothing. As Elena put it, Marcello and Michele were "part of us, just as Pasquale was" (SLC, 376). Pondering the progress of the Solara bothers in turning at least some of their ill-gotten gains into legitimate business endeavors, Elena wondered how much difference there was between the wealth of the elite and that of the Solara: "How many hidden turns does money take before becoming high salaries and hidden fees?" She may not have known the mechanisms by which this occurred or the point at which good money became bad, but she was well aware that the dividing line was not clear and that much of the Neapolitan elite, as well as her family and friends from the neighborhood, were all to some extent part of the world of the Solaras.

In one of those coincidences that might seem ridiculous in a plot summary but work in the context of Ferrante's powerful, evocative prose, Elena's silver bracelet is once again broken by one of the Solara brothers. This time it is Michele who grabs Elena's wrist; when she tries to free herself, the bracelet is broken. Marcello then promised to have the bracelet repaired; Lila with her usual deep-seated distrust of the Solaras told Elena she would never see that bracelet again. Some time after the brothers were murdered, Elena received a package with her silver bracelet, highly polished and looking as if it were new. The note, signed with an elaborate M, contained one word—"Sorry." Marcello had in a sense affirmed Elena's belief that the Solara brothers were indeed part of the community, just as Pasquale was.

When Lila's daughter Tina disappeared, the Solaras did more than anyone else in the neighborhood in the effort to find her. Although expecting to be treated with hostility, they appeared one evening at Lila's house with the demeanor of those who are speaking for the entire community, and promised they would do everything in their power to return Tina safe and sound to her parents. Antonio put off his departure for Germany because his boss Michele Solara ordered him to track down Tina. Ferrante does not identify the abductor of Tina, but she lets the reader know the culprits were not the Solaras. When years later Elena visited Pasquale in prison, she asked him who took Tina. He answered "The Solaras," and she responded by asking him if he was certain the Solaras were the kidnappers. Pasquale merely smiled, and Elena understood that he was not telling the truth and that he might not know who was responsible.

Ferrante leaves open the question of Tina's disappearance, although she does provide some clues. In the final pages of the Neapolitan Quartet, many years after the disappearance of Tina, Lila tells Elena, that she doesn't understand why Elena never once considered that a newspaper photo of Elena and Tina that misidentified Tina as Elena's daughter might have been the reason Tina was abducted. Lila speculated that the kidnappers thought they were stealing Elena's daughter and instead stole Lila's. Lila noted that Elena at that time was often in the newspapers and on television, and that maybe the kidnappers wanted money from Elena rather than from Lila. Elena emphatically rejected the idea the kidnappers would have hoped to extort money from her. She apparently saw no connection between her articles exposing the crimes of the Camorra and the abduction of a child perhaps mistakenly thought to be hers.

The Camorra has had a long history of taking revenge on the relatives of those who have exposed their activities. Roberto Saviano in *Gomorrah* described the courage of Renato Natale, the Communist Mayor of Casal di Principe, who spoke out against the Casalese Camorra families' waste management operations. The Camorra "threatened his life, told him that if he didn't stop his family would be made to pay for his choices."[26] Ferrante's Italian readers would certainly have been aware that the Camorra often took revenge on family members of their enemies. However, Ferrante does not offer any more information about what might be behind the abduction of Tina, and the reader, like her characters, must live with the unresolved mystery.

Saviano, who himself has received numerous death threats, described the Camorra's lack of qualms about saturating their towns and the surrounding lands with toxins: "The life of a boss is short. To flood an area with toxic waste and circle one's city with poisonous mountain ranges is a problem only for someone who has a sense of social responsibility and a long-term concept of power."[27] Growing concern about the environmental impact of the Camorra's involvement in waste disposal prompted Elena Ferrante in 2008 to write an op-ed in the *New York Times* about her "Fetid City." She described a city where the Camorra controlled the waste disposal industry, running illegal dumps with the complicity of local politicians, where "at night the mice and the dogs are masters. The garbage is piled up to the second floor of the houses, and in the darkness it comes alive. Plastic bags and sacks vibrate, emitting the sounds of things pulled apart, scavenged.... The garbage—thousands of tons of it—has gone uncollected for three weeks, because all the available landfills are full. The evil odor of decomposition and burning waste moves down the hills of refuse and slides along the streets, enters shops, doorways, houses."[28] What Ferrante has called the "daily standard of unlivability"[29] is a theme recurring throughout the Neapolitan Quartet. Ferrante began to see the corruption in Naples as a sign of something deeper, broader: "Here the rot is not only visible; it has the power of portent.... This stinking, polluted filth, generator of profits both legal and illegal, is not some ancient relic but very modern, and it underlines the precariousness of every sort of order, in every part of the planet."[30]

Conclusion

I wrote this book to try to understand why the Neapolitan Quartet has had such a hold over me. The answer is no surprise; Ferrante has created truly memorable characters. Great novelists owe their place in the literary pantheon to the creation of characters such as David Copperfield, Anna Karenina, Elizabeth Bennet, Jane Eyre, Heathcliff, and Raskolnikov; for many readers, these are real people. I was struck by novelist Jonathan Franzen's response when asked by an interviewer what question he would ask Elena Ferrante if he had the opportunity. Franzen replied: "I might ask her what she imagines happened to the eponymous lost child of the fourth Neapolitan novel."[1] For Franzen, like many other readers, Tina is on some level a real person and we want very much to know her fate. I had a similar experience when reading that, despite the passage of a 1981 referendum to retain sentences of life imprisonment, as the result of a 1986 prison reform law, life in prison was effectively abolished in Italy.[2] My initial reaction was to think that just maybe Pasquale would not spend his entire life in prison, as if Pasquale were a real person rotting away in Poggioreale prison, rather than a fictional character.

We know the great characters of world literature in a way we can't possibly know our close friends and family members. In an article about implicit bias published in *Scientific American*, science writer Michael Shermer opens with the observation that "novelists often offer deep insights into the human psyche that take psychologists years to test," and by way of illustration includes a quotation from Dostoyevsky's *Notes from the Underground*: "Every man has reminiscences which he would not tell to everyone, but only to his friends. He has other matters in his mind, which he would not reveal even to his friends, but only to himself, and that in secret. But there are other things which a man is afraid to tell even to himself and every decent man has a number of such things stored away in his mind."[3]

Conclusion

Dostoyevsky's observation reminds me of Elena Greco. She has thoughts she would not reveal to anyone including: her fear of being overshadowed by Lila; her envy of Lila's talent and belief that Lila is somehow the source of everything she has achieved; her bitterness about Lila's having "stolen" Nino leading her to wish at times that Lila would die. Elena acknowledged and wrestled with these ugly feelings, the inner demons that have tormented her over the course of a lifetime. Ferrante also allows the reader to see the things Elena cannot admit to herself: principally her guilt about having neglected her children and her resistance to looking honestly at her relationship with her daughters. She steadfastly insists, to herself and to others, that she has been a consistently good mother. Great novelists, and I certainly include Ferrante in this category, allow us to understand their characters' inner lives on all the levels Dostoyevsky includes in his anatomy of mental life. This access to the interior life of fictional characters is what the novel can provide in a way film cannot. Film may have replaced the novel as the principal story-telling medium of our age, but great novels like Ferrante's Neapolitan Quartet remind us of what only literature can do.

In the Neapolitan novels, Ferrante examines the lives of her characters over a span of six decades, thus exploring the extent to which personality changes over time and the extent to which it remains constant. Elena Greco grapples with this question as she tries to understand the man she once loved and who caused her such great pain. Was Nino, the young man she had loved since childhood the same person as the serial womanizer who betrayed her? To what extent is the child the father of the man? With some characters, Ferrante suggests that personality is deeply rooted in childhood experience with Nino, for example, becoming an incarnation of his father Donato; others such as Lila seem radically different from any of her family members. In literature as in life, such questions regarding the origins and continued existence of a stable core of personality traits can never be fully answered. An element of mystery persists.

Elena and Lila are as complicated and as fully alive as any fictional characters I have encountered, and like all great fictional characters they evoke very different responses in readers. As I read reviews of the Neapolitan novels, I sometimes thought the reviewer had read a different series of novels from the ones I had. I find Elena Greco, warts and all, a sympathetic character, and profoundly disagree with assessments such as that of GD Dess who considers Elena Greco the least interesting of all Ferrante's female protagonists. Dess writes: "What is deeply disappointing about Elena is her inability to transform herself—even though she seemingly has the intellectual capacity for it.... Ferrante keeps us teetering with anticipation of change as we read page after page of Elena's ruthless psychological insights, and witness her pathological excavation of her feelings. We keep hoping for a catharsis that never comes."[4] The books I read trace Elena's struggle for transformation—first to escape her background, then to reconcile the different worlds she inhabits and accept the consequences of her choices. She achieves a genuine measure of self-acceptance when in her sixties—perhaps not the catharsis Dess hoped for, but a kind of equilibrium nonetheless.

With Elena, Ferrante ties up the loose ends, but with Lila the mystery remains. Like Jonathan Franzen, I too would like to ask Ferrante a question about her characters' fate; in my case I would like to know what Ferrante imagines for Lila. Yet Ferrante has brought the saga of Elena and Lila to a deeply satisfying conclusion and in the last analysis I'm not sure I would want to dispel the mystery. I have sometimes wished that Ferrante would retell the story from Lila's perspective, but acknowledge that despite narrating the Neapolitan Quartet from Elena's vantage point, Ferrante has managed to convey a good deal about Lila. We have Lila's diaries, albeit summarized by Elena, Lila's long letter to Elena, and the reactions of other characters to Lila—many pieces of the puzzle.

We know much less about the other characters. I would like to read Nino's story: how did he justify his callous behavior towards the women in his life; his irresponsibility towards his children; the rightward drift of his politics; the political wrongdoing that cost him his seat in parliament? I would also like to read Pietro's story: his perspective on his failed marriage to Elena and his changing behavior towards the women in his life. Pietro is a different man at the end of the Neapolitan Quartet; unlike Nino whose story is one of moral decline, Pietro's is one of growth. I would like to read Alfonso's story about growing up in a homophobic society, his coming to terms with his sexuality and his doomed relationship with Michele. I would like to read Pasquale's story—how his political passion for justice and equality took a murderous turn. And finally, I would like to read the story of Michele Solara—the enigmatic Camorrist consumed by an unrequited love for Lila.

It's not just the principal characters (Elena, Lila and Nino) and those we might consider second tier characters (for example, Pietro, Pasquale,

Alfonso and Michele) that many of Ferrante's readers would like to know better. Ferrante's genius is also expressed in her portrayal of third tier characters who arouse our interest such as Maestra Oliviero, a woman of intense emotion, passionately devoted to those few students she believes have exceptional promise and no doubt doing incalculable damage to those she dismisses as dunces. Also, Lila's father Fernando, a conventional man, who unthinkingly accepts the gender biases of his culture, who briefly comes alive with a story of repressed ambitions and desires, regretting that he had not married Inés a flame of his youth who might have been able to help him realize his dreams. We get to know some of these minor characters better than others, but Ferrante's genius is that even those who make only a fleeting appearance are always more than mere caricatures. So many of her characters deserve a book, or at least a short story, in their own right.

These books will probably not be written, but for anyone like me, desperately wanting more of Elena and Lila's world, I recommend re-reading the novels. There is so much one misses on a first reading. For example, on a first reading of *My Brilliant Friend*, we lack the information to understand the source of Nino's confusion when the children in Elena and Lila's elementary school were engaged in a scholastic competition. Nino, who had a reputation as an excellent student, seemed disoriented for some inexplicable reason. He seemed unable to respond to the teachers' questions, and appeared distracted as if he didn't understand what they were asking. It is not until book two, *The Story of a New Name*, that we learn that Nino as a child was hopelessly in love with Lila, which explains his disorientation during the competition. His love for Lila did not start during their summer of love on Ischia, but extended back to childhood. When I re-read *My Brilliant Friend* in the light of the love story in *The Story of a New Name*, I understood the significance of Nino's behavior during the scholastic competition and the depth of his love for Lila.

Similarly, most readers of *My Brilliant Friend* would not understand the significance of Don Achille's reaction when Elena and Lila accuse him of having stolen their dolls. It is not until we learn Alfonso's story in *Story of the Lost Child* that we understand Don Achille's response—"unexpectedly pained as if he were receiving confirmation of something he already knew" (BF, 67). Once again, when I re-read *My Brilliant Friend*, with the knowledge of Alfonso's sexuality gleaned from *Story of the Lost*

Child, I understood Don Achille's reaction and grasped the significance of the scene. Unless we are exceptionally attentive and perceptive readers, only on a second reading of the Neapolitan Quartet can we fully appreciate the complicated interplay of themes and the seamless interweaving of historical material. It is almost as if Ferrante wrote the Neapolitan Quartet with the re-reader in mind.

The Neapolitan Quartet is sometimes compared to the vast canvas of the 19th- and early 20th-century novels of Dickens, Balzac, Tolstoy and Proust. As carefully plotted as *Remembrance of Things Past*, the Neapolitan novels are an intricate tapestry of recurring characters, themes and symbols such as the dolls and Elena's silver bracelet. Ferrante acknowledges employing some literary conventions that might be considered old-fashioned and no longer much used in serious literary fiction. In an interview with the *Paris Review* Ferrante observes: "I think of literary tradition as a single, large depository, where anyone who wants to write goes to choose what is useful to him.... I renounce nothing that can give pleasure to the reader, not even what is considered old, trite, vulgar, not even the devices of genre fiction."[5]

Towards the conclusion of the Neapolitan Quartet, Ferrante alludes to her use of recurrent patterns and of coincidence, a staple of 19th-century fiction. Elena speculates that Lila may have repudiated her book about their friendship because of her portrayal of the episode of the lost dolls. Elena had exaggerated the trauma of the loss of the dolls and to further heighten the emotional impact had given one of the dolls and the lost child the same name. Elena had encouraged her reader to connect the childhood loss of the dolls, the make-believe daughters, to the adult loss of the real daughter. Elena worried that "Lila found it cynical, dishonest" (SLC, 465). Is Elena (or Ferrante) suggesting that the recurrent scenes and images, the careful patterning of the Neapolitan novels is in some sense a falsification? Elena makes a similar point when responding to Lila's criticism of her book on life of the neighborhood; perhaps her book, despite its commercial success, was an artistic failure precisely because it was well-organized and carefully written, because she had been unable to imitate the "shapeless banality of things" (SLC, 311).

There is a strand in feminist theory that sees traditional literary structures and techniques as a falsification of the complexity of experience and rejects their use, privileging formal experimentation as the best vehicle for feminist thought. Literary theorist Rita Felski has challenged this preference for formal experimentation, and has questioned whether a text "that employs experimental techniques is therefore more radical in its effects than one which relies on established structures."[6] She has argued against "a 'purist" tendency in feminist theory, which assumes that that the only legitimate feminist cultural activity renounces all popular conventions and is situated outside existing commercial cultural institutions."[7] Felski's theoretical work in a sense anticipates the commercially successful Neapolitan novels, which do rely on established structures, and employ popular conventions and narrative techniques associated with the 19th-century novel to convey a powerful 21st-century feminist vision.

For now, I am contenting myself with re-reading the Neapolitan novels, but I want more of Ferrante, or more accurately, more of the Starnone/Raja collaboration. My guess is they collaborate on themes and on structure, but that Starnone may be the principal writer. To my knowledge there are four separate teams of linguists whose text analysis software has pointed to Starnone as the principal author. Also, I have read the two of his books which have been translated into English, *First Execution* and *Ties*, and have found thematic, structural, and linguistic similarities to Ferrante's work. Starnone has apparently published thirteen works of fiction, eleven of which have not been translated into English, and which I would very much like to read. If Starnone were publicly identified as the co-author of the Neapolitan Quartet, I expect some of these books would be translated and made available to the English speaking reader.

Ferrante's publishers may fear that if a male author is acknowledged as the co-author of Ferrante's books, many of Ferrante's readers will be disappointed, may feel deceived and book sales will plummet. My guess is that many readers will be intrigued by the collaboration of a man and woman on books that so powerfully explore gender roles. Many second wave feminists have (in some cases reluctantly) moved beyond the idea that there is an authentic female voice that can be recognized as such. Queer theory and intersectional feminism have emphasized the fluidity of gender and undermined the notion of a stable female identity.

Perhaps Starnone and Raja are uncomfortable about what might be viewed as a web of lies rather than the artful creation of the literary person of Elena Ferrante. Or perhaps they worry that interest in their dual authorship would in some way detract from serious interest in the texts. However, since thanks to Claudio Gatti's investigations and the text analysis software identifying Starnone as the likely co-author, there seems to be little to be gained from denying what is widely known. And readers would certainly benefit from the translations of Starnone's works, which would in all probability follow from acknowledgment of his role in the creation of the Neapolitan Quartet.

However, what I think most readers long for is more novels from "Ferrante," whoever she might be. Sandro Ferri, Ferrante's publisher, has held out a ray of hope for Ferrante fans, telling an Italian literary newsletter, "I know she is writing, but at the moment I cannot say anything more."[8] We just have to hope.

Chapter Notes

Introduction

1. James Wood, "Women on the Verge: The Fiction of Elena Ferrante," *The New Yorker*, January 21, 2013, http://www.newyorker.com/magazine/2013/01/21/women-on-the-verge.
2. Lisa Mullenneaux, *Naples' Little Women: The Fiction of Elena Ferrante* (New York: Pennington Press, 2016).
3. Grace Bullaro and Stephanie Love, *The Works of Elena Ferrante: Reconfiguring the Margins* (New York: Palgrave Macmillan, 2017).
4. Ibid.
5. Claudio Gatti, "Elena Ferrante: An Answer?" *The New York Review of Books*, October 2, 2016, http://www.nybooks.com/daily/2016/10/02/elena-ferrante-an-answer/.
6. Elena Ferrante, "Narrating What Escapes the Narrative: Answers to Questions from Yasemin Congar," *Frantumaglia: A Writer's Journey* (New York: Europa Editions, 2016), 306.
7. Leonardo Sciascia, *The Moro Affair* (Manchester: Carcanet, 1987).
8. Elissa Schappell, "The Mysterious, Anonymous Author Elena Ferrante on the Conclusion of Her Neapolitan Novels," *Vanity Fair*, August 27, 2015, http://www.vanityfair.com/culture/2015/08/elena-ferrante-interview-the-story-of-the-lost-child (reprinted in *Frantumaglia*, 332).
9. Simone de Beauvoir, *The Second Sex*, trans. H.M. Parshley (New York: Knopf, 1953).

Chapter 1

1. Alexandra Alter, "'Ferrante Fever' Continues to Spread," *New York Times*, December 7, 2016, http://www.nytimes.com/2016/12/07/arts/ferrante-fever-continues-to-spread.html?_r=0.
2. Binah Shaw, "The women who do," *DAWN*, August 14, 2016, http://www.dawn.com/news/1277487/the-women-who-do?fromNewsdog=1.
3. Elizabeth Mitchell, "Who is the mysterious author spreading #FerranteFever?" *New York Daily News*, December 31, 2015, http://www.nydailynews.com/entertainment/mysterious-author-spreading-ferrantefever-article-1.2480313.
4. Adam Kirsch, *The Global Novel: Writing the World in the 21st Century* (New York: Columbia Global Reports, 2017), 25.
5. Rachel Donadio, "'Writing Has Always Been a Great Struggle for Me': Q. and A.: Elena Ferrante," *New York Times*, December 9, 2014, http://www.nytimes.com/2014/12/10/books/writing-has-always-been-a-great-struggle-for-me.html? (reprinted in *Frantumaglia*, 249).
6. Michael Reynolds quoted in Patti Hartigan, "Success of 'Neapolitan Novels' stranger than fiction," *Boston Globe*, April 11, 2016, https://www.bostonglobe.com/metro/2016/04/\10/success-neapolitan-novels-stranger-than-fiction/3GHNc3Doc0jT2XhACcjpWO/story.html.

Notes. Chapter 1

7. Rachel Donadio, "Elena Ferrante, Author of Naples Novels, Stays Mysterious," *New York Times*, December 10, 2014, https://www.nytimes.com/2014/12/10/books/elena-ferrante-author-of-naples-novels-stays-mysterious.html?_r=0.

8. Daniela Petracco quoted in Gaby Wood, "How Karl Ove Knausgaard and Elena Ferrante won us over," *The Telegraph*, February 28, 2016, http://www.telegraph.co.uk/books/what-to-read/how-karl-ove-knausgaard-and-elena-ferrante-won-us-over/.

9. Sonya Gellert, "*My Brilliant Friend* by Elena Ferrante," *Shelf Esteem*, August 10, 2016, https://shelfesteemsite.com/2016/08/10/my-brilliant-friend-by-elena-ferrante/.

10. Deidre Lynch, ed., *Janeites: Austen's Disciples and Devotees* (Princeton: Princeton University Press, 2000).

11. Anna, "Bookish musings: Diving into the world of Elena Ferrante's Neapolitan Series," *Imaginary Book Club*, August 29, 2016, http://imaginarybookclub.com/bookish-musings-diving-into-the-world-of-elena-ferrantes-neapolitan-series.

12. Madeline Gressel, "The Quotidian Ephemera of Women's Lives," *The Brooklyn Rail*, October 5, 2015, http://www.brooklynrail.org/2015/10/books/the-quotidian-ephemera-of-womens-lives.

13. Joanna Biggs, "I was blind, she a falcon," *The London Review of Books*, September 10, 2015, http://www.lrb.co.uk/v37/n17/joanna-biggs/i-was-blind-she-a-falcon.

14. Francesca Pellas, "Michael Reynolds on Ferrante's Class Consciousness," *Literary Hub*, May 10, 2016, http://lithub.com/michael-reynolds-on-ferrantes-class-consciousness-and-rome-vs-nyc/.

15. Patti Hartigan, "Success of 'Neapolitan Novels' stranger than fiction," *Boston Globe*, April 11, 2016, https://www.bostonglobe.com/metro/2016/04/10/success-neapolitan-novels-stranger-than-fiction/3GHNc3Doc0jT2XhACcjpWO/story.html.

16. Damien, "Naples: The Neapolitan Novels by Elena Ferrante," *Travel Readings*, April 18, 2016, http://www.travelreadings.com/2016/04/18/naples-the-neapolitan-novels-by-elena-ferrante/.

17. Anna Silliman, "Make Your Dad Read Elena Ferrante!" *New York Magazine*, June 17, 2016, http://nymag.com/thecut/2016/06/reading-elena-ferrante-with-my-dad.html.

18. Miriam Krule, "Dressing a Refined Story with a Touch of Vulgarity, an Interview with Elena Ferrante's Art Director," *Slate*, August 28, 2015, http://www.slate.com/blogs/browbeat/2015/08/28/elena_ferrante_neapolian_novels_cover_design_an_interview_with_the_publisher.html.

19. Emily Harnett, "The Subtle Genius of Elena Ferrante's Bad Book Covers," *The Atlantic*, July 3, 2016, https://www.theatlantic.com/entertainment/archive/2016/07/elena-ferrante-covers-bad-no-good/488732/.

20. Georgiana, "Book Covers Around the World," *Readers' High Tea*, https://readershightea.wordpress.com/2017/07/20/book-covers-around-the-world-the-neapolitan-novels-by-elena-ferrante/.

21. Catherine Bennett, "Modern tribes; the Elena Ferrante fan," *The Guardian*, April 30, 2016, https://www.theguardian.com/lifeandstyle/2016/apr/30/elena-ferrante-fan-girl-modern-tribes.

22. Claire Messud, "Elena Ferrante's Neapolitan Quartet," *The Financial Times*, August 28, 2015, http://www.ft.com/intl/cms/s/0/0b7a4200-4bd3-11e5-b558-8a9722977189.html.

23. Fernanda Moore, "Neapolitan Nonsense *Commentary Magazine*, December 1, 2015, https://www.commentarymagazine.com/articles/neapolitan-nonsense/.

24. Tim Parks, "How Could You Like That Book?" *New York Review of Books*, November 10, 2015, http://www.nybooks.com/daily/2015/11/10/how-could-you-like-that-book/.

25. Elizabeth Mitchell, "Who is the mysterious author spreading #FerranteFever?" *New York Daily News*, December 31, 2015, http://www.nydailynews.com/entertainment/mysterious-author-spreading-ferrantefever-article-1.2480213.

26. Michael Reynolds quoted in Francesca Pellas.

27. Elena Ferrante, "Correspondence with Mario Martone," *Frantumaglia*, 26.
28. *Ibid.*, 32.
29. *Ibid.*, 38.
30. *Ibid.*, 55–57.
31. Kate Chisholm, "Why Elena Ferrante doesn't work on radio," *The Spectator*, August 6, 2016, http://www.spectator.co.uk/2016/08/why-elena-ferrante-doesnt-work-on-radio/.
32. Alex O'Connell, "Elena Ferrante was more challenging than Tolstoy," *The Times*, January 13 2017, http://www.thetimes.co.uk/edition/times2/elena-ferrante-was-more-challenging-than-tolstoy-6c7zbq6tf.
33. Lynn Enright, "April De Angelis, the woman tasked with bringing Elena Ferrante's vision to life," *The Pool*, March 3, 2017, https://www.the-pool.com/arts-culture/things-to-do/2017/9/april-de-angelis-on-adapting-elena-ferrante-s-neapolitan-novels/april-de-angelis-on-adapting-elena-ferrante-s-neapolitan-novels.
34. Laura Freeman, "How on earth do you put 1,600 pages of Elena Ferrante on stage?" *The Spectator*, March 4, 2017, http://www.spectator.co.uk/2017/03/how-on-earth-do-you-put-1600-pages-of-elena-ferrante-on-stage/.
35. Patrick Marmion, "Ambitious Italian saga winds up in a dead-end," *The Daily Mail*, March 16, 2017, http://www.dailymail.co.uk/tvshowbiz/article-4322464/My-Brilliant-Friend-Italian-saga-winds-dead-end.html.
36. Gary Naylor, "BWW Review: *My Brilliant Friend*," *Broadway World*, March 20, 2017, http://www.broadwayworld.com/westend/article/BWW-Review-MY-BRILLIANT-FRIEND-PARTS-1-2-Rose-Theatre-20170320#.
37. Susannah Clapp, "My Brilliant friend review—intensity wins through," *The Guardian*, March 19, 2017, https://www.theguardian.com/stage/2017/mar/19/my-brilliant-friend-niamh-cusack-catherine-mccormack-elena-ferrante-review.

Chapter 2

1. Charlotte Shane, "The Sexist Big Reveal," *The New Republic*, October 3, 2016, https://newrepublic.com/article/137400/sexist-big-reveal.
2. Editorial Board, "Why we should celebrate the Elena Ferrante firestorm," *Washington Post*, October 6, 2016, https://www.washingtonpost.com/opinions/why-we-should-celebrate-the-elena-ferrante-firestorm/2016/10/06/b26e3fc2-8a79-11e6-875e-2c1bfe943b66_story.html?tid=a_inl&utm_term=.2e754b40cb33.
3. Rachel Donadio, "Elena Ferrante, Author of Naples Novels, Stays Mysterious," *New York Times*, December 9, 2014, http://www.nytimes.com/2014/12/10/books/elena-ferrante-author-of-naples-novels-stays-mysterious.html.
4. Sandro and Sandra Ferri, interviewers, "Elena Ferrante, Art of Fiction No. 228," *The Paris Review*, Issue 212, Spring 2015, http://www.theparisreview.org/interviews/6370/art-of-fiction-no-228-elena-ferrante (reprinted in *Frantumaglia*, 270).
5. Roland Barthes, "The Death of the Author," 1968, http://www.ubu.com/aspen/aspen5and6/threeEssays.html#barthes.
6. Alison Flood, "Elena Ferrante pours scorn on speculation she could be a man," *The Guardian*, September 2, 2015, https://www.theguardian.com/books/2015/sep/02/elena-ferrante-speculation-she-could-be-man-italian-novelist.
7. Elena Ferrante, "The Gift of the Befana" (1991), *Frantumaglia*, 15.
8. Elena Ferrante, "Without Keeping a Safe Distance: Answers to Questions from Stefania Scateni" (2002), *Frantumaglia*, 81.
9. Grace Bullaro and Stephanie Love, *The Works of Elena Ferrante: Reconfiguring the Margins* (New York: Palgrave Macmillan, 2017).
10. Tiziana de Rogatis, "Uncovering' Elena Ferrante, and the importance of a woman's

Notes. Chapter 2

voice," *The Conversation*, October 5, 2016, https://theconversation.com/uncovering-elena-ferrante-and-the-importance-of-a-womans-voice-66456.

11. Ann Goldstein quoted in Meghan O'Rourke, "Elena Ferrante; The Global Sensation Nobody Knows," *The Guardian*, October 31, 2014, http://www.theguardian.com/books/2014/oct/31/elena-ferrante-literary-sensation-nobody-knows.

12. Veronique Darwin, "Book Review: Elena Ferrante's Neapolitan novels," *a novel journal*, September 25, 2016, https://anoveljournal.wordpress.com/2016/09/25/book-review-elena-ferrantes-neapolitan-novels/.

13. John Mullan, *Anonymity: A Secret History of English Literature* (Princeton: Princeton University Press, 1980).

14. Elena Ferrante, "Elena Ferrante on Sense and Sensibility: I was passionate about Austen's anonymity," *The Guardian*, October 16, 2015, https://www.theguardian.com/books/2015/oct/16/sense-and-sensibility-jane-austen-elena-ferrante-anonymity.

15. Jennifer Levasseur, "Exclusive Elena Ferrante interview: The full transcript," The *Sydney Morning Herald*, December 21, 2015, http://www.smh.com.au/entertainment/books/exclusive-elena-ferrante-interview-the-full-transcript-20151221-glt1op#ixzz3vfFeUUaj.

16. Dayna Tortorici, "Those Like Us: On Elena Ferrante," *n+1*, Issue 22, Spring 2015, https://nplusonemag.com/issue-22/reviews/those-like-us/.

17. Claudio Gatti, "Elena Ferrante: An Answer?" *New York Review of Books*, October 2, 2016, http://www.nybooks.com/daily/2016/10/02/elena-ferrante-an-answer/.

18. Elena Ferrante, "Letter to Sandra Ozzola" (2003), *Frantumaglia*, 99.

19. Maria Laurino, "Q&A: The reporter who may have unmasked Ferrante: I have no regrets," *The National Book Review*, November 16, 2016, http://www.thenationalbookreview.com/features/2016/11/16/qa-the-reporter-who-may-have-unmasked-elena-ferrante-i-have-no-regrets.

20. Elissa Schappell, "The Mysterious, Anonymous Author Elena Ferrante on the Conclusion of Her Neapolitan Novels," *Vanity Fair*, August 27, 2015, http://www.vanityfair.com/culture/2015/08/elena-ferrante-interview-the-story-of-the-lost-child (reprinted in *Frantumaglia*, 328).

21. Elena Ferrante, "Letter to Sandra Ozzola" (2003), 124.

22. Claudio Gatti, "The Story Behind a Name," *New York Review*, October 2, 2016, http://www.nybooks.com/daily/2016/10/02/story-behind-a-name-elena.

23. "Systematic Discontent: Answers to Questions from Andrea Aguilar" (2015), *Frantumaglia*, 345.

24. Adam Kirsch, "Elena Ferrante and the power of appropriation," *New York Times*, October 3, 2016, https://www.nytimes.com/2016/10/04/opinion/elena-ferrante-and-the-power-of-appropriation.html?_r=1.

25. Alyssa Rosenberg, "Elena Ferrante and the tensions between authenticity and privacy," *Washington Post*, October 4, 2016, https://www.washingtonpost.com/news/act-four/wp/2016/10/04/elena-ferrante-and-the-tensions-between-authenticity-and-privacy/?utm_term=.e7b8df5250e3.

26. Maria Laurino, "Review: Elena Ferrante's New Book: Frantumaglia," *Huffington Post*, November 3, 2017, https://www.huffingtonpost.com/maria-laurino/review-elena-ferrantes-ne_b_12775280.html.

27. Elena Ferrante, "Complicit Even Though Absent: Answers to Questions from Simonetta Fiori" (2014), *Frantumaglia*, 246.

28. Michiko Kakutani, "Elena Ferrante Wants Privacy. Her New Book Implies Otherwise," *New York Times*, October 10, 2016, https://www.nytimes.com/2016/10/11/books/review-elena-ferrante-frantumaglia.html?_r=2

29. Dalya Alberge, "Christopher Marlowe credited as one of Shakespeare's co-writers," *The Guardian*, October 23, 2016, https://www.theguardian.com/culture/2016/oct/23/christopher-marlowe-credited-as-one-of-shakespeares-co-writers.

30. Sandro and Sandra Ferri, interviewers, "Elena Ferrante, Art of Fiction No. 228," *The Paris Review*, Issue 212, Spring 2015, http://www.theparisreview.org/interviews/6370/art-of-fiction-no-228-elena-ferrante (reprinted in *Frantumaglia*, 271).

31. Elena Ferrante, "Letter to Sandra Ozzola" (2003), *Frantumaglia*, 146.

32. Elena Ferrante, "Narrating What Escapes the Narrative: Answers to Questions from Yasemin Congar (2015)," *Frantumaglia*, 306.

33. Tiziana de Rogatis, "Uncovering' Elena Ferrante, and the importance of a woman's voice," *The Conversation*, October 5, 2016, https://theconversation.com/uncovering-elena-ferrante-and-the-importance-of-a-womans-voice-66456.

34. Claudio Gatti, "Elena Ferrante: An Answer?" *New York Review of Books*, October 2, 2016, http://www.nybooks.com/daily/2016/10/02/elena-ferrante-an-answer/.

35. Guy Genilloud and Claude-Alain Roten, "Determination by stylometry of the probable author of the Ferrante corpus: Domenico Starnone," *OrphAnalytics*, October 11, 2016, http://www.orphanalytics.com/media/press-release-elena-ferrante.

36. Expert System Semantic Intelligence, "Who is Elena Ferrante?" February 2017, http://www.expertsystem.com/wp-content/uploads/2017/02/Report-Who-is-Elena-Ferrante.pdf.

37. Gabriella DiPietro, "Computer Science professor investigates author's true identity," *The Duquesne Duke*, October 16, 2017, http://www.duqsm.com/computer-science-professor-investigates-authors-true-identity/.

38. Julie Kosin, "Why isn't a woman directing *My Brilliant Friend*?" *Harper's Bazaar*, April 5, 2017, http://www.harpersbazaar.com/culture/art-books-music/a21803/my-brilliant-friend-tv-show-male-director/.

39. Michael Sheridan, "Finding Ferrante," *The Australian*, April 22, 2017, http://www.theaustralian.com.au/life/weekend-australian-magazine/finding-elena-ferrante-who-wrote-the-naples-novels/news-story/f218c96ef602e0d9ff2e6fe2c9d90449.

40. Domenico Starnone, *First Execution*, trans. Anthony Shugaar (New York: Europa Editions, 2009).

41. Domenico Starnone, *Ties*, trans. Jhumpa Lahiri (New York: Europa Editions, 2017).

42. *Ibid.*, 140.

43. Aaron Bady, "A novel of infidelity in dialogue with Elena Ferrante's *The Days of Abandonment*," *The New Yorker*, March 11, 2017, http://www.newyorker.com/books/page-turner/a-novel-of-infidelity-in-dialogue-with-elena-ferrantes-the-days-of-abandonment.

44. Dayna Tortorici, "Those Like Us: On Elena Ferrante," *n+1*, Issue 22, Spring 2015, https://nplusonemag.com/issue-22/reviews/those-like-us/.

Chapter 3

1. Daniel Hahn, "The Man Booker International Prize: A celebration of translation," *The Guardian*, May 16, 2016, https://www.theguardian.com/books/booksblog/2016/may/16/man-booker-international-prize-celebration-translation.

2. Adam Kirsch, *The Global Novel: Writing the World in the 21st Century* (New York: Columbia Global Reports, 2016), 92–92.

3. "About the prize," *Warwick Prize for Women in Translation*, March 2017, https://www2.warwick.ac.uk/fac/cross_fac/womenintranslation/.

4. Wyatt Mason, "The first woman to translate the Odyssey into English," *New York Times*, November 2, 2017, https://www.nytimes.com/2017/11/02/magazine/the-first-woman-to-translate-the-odyssey-into-english.html?_r=0.

5. Barbara Alfano, "Ann Goldstein Wanted (Really, Really Wanted) to Bring Elena Ferrante to America," *Arcade: Literature Humanities and the World*, October 14, 2016, http://arcade.stanford.edu/content/ann-goldstein-wanted-really-really-wanted-bring-elena-ferrante-america-0.

6. Liesel Schillinger, "Multilingual Wordsmiths, Part 4: Anne Goldstein on 'Ferrante Fever,'" *LA Review of Books*, May 29, 2016, https://lareviewofbooks.org/article/multilingual-wordsmiths-part-4-ann-goldstein-ferrante-fever/.

7. Richard Bojar, "Fidelity to the original: What does it mean?" *Translation: Treason or Trust*, unpublished manuscript, 2017.

8. Richard Bojar, "A comparison of the titles of the Neapolitan novels in Ferrante's Italian and Goldstein's English," *Translation: Treason or Trust*, unpublished manuscript, 2017.

9. Naomi Skwarna, "It's about making a person more herself: translating Elena Ferrante," March 16, 2017, http://hazlitt.net/feature/its-about-making-person-more-herself-translating-elena-ferrante.

10. Liesel Schillinger, "Multilingual Wordsmiths, Part 4: Anne Goldstein on 'Ferrante Fever,'" *LA Review of Books*, May 29, 2016, https://lareviewofbooks.org/article/multilingual-wordsmiths-part-4-ann-goldstein-ferrante-fever/.

11. Richard Bojar, "Fidelity to the original: What does it mean?" *Translation: Treason or Trust*, unpublished manuscript, 2017.

12. Melinda Harvey, "Ann Goldstein on translating Elena Ferrante and the inner workings of *The New Yorker*," *Lithub*, September 1, 2016, http://lithub.com/ann-goldstein-on-translating-elena-ferrante-and-the-inner-workings-of-the-new-yorker/.

13. Megan O'Rourke, "Elena Ferrante: The global literary sensation nobody knows," *The Guardian*, October 31, 2014, https://www.theguardian.com/books/2014/oct/31/elena-ferrante-literary-sensation-nobody-knows.

14. Neena Bhandari, "I don't become the writer, I inhabit the writer's words: Ann Goldstein, Elena Ferrante's translator," *Scroll.in*, May 22, 2016, https://scroll.in/article/808521/i-dont-become-the-writer-i-inhabit-the-writers-words-ann-goldstein-elena-ferrantes-translator.

15. Michelle Langstone, "New Yorker editor and translator Ann Goldstein—interview," *The Listener*, May, 13, 2016, http://www.noted.co.nz/currently/profiles/new-yorker-editor-and-translator-ann-goldstein-interview/.

16. Melinda Harvey, "Ann Goldstein on translating Elena Ferrante and the inner workings of *The New Yorker*," *Lithub*, September 1, 2016, http://lithub.com/ann-goldstein-on-translating-elena-ferrante-and-the-inner-workings-of-the-new-yorker/.

17. Michelle Langstone, "New Yorker editor and translator Ann Goldstein—interview," *The Listener*, May, 13, 2016, http://www.noted.co.nz/currently/profiles/new-yorker-editor-and-translator-ann-goldstein-interview/.

18. Melinda Harvey, "Ann Goldstein on translating Elena Ferrante and the inner workings of *The New Yorker*," *Lithub*, September 1, 2016, http://lithub.com/ann-goldstein-on-translating-elena-ferrante-and-the-inner-workings-of-the-new-yorker/.

19. Roberta Falkoff quoted in Sarah Begley, "The Historical Truth Behind Elena Ferrante's Neapolitan Novels," *Time*, August 31, 2015, http://time.com/4010504/neapolitan-novels-history/.

20. Naomi Skwarna, "It's about making a person more herself: translating Elena Ferrante," March 16, 2017, http://hazlitt.net/feature/its-about-making-person-more-herself-translating-elena-ferrante.

21. Jillian R. Cavanaugh, "Indexicalities of Language in Ferrante's Neapolitan Novels," *The Works of Elena Ferrante: Reconfiguring the Margins*, ed. Grace Bullaro and Stephanie Love (New York: Palgrave Macmillan, 2017), 66–67.

22. See the discussion of Eleanor Marx and Lydia Davis's observations about translating *Madame Bovary* in Emily Apter, *Against World Literature: On the Politics of Untranslatability* (New York: Verso, 2013), 265–97.

23. Gregory Rabassa, *If This Be Treason: Translation and its Discontents* (New York: New Directions, 2005).

Chapter 4

1. James Wood, quoted in Dayna Tortorici, "Those Like Us: On Elena Ferrante," *n+1*, Issue 22, Spring 2015, https://nplusonemag.com/issue-22/reviews/those-like-us/.
2. Elena Ferrante, "A Conversation with the Listeners of Fahrenheit," Radio 3, Italy (2006), *Frantumaglia*, 203.
3. Rachel Donadio, "'Writing Has Always Been a Great Struggle for Me': Q. and A.: Elena Ferrante," *New York Times*, December 9, 2014, https://www.nytimes.com/2014/12/10/books/writing-has-always-been-a-great-struggle-for-me.html?_r=1 (reprinted in *Frantumaglia*, 251).
4. Dayna Tortorici, "Those Like Us: On Elena Ferrante," *n+1*, Issue 22, Spring 2015, https://nplusonemag.com/issue-22/reviews/those-like-us/.
5. Ibid.
6. Sandro and Sandra Ferri, interviewers, "Elena Ferrante, Art of Fiction No. 228," *The Paris Review*, Issue 212, Spring 2015, http://www.theparisreview.org/interviews/6370/art-of-fiction-no-228-elena-ferrante (reprinted in *Frantumaglia*, 259).
7. *Ibid.* (reprinted in *Frantumaglia*, 268).
8. Michelle Langstone, "New Yorker editor and translator Ann Goldstein—interview," *The Listener*, May, 13, 2016, http://www.noted.co.nz/currently/profiles/new-yorker-editor-and-translator-ann-goldstein-interview/.
9. Elizabeth Mitchell, "Who is the mysterious author spreading #FerranteFever?" *New York Daily News*, December 31, 2015, http://www.nydailynews.com/entertainment/mysterious-author-spreading-ferrantefever-article-1.2480313.
10. Stefania Lucamante, *A Multitude of Women: The Challenges of the Contemporary Italian Novel* (Toronto: University of Toronto Press, 2008), 86.
11. Elena Ferrante, "Letter to Sandra Ozzolo" (2003), *Frantumaglia*, 138.
12. Elena Ferrante, "A Story of Disintegration: Answers to Questions from Jesper Storgaard Jensen" (2003), *Frantumaglia*, 89.
13. James Wood, "Women on the Verge: The Fiction of Elena Ferrante," *The New Yorker*, January 21, 2013, http://www.newyorker.com/magazine/2013/01/21/women-on-the-verge.
14. Elena Ferrante, "Without Keeping a Safe Distance: Answers to Questions from Stefania Scateni" (2002), *Frantumaglia*, 83.
15. Sandro and Sandra Ferri, interviewers, "Elena Ferrante, Art of Fiction No. 228," *The Paris Review*, Issue 212, Spring 2015, http://www.theparisreview.org/interviews/6370/art-of-fiction-no-228-elena-ferrante (reprinted in *Frantumaglia*, 269).
16. Simone de Beauvoir, *The Woman Destroyed*, trans. Patrick O'Brien (New York: Pantheon, 1969).
17. Lisa Mullenneaux, *Naples' Little Women: The Fiction of Elena Ferrante* (New York: Pennington Press, 2016).

Chapter 5

1. Margaret Drabble, "My hero, Elena Ferrante," *The Guardian*, March 11, 2016, https://www.theguardian.com/books/2016/mar/11/my-hero-elena-ferrante-margaret-drabble?CMP=twt_gu.
2. Elena Ferrante, "Women Who Write: Answers to Questions from Sandra, Sandro, and Eva," *Frantumaglia*, 274. (This reference is included in the expanded version of the 2015 *Paris Review* interview reprinted in *Frantumaglia*, 274.)
3. Claire Messud, "Elena Ferrante's Neapolitan quartet," *The Financial Times*, August 28, 2015, http://www.ft.com/intl/cms/s/0/0b7a4200-4bd3-11e5-b558-8a9722977189.html.

4. Cary Knapp, "#FerranteFever is raging," *Coastal Illustrated*, December 23, 2015, http://www.coastalillustrated.com/columns/coastal_columns/article_1aba9ec2-a821-11e5-88d8-c3f3049590c5.html.

5. Elena Ferrante, "The Brilliant Subordinate: Answers to Questions from Paolo di Stefano" (2011), *Frantumaglia*, 232.

6. Sandro and Sandra Ferri, interviewers, "Elena Ferrante, Art of Fiction No. 228," *The Paris Review*, Issue 212, Spring 2015, http://www.theparisreview.org/interviews/6370/art-of-fiction-no-228-elena-ferrante (reprinted in *Frantumaglia*, 284).

7. Toni Morrison, *Sula* (New York: Knopf, 1973).

8. Sandro and Sandra Ferri, interviewers, "Elena Ferrante, Art of Fiction No. 228," *The Paris Review*, Issue 212, Spring 2015, http://www.theparisreview.org/interviews/6370/art-of-fiction-no-228-elena-ferrante (reprinted in *Frantumaglia*, 284).

9. Zadie Smith, *Swing Time* (New York: Random House, 2016).

10. Alex Clark, "Female friendship in fiction from Wolf to Ferrante and Zadie Smith," *The Guardian*, August 6, 2016, https://www.theguardian.com/books/2016/aug/06/women-friendship-wold-ferrante-zadie-smith-fiction-alex-clark.

11. Claire Messud, *The Burning Girl* (New York: W.W. Norton, 2017).

12. Elena Ferrante, "Extreme People: Answers to Questions from Gudmund Skjeldal" (2015), *Frantumaglia*, 293.

13. Elissa Schappell, "The Mysterious, Anonymous Author Elena Ferrante on the Conclusion of Her Neapolitan Novels," *Vanity Fair*, August 27, 2015, http://www.vanityfair.com/culture/2015/08/elena-ferrante-interview-the-story-of-the-lost-child (reprinted in *Frantumaglia*, 329).

14. Sandro and Sandra Ferri, interviewers, "Elena Ferrante, Art of Fiction No. 228," *The Paris Review*, Issue 212, Spring 2015, http://www.theparisreview.org/interviews/6370/art-of-fiction-no-228-elena-ferrante.

15. Elissa Schappell, "The Mysterious, Anonymous Author Elena Ferrante on the Conclusion of Her Neapolitan Novels," *Vanity Fair*, August 27, 2015, http://www.vanityfair.com/culture/2015/08/elena-ferrante-interview-the-story-of-the-lost-child (reprinted in *Frantumaglia*, 328).

16. Jennifer Levasseur, "Exclusive Elena Ferrante interview: The full transcript," *The Sydney Morning Herald*, December 21, 2015, http://www.smh.com.au/entertainment/books/exclusive-elena-ferrante-interview-the-full-transcript-20151221-glt1op#ixzz3vfGQo1uC.

17. Lily Tuck, *Woman of Rome: A Life of Elsa Morante* (New York: HarperCollins, 2008), 23.

18. *Ibid.*, 24.

19. Rachel Cusk, "'The Story of the Lost Child,' by Elena Ferrante," *The New York Times*, August 26, 2015, http://www.nytimes.com/2015/08/30/books/review/the-story-of-the-lost-child-by-elena-ferrante.html?_r=1.

20. Jennifer Levasseur, "Exclusive Elena Ferrante interview: The full transcript," *The Sydney Morning Herald*, December 21, 2015, http://www.smh.com.au/entertainment/books/exclusive-elena-ferrante-interview-the-full-transcript-20151221-glt1op#ixzz3vfGQo1uC.

21. Deborah Orr, "Elena Ferrante's anonymity lets me concentrate exclusively on writing," *The Guardian*, February 19, 2016, http://www.theguardian.com/books/2016/feb/19/elena-ferrante-anonymity-lets-me-concentrate-exclusively-on-writing (reprinted in *Frantumaglia*, 360).

22. Elena Ferrante, "Letter to Sandra Ozzolo" (2013), *Frantumaglia*, 113.

23. Tommaso Astarito, *Between Salt Water and Holy Water: A History of Southern Italy* (New York: Norton, 2005), 275–77.

24. Sandro and Sandra Ferri, interviewers, "Elena Ferrante, Art of Fiction No. 228," *The Paris Review*, Issue 212, Spring 2015, http://www.theparisreview.org/interviews/6370/art-of-fiction-no-228-elena-ferrante (reprinted in *Frantumaglia*, 271).

Chapter 6

1. Charlotte Perkins Gilman, "Why I Wrote 'The Yellow Wallpaper,'" *Feminist Literary Theory and Criticism*, ed. Sandra M. Gilbert and Susan Gubar (New York: Norton, 2007), 119.

2. Adrienne Rich, *Of Woman Born: Motherhood as Experience and Institution* (New York: Norton, 1976), 21.

3. Adrienne Rich, "When We Dead Awaken," *Feminist Literary Theory and Criticism*, ed. Sandra M. Gilbert and Susan Gubar (New York: Norton, 2007), 196.

4. Tillie Olsen, "One Out of Twelve: Writers Who Are Women in Our Century," *Feminist Literary Theory and Criticism*, ed. Sandra M. Gilbert and Susan Gubar (New York: Norton, 2007), 179.

5. Rachel Donadio, "'Writing Has Always Been a Great Struggle for Me': Q. and A.: Elena Ferrante," *New York Times*, December 9, 2014, http://www.nytimes.com/2014/12/10/books/writing-has-always-been-a-great-struggle-for-me.html? (reprinted in *Frantumaglia*, 251–52).

6. Laura Benedetti, *Tigress in the Snow: Motherhood and Literature in Twentieth Century Italy* (Toronto: University of Toronto Press, 2007), 6.

7. Joan Acocella, "Elena Ferrante's New Book: Art Wins," *The New Yorker*, September 1, 2015, http://www.newyorker.com/culture/cultural-comment/elena-ferrantes-new-book-art-wins.

8. Elissa Schappell, "The Mysterious, Anonymous Author Elena Ferrante on the Conclusion of Her Neapolitan Novels," *Vanity Fair*, August 27, 2015, http://www.vanityfair.com/culture/2015/08/elena-ferrante-interview-the-story-of-the-lost-child (reprinted in *Frantumaglia*, 329).

9. Liz Jobey, "Women of 2015: Elena Ferrante, writer," *Financial Times*, December 11, 2015, https://www.ft.com/content/1f019b5c-9d18-11e5-b45d-4812f209f861 (reprinted in *Frantumaglia*, 350).

Chapter 7

1. Amalia Signorelli, "Women in Italy in the 1970s," *Speaking Out and Silencing: Culture, Society and Politics in Italy in the 1970's*, ed. Anna Cento Bull and Adalgisa Giorgio (London: Modern Humanities Research Association, 2006), 5.

2. Laura Benedetti, *Tigress in the Snow: Motherhood and Literature in Twentieth Century Italy* (Toronto: University of Toronto Press, 2007). See chapter 2, "Resilience and Resistance: The Fascist Years."

3. Elena Ferrante, "The Brilliant Subordinate: Answers to Questions from Paolo di Stefano" (2011), *Frantumaglia*, 235.

4. Deborah Orr, "Elena Ferrante's anonymity lets me concentrate exclusively on writing," *The Guardian*, February 19, 2016, http://www.theguardian.com/books/2016/feb/19/elena-ferrante-anonymity-lets-me-concentrate-exclusively-on-writing (reprinted in *Frantumaglia*, 358).

5. Lorenzo DaPonte, "Libretto to Mozart's *Don Giovanni*," trans. William Murray (1961), DM's Opera Site, http://www.murashev.com/opera/Don_Giovanni_libretto_Italian_English.

6. Rebecca Traister, *All the Single Ladies: Unmarried Women and the Rise of an Independent Nation* (New York: Simon & Schuster, 2016), 239.

Chapter 8

1. Jennifer Levasseur, "Exclusive Elena Ferrante interview: The full transcript," *The Sydney Morning Herald*, December 21, 2015, http://www.smh.com.au/entertainment/books/exclusive-elena-ferrante-interview-the-full-transcript-20151221-glt1op#ixzz3vfFeUUaj.

2. Liz Jobey, "Women of 2015: Elena Ferrante, writer," *Financial Times*, December 11, 2015, https://www.ft.com/content/1f019b5c-9d18-11e5-b45d-4812f209f861 (reprinted in *Frantumaglia*, 349).

3. Elena Ferrante, *The Beach at Night*, trans. Ann Goldstein (New York: Europa Editions, 2016), 34.

4. Noreen Malone, "Elena Ferrante's 'Unmasking' Wasn't the End of the World," *New York Magazine*, October 4, 2016, http://nymag.com/thecut/2016/10/elena-ferrantes-unmasking-wasnt-the-end-of-the-world.html.

Chapter 9

1. Thomas Piketty, *Capital in the Twenty First Century*, trans. Arthur Goldhammer (Cambridge: Harvard University Press, 2014).

2. Nicola Lagioia, "Writing is an Act of Pride: A Conversation with Elena Ferrante," *The New Yorker*, May 19, 2016, http://www.newyorker.com/books/page-turner/writing-is-an-act-of-pride-a-conversation-with-elena-ferrante (reprinted in *Frantumaglia*, 371).

3. John Hooper, *The Italians* (New York: Viking, 2015), 144.

4. Roxanna Robinson quoted in Angela Chen, "Ferrante fever in full swing at the PEN World Voices Festival," *The Guardian*, April 29, 2016, https://www.theguardian.com/books/2016/apr/29/elena-ferrante-fever-pen-world-voices-festival.

5. Elena Ferrante, "Extreme People: Answers to Questions from Gudmund Skjeldal" (2015), *Frantumaglia*, 296.

6. Deborah Orr, "Elena Ferrante's anonymity lets me concentrate exclusively on writing," *The Guardian*, February 19, 2016, http://www.theguardian.com/books/2016/feb/19/elena-ferrante-anonymity-lets-me-concentrate-exclusively-on-writing (reprinted in *Frantumaglia*, 356).

7. Sandro and Sandra Ferri, interviewers, "Elena Ferrante, Art of Fiction No. 228," *The Paris Review*, Issue 212, Spring 2015, http://www.theparisreview.org/interviews/6370/art-of-fiction-no-228-elena-ferrante (Reprinted in *Frantumaglia*, 283. The wording of the quotation is slightly different from that in the *Paris Review* article.)

Chapter 10

1. Elizabeth Mitchell, "#FerranteFever: What's fueling the passion for these captivating novels?" *New York Daily News*, December 21, 2015, http://www.nydailynews.com/entertainment/mysterious-author-spreading-ferrantefever-article-1.2480313.

2. Deborah Orr, "Elena Ferrante's anonymity lets me concentrate exclusively on writing," *The Guardian*, February 19, 2016, http://www.theguardian.com/books/2016/feb/19/-elena-ferrante-anonymity-lets-me-concentrate-exclusively-on-writing (reprinted in *Frantumaglia*, 356).

3. Michael Sheridan, "Finding Ferrante," *The Australian*, April 22, 2017, http://www.theaustralian.com.au/life/weekend-australian-magazine/finding-elena-ferrante-who-wrote-the-naples-novels/news-story/f218c96ef602e0d9ff2e6fe2c9d90449.

4. Alessandro Orsini, *Anatomy of the Red Brigades*, trans. Sarah J. Nodes (Ithaca: Cornell University Press, 2011), 103.

5. Roberto Batali, "The Red Brigades and the Moro Kidnapping," *Society and Politics in Italy in the 1970's*, ed. Anna Cento Bull and Adalgisa Giorgio (London: Modern Humanities Research Association, 2006), 147.

6. Leonardo Sciascia, *The Moro Affair* (Manchester: Carcanet, 1987).

7. Roberto Batali, "The Red Brigades and the Moro Kidnapping," *Society and Politics in Italy in the 1970's*, ed. Anna Cento Bull and Adalgisa Giorgio (London: Modern Humanities Research Association, 2006), 147.

8. Susannah Clapp, "My Brilliant friend review—intensity wins through," *The Guardian*, March 19, 2017, https://www.theguardian.com/stage/2017/mar/19/my-brilliant-friend-niamh-cusack-catherine-mccormack-elena-ferrante-review.

9. David Moss, *The Politics of Left-Wing Violence in Italy* (New York: St. Martin's Press, 1989), 47.

10. Nanni Balestrini, *We Want Everything* (New York: Verso, 2016), 87. (First published as *Vogliamo tutto* in 1971.)

11. *Ibid.*, 199–200.

12. Sylvere Lotringer and Christian Marazzi, "The Return of Politics," *Autonomia: Post Political Politics*, ed. Sylvere Lotringer and Christian Marazzi (Los Angeles: Semiotexte, 2007), 19.

13. Tom Behan, *Dario Fo: Revolutionary Theater* (London: Pluto Press, 2000), 117.

14. Tom Behan, "Allende, Berlinguer, Pinochet, and Dario Fo," *Society and Politics in Italy in the 1970's*, ed. Anna Cento Bull and Adalgisa Giorgio (London: Modern Humanities Research Association, 2006), 168–69.

15. Nicola Lagioia, "Writing is an Act of Pride": A Conversation with Elena Ferrante," *The New Yorker*, May 19, 2016, http://www.newyorker.com/books/page-turner/writing-is-an-act-of-pride-a-conversation-with-elena-ferrante (reprinted in *Frantumaglia*, 376–77).

Chapter 11

1. Simone de Beauvoir, Introduction, *The Second Sex*, trans. H.M. Parshley (New York: Knopf, l953), xix.

2. Ann Snitow, "Pages from A Gender Diary," *Dissent*, Spring l989, 205.

3. Joan Acocella, "Elena Ferrante's New Book: Art Wins," *The New Yorker*, September 1, 2015, http://www.newyorker.com/culture/cultural-comment/elena-ferrantes-new-book-art-wins.

4. Elena Ferrante, "The City without Love: Answers to Questions from Goffredo Fofi" (2002), *Frantumaglia*, 77.

5. Amalia Signorelli, "Women in Italy in the 1970s," *Society and Politics in Italy in the 1970's*, ed. Anna Cento Bull and Adalgisa Giorgio (London: Modern Humanities Research Association, 2006), 53.

6. Susan Faludi, "Death of a Revolutionary," *New Yorker Magazine*, April 15, 2013, http://www.newyorker.com/magazine/2013/04/15/death-of-a-revolutionary.

7. Sandra Kemp and Paolo Bono, "Introduction," *The Lonely Mirror: Italian Perspectives on Feminist Theory*, ed. Sandra Kemp and Paolo Bono (New York: Routledge, 1993), 6.

8. Shirley Geok-lin Lim, "'Ain't I a Feminist?' Reforming the Circle," *The Feminist Memoir Project: Voices from Women's Liberation*, ed. Rachel duPlessis and Ann Snitow (New York: Three Rivers Press, 1998), 452–53.

9. Elena Ferrante, "Letter to Sandra Ozzolo" (2003), *Frantumaglia*, 103.

10. Elissa Schappell, "The Mysterious, Anonymous Author Elena Ferrante on the Conclusion of Her Neapolitan Novels," *Vanity Fair*, August 27, 2015, http://www.vanityfair.com/culture/2015/08/elena-ferrante-interview-the-story-of-the-lost-child (reprinted in *Frantumaglia*, 332).

11. Dayna Tortorici, "Those Like Us: On Elena Ferrante," *n+1*, Issue 22, Spring 2015, https://nplusonemag.com/issue-22/reviews/those-like-us/.

12. Adrienne Rich, *Of Woman Born: Motherhood as Experience and Institution* (New York: W.W. Norton, 1976), 247.

13. Laura Benedetti, *The Tigress in the Snow: Motherhood and Literature in Twentieth Century Italy* (Toronto: University of Toronto Press, 2007), 85.
14. *Ibid.*, 87.
15. Patricia Hill Collins, *Black Feminist Thought* (New York: Routledge, 1990), 115–16.
16. Alice Walker, *In Search of our Mothers' Gardens* (New York: Harcourt-Brace, 1983), 240.
17. Patricia Hill Collins, *Black Feminist Thought* (New York: Routledge, 1990), 131.
18. Elena Ferrante, "Narrating What Escapes the Narrative: Answers to Questions from Yasemin Congar" (2015), *Frantumaglia*, 307.
19. Elissa Schappell, "The Mysterious, Anonymous Author Elena Ferrante on the Conclusion of Her Neapolitan Novels," *Vanity Fair*, August 27, 2015, http://www.vanityfair.com/culture/2015/08/elena-ferrante-interview-the-story-of-the-lost-childell (reprinted in *Frantumaglia*, 330).
20. Jennifer Levasseur, "Exclusive Elena Ferrante interview: The full transcript," The *Sydney Morning Herald*, December 21, 2015, http://www.smh.com.au/entertainment/books/exclusive-elena-ferrante-interview-the-full-transcript-20151221-glt1op#ixzz3vfFeUUaj.
21. Rachel Donadio, "'Writing Has Always Been a Great Struggle for Me': Q. and A.: Elena Ferrante," *New York Times*, December 9, 2014, http://www.nytimes.com/2014/12/10/books/writing-has-always-been-a-great-struggle-for-me.html? (reprinted in *Frantumaglia*, 250).
22. Marco Bardini, "House of Liars: The American Translation, " *Under Arturo's Star: The Cultural Legacies of Elsa Morante*, ed. Sharon Wood and Stefania Lucamante (West Lafayette: Purdue University Press, 2005), 123.
23. Megan O'Grady, "Elena Ferrante on the Origins of her Neapolitan Novels," *Vogue*, August 19, 2014, http://www.vogue.com/article/elena-ferrante-neapolitan-novels-origin-those-who-leave-and-those-who-stay.
24. Lily Tuck, *Woman of Rome: A Life of Elsa Morante* (New York: Harper Collins, 2008), 1.
25. See Stefania Lucamante, *A Multitude of Women: The Challenges of the Contemporary Italian Novel* (Toronto: University of Toronto Press, 2008) and Lisa Mullenneaux, *Naples' Little Women: The Fiction of Elena Ferrante* (New York: Pennington Press, 2016).
26. Claudio Gatti, "Elena Ferrante: An Answer?" *The New York Review of Books*, October 2, 2016, http://www.nybooks.com/daily/2016/10/02/elena-ferrante-an-answer/.
27. Christa Wolf, *The Quest for Christa T.*, trans. Christopher Middleton (New York: Farrar, Straus and Giroux, 1970), 11.
28. *Ibid.*
29. Stefania Lucamante, *A Multitude of Women: The Challenges of the Contemporary Italian Novel* (Toronto: University of Toronto Press, 2008), 86.
30. Christa Wolf, *Cassandra: A Novel and Four Essays* (New York: Farrar, Straus and Giroux, 1984), 259.
31. Sandro and Sandra Ferri, interviewers, "Elena Ferrante, Art of Fiction No. 228," *The Paris Review*, Issue 212, Spring 2015, http://www.theparisreview.org/interviews/6370/art-of-fiction-no-228-elena-ferrante (reprinted in *Frantumaglia*, 271).
32. Dayna Tortorici, "Those Like Us: On Elena Ferrante," *n+1*, Issue 22, Spring 2015, https://nplusonemag.com/issue-22/reviews/those-like-us/.
33. Sandro and Sandra Ferri, interviewers, "Elena Ferrante, Art of Fiction No. 228," *The Paris Review*, Issue 212, Spring 2015, http://www.theparisreview.org/interviews/6370/art-of-fiction-no-228-elena-ferrante (reprinted in *Frantumaglia*, 265).
34. *Ibid.* (reprinted in *Frantumaglia*, 266).
35. Gerda Lerner, *The Creation of Feminist Consciousness* (New York: Oxford University Press, 1993), 261.
36. Elissa Schappell, "The Mysterious, Anonymous Author Elena Ferrante on the Con-

clusion of Her Neapolitan Novels," *Vanity Fair*, August 27, 2015, http://www.vanityfair.com/culture/2015/08/elena-ferrante-interview-the-story-of-the-lost-childell (reprinted in *Frantumaglia*, 332).

37. Amalia Signorelli, "Women in Italy in the 1970s," *Society and Politics in Italy in the 1970's*, ed. Anna Cento Bull and Adalgisa Giorgio (London: Modern Humanities Research Association, 2006), 65.

38. Rachel Donadio, "Elena Ferrante, Author of Naples Novels, Stays Mysterious," *New York Times*, December 9, 2014, http://www.nytimes.com/2014/12/10/books/elena-ferrante-author-of-naples-novels-stays-mysterious.html.

39. Elena Ferrante, "Extreme People: Answers to Questions from Gudmund Skjedal" (2015), *Frantumaglia*, 293.

40. Elena Ferrante, "Every Individual Is a Battlefield: Answers to Questions from Giulia Calligaro" (2014), *Frantumaglia*, 241.

Chapter 12

1. "Interview with Francesca Siniscalchi: Foreigners appreciate Naples more than the Italians," *Il Napolista*, March 15, 2016, http://www.ilnapolista.it/2016/03/nyt-elena-ferrante-francesca-siniscalchi/.

2. Roisin Agnew, "In search of Elena Ferrante's Naples," *The Irish Times*, May 21, 2016, http://www.irishtimes.com/life-and-style/travel/in-search-of-elena-ferrante-s-naples-1.2651954.

3. Elissa Schappell, "The Mysterious, Anonymous Author Elena Ferrante on the Conclusion of Her Neapolitan Novels," *Vanity Fair*, August 27, 2015, http://www.vanityfair.com/culture/2015/08/elena-ferrante-interview-the-story-of-the-lost-child (reprinted in *Frantumaglia*, 328).

4. Posted by FerranteEvent Ischia, August 28, 2016, https://www.facebook.com/ferranteevent.ischia/posts/150778075365658?comment_id=150955848681214&comment_tracking=%7B%22tn%22%3A%22R1%22%D.

5. Katherine Wilson, "How Elena Ferrante made the neglected Naples a must-visit destination," *The Pool*, February 6, 2016, https://www.the-pool.com/arts-culture/books/2016/22/how-elena-ferrante-made-the-neglected-naples-a-must-visit-destination.

6. Tommaso Astarito, *Between Salt Water and Holy Water: A History of Southern Italy* (New York: W.W. Norton, 2005), 243.

7. Johann Wolfgang von Goethe, journal entry (3 March 1787), in *Italian Journey [1786–1788]*, Trans. W. H. Auden and Elizabeth Mayer (New York: Penguin,1962).

8. Francine Prose, "Sensory Overload In Naples," *New York Times*, June 15, 2003, http://www.nytimes.com/2003/06/15/travel/sensory-overload-in-naples.html.

9. Dan Hofstadter, *Falling Palace: A Romance of Naples* (New York: Random House, 2010).

10. Shirley Hazzard and Francis Steegmuller, *The Ancient Shore: Dispatches from Naples* (Chicago: University of Chicago Press, 2009).

11. Benjamin Taylor, *Naples Declared: A Walk Around the Bay* (New York: Penguin, 2013).

12. Paola Gambarota quoted in Sarah Begley, "The Historical Truth Behind Elena Ferrante's Neapolitan Novels," *Time*, August 31, 2015, http://time.com/4010504/neapolitan-novels-history/.

13. Tom Behan, *See Naples and Die: The Camorra and Organized Crime* (London: I.B. Tauris, 2002), 48.

14. Tommaso Astarito, *Between Salt Water and Holy Water: A History of Southern Italy* (New York: W.W. Norton, 2005), 314.

15. Paola Gambarota quoted in Sarah Begley, "The Historical Truth Behind Elena Fer-

rante's Neapolitan Novels," *Time*, August 31, 2015, http://time.com/4010504/neapolitan-novels-history/.

16. John Hooper, *The Italians* (New York: Viking, 2015), 238.

17. Paul Ginsborg, *Italy and Its Discontents: Family, Civil Society, State: 1980–2001* (New York: Palgrave Macmillan, 2003), 179–82.

18. *Ibid.*, 186.

19. *Ibid.*, 150.

20. John Hooper, *The Italians* (New York: Viking, 2015), 256.

21. Roberto Saviano, *Gomorrah: A Personal Journey into the Violent International Empire of Naples' Organized Crime System* (New York: Farrar, Straus and Giroux, 2007), 38.

22. Paul Ginsborg, *Italy and Its Discontents: Family, Civil Society, State: 1980–2001* (New York: Palgrave Macmillan, 2003), 200.

23. Tom Behan, *See Naples and Die: The Camorra and Organized Crime* (London: I.B. Tauris, 2002), 85.

24. *Ibid.*, 225.

25. Paul Ginsborg, *Italy and Its Discontents: Family, Civil Society, State: 1980–2001* (New York: Palgrave Macmillan, 2003), 201.

26. Roberto Saviano, *Gomorrah: A Personal Journey into the Violent International Empire of Naples' Organized Crime System* (New York: Farrar, Straus and Giroux, 2007), 231–32.

27. *Ibid.*, 284.

28. Elena Ferrante, "Our Fetid City," *New York Times*, January 15, 2008.

29. Elena Ferrante, "Stages in a Unique Quest: Answers to Questions from Francesco Erbani," *La Repubblica*, December 4, 2006 (reprinted in *Frantumaglia*, 201).

30. Elena Ferrante, "Our Fetid City," *New York Times*, January 15, 2008.

Conclusion

1. Elizabeth Mitchell, "The Question for Elena Ferrante," *New York Daily News*, Monday, January 4, 2016, http://www.nydailynews.com/blogs/pageviews/question-elena-ferrante-blog-entry-1.2485045.

2. David Moss, *The Politics of Left-Wing Violence in Italy* (New York: St. Martin's Press, 1989), 265.

3. Michael Shermer, "Are We All Racists? Private thoughts and public acts," *Scientific American*, August 2017, 81.

4. G.D. Dess, "Elena Ferrante: The Mad Adventures of Serious Ladies," *Los Angeles Review of Books*, July 29, 2017, https://lareviewofbooks.org/article/elena-ferrante-the-mad-adventures-of-serious-ladies#!.

5. Sandro and Sandra Ferri, interviewers, "Elena Ferrante, Art of Fiction No. 228," *The Paris Review*, Issue 212, Spring 2015, http://www.theparisreview.org/interviews/6370/art-of-fiction-no-228-elena-ferrante (reprinted in *Frantumaglia*, 270. The wording of the quotation in *Frantumaglia* is slightly different from that in the *Paris Review* article).

6. Rita Felski, *Beyond Feminist Aesthetics: Feminist Literature and Social Change* (Cambridge: Harvard University Press, 1989), 161.

7. *Ibid.*, 173–74.

8. Stephanie Kirchgaessner, "Elena Ferrante is writing again," *The Guardian*, November 29, 2017, https://www.theguardian.com/books/2017/nov/29/elena-ferrante-writing-again-publisher-says-neopolitan-series-novel.

Bibliography

Acocella, Joan. "Elena Ferrante's New Book: Art Wins." *New Yorker*, September 1, 2015, http://www.newyorker.com/culture/cultural-comment/elena-ferrantes-new-book-art-wins.
Agnew, Roisin. "In Search of Elena Ferrante's Naples." *The Irish Times*, May 21, 2016, http://www.irishtimes.com/life-and-style/travel/in-search-of-elena-ferrante-s-naples-1.2651954/.
Alberge, Dalya. "Christopher Marlowe Credited as One of Shakespeare's Co-writers." *The Guardian*, October 23, 2016, https://www.theguardian.com/culture/2016/oct/23/christopher-marlowe-credited-as-one-of-shakespeares-co-writers.
Alfano, Barbara. "Ann Goldstein Wanted (Really, Really Wanted) to Bring Elena Ferrante to America." *Arcade: Literature Humanities and the World*, October 14, 2016, http://arcade.stanford.edu/content/ann-goldstein-wanted-really-really-wanted-bring-elena-ferrante-america-0.
Alter, Alexandra. "'Ferrante Fever' Continues to Spread." *New York Times*, December 7, 2016, http://www.nytimes.com/2016/12/07/arts/ferrante-fever-continues-to-spread.html?_r=0.
Apter, Emily. *Against World Literature: On the Politics of Untranslatability*. New York: Verso, 2013.
Astarito, Tommaso. *Between Salt Water and Holy Water: A History of Southern Italy*. New York: Norton, 2005.
Bady, Aaron. "A Novel of Infidelity in Dialogue with Elena Ferrante's *The Days of Abandonment*." *The New Yorker*, March 11, 2017, http://www.newyorker.com/books/page-turner/a-novel-of-infidelity-in-dialogue-with-elena-ferrantes-the-days-of-abandonment.
Balestrini, Nanni. *We Want Everything*. New York: Verso, 2016. (First published as *Vogliamo tutto* in 1971.)
Bardini, Marco. "House of Liars: The American Translation of Menzogna e Sortilegio." In *Under Arturo's Star: The Cultural Legacies of Elsa Morante*, ed. Sharon Wood and Stefania Lucamante. West LafayetteL Purdue University Press, 2005, 112–23.
Barthes, Roland Barthes. "The Death of the Author." 1968. http://www.ubu.com/aspen/aspen5and6/threeEssays.html#barthes.
Batali, Roberto. "The Red Brigades and the Moro Kidnapping." In *Society and Politics in Italy in the 1970's*, ed. Anna Cento Bull and Adalgisa Giorgio. London: Modern Humanities Research Association, 2006, 147–60.
Beauvoir, Simone de. *The Second Sex*. Trans. H.M. Parshley. New York: Knopf, l953.
Beauvoir, Simone de. *The Woman Destroyed*. Trans. Patrick O'Brien. New York: Pantheon, 1969.
Begley, Sarah. "The Historical Truth Behind Elena Ferrante's Neapolitan Novels." *Time Magazine*, August 31, 2015, http://time.com/4010504/neapolitan-novels-history/.

Bibliography

Behan, Tom. "Allende, Berlinguer, Pinochet, and Dario Fo." In *Society and Politics in Italy in the 1970's*, ed. Anna Cento Bull and Adalgisa Giorgio. London: Modern Humanities Research Association, 2006, 160–70.
Behan, Tom. *Dario Fo: Revolutionary Theater*. London: Pluto Press, 2000.
Behan, Tom. *See Naples and Die: The Camorra and Organized Crime*. London: I.B. Tauris, 2002.
Benedetti, Laura. *Tigress in the Snow: Motherhood and Literature in Twentieth Century Italy*. Toronto: University of Toronto Press, 2007.
Bennett, Catherine. "Modern Tribes; the Elena Ferrante Fan." *The Guardian*, April 30, 2016, https://www.theguardian.com/lifeandstyle/2016/apr/30/elena-ferrante-fan-girl-modern-tribes.
Bhandari, Neena. "I Don't Become the Writer, I Inhabit the Writer's Words: Ann Goldstein, Elena Ferrante's translator." *Scroll.in*, May 22, 2016, https://scroll.in/article/808521/i-dont-become-the-writer-i-inhabit-the-writers-words-ann-goldstein-elena-ferrantes-translator.
Biggs, Joanna. "I Was Blind, She a Falcon." *The London Review of Books*, September 10, 2015, http://www.lrb.co.uk/v37/n17/joanna-biggs/i-was-blind-she-a-falcon.
Bojar, Richard. "A Comparison of the Titles of the Neapolitan Novels in Ferrante's Italian and Goldstein's English," *Translation: Treason or Trust*. Unpublished manuscript, 2017.
Bojar, Richard. "Fidelity to the Original: What Does It Mean?" *Translation: Treason or Trust*. Unpublished manuscript, 2017.
"Bookish Musings: Diving into the World of Elena Ferrante's Neapolitan Series." *Imaginary Book Club*, August 29, 2016, http://imaginarybookclub.com/bookish-musings-diving-into-the-world-of-elena-ferrantes-neapolitan-series.
Bullaro, Grace, and Stephanie Love, eds. *The Works of Elena Ferrante: Reconfiguring the Margins*. New York: Palgrave Macmillan, 2017.
Cavanaugh, Jillian R. "Indexicalities of Language in Ferrante's Neapolitan Novels." In *The Works of Elena Ferrante: Reconfiguring the Margin*, ed. Grace Bullaro and Stephanie Love. New York: Palgrave Macmillan, 2017, 45–70.
Chen, Angela. "Ferrante Fever in Full Wwing at the PEN World Voices Festival." *The Guardian*, April 29, 2016, https://www.theguardian.com/books/2016/apr/29/elena-ferrante-fever-pen-world-voices-festival.
Chisholm, Kate. "Why Elena Ferrante Doesn't Work on Radio." *The Spectator*, August 6, 2016, http://www.spectator.co.uk/2016/08/why-elena-ferrante-doesnt-work-on-radio/.
Clapp, Susannah. "My Brilliant Friend Review—Intensity Wins Through." *The Guardian*, March 19, 2017, https://www.theguardian.com/stage/2017/mar/19/my-brilliant-friend-niamh-cusack-catherine-mccormack-elena-ferrante-review.
Clark, Alex. "Female Friendship in Fiction from Wolf to Ferrante and Zadie Smith." *The Guardian*, August 6, 2016, https://www.theguardian.com/books/2016/aug/06/women-friendship-wold-ferrante-zadie-smith-fiction-alex-clark.
Collins, Patricia Hill. *Black Feminist Thought*. New York: Routledge, 1990.
Cusk, Rachel. "'The Story of the Lost Child,' by Elena Ferrante." *New York Times*, August 26, http://www.nytimes.com/2015/08/30/books/review/the-story-of-the-lost-child-by-elena-ferrante.html?_r=1.
Damien. "Naples: The Neapolitan Novels by Elena Ferrante." *Travel Readings*, April 18, 2016, http://www.travelreadings.org/2016/04/18/naples-the-neapolitan-novels-by-elena-ferrante/.
DaPonte, Lorenzo. "Libretto to Mozart's *Don Giovanni*." Trans. William Murray, 1961. *DM's Opera Site*, http://www.murashev.com/opera/Don_Giovanni_libretto_Italian_English.
Dess, G.D. "Elena Ferrante: The Mad Adventures of Serious Ladies." *Los Angeles Review of Books*, July 29, 2017, https://lareviewofbooks.org/article/elena-ferrante-the-mad-adventures-of-serious-ladies#!.

Bibliography

DiPietro, Gabriella. "Computer Science Professor Investigates Author's True Identity." *The Duquesne Duke*, October 16, 2017, http://www.duqsm.com/computer-science-professor-investigates-authors-true-identity.

Donadio, Rachel. "Elena Ferrante, Author of Naples Novels, Stays Mysterious." *New York Times*, December 10, 2014, https://www.nytimes.com/2014/12/10/books/elena-ferrante-author-of-naples-novels-stays-mysterious.html?_r=0.

Donadio, Rachel. "'Writing Has Always Been a Great Struggle for Me': Q. and A.: Elena Ferrante." *New York Times*, December 9, 2014, http://www.nytimes.com/2014/12/10/books/writing-has-always-been-a-great-struggle-for-me.html? (reprinted in *Frantumaglia*).

Drabble, Margaret. "My Hero, Elena Ferrante." *The Guardian*, March 11, 2016, https://www.theguardian.com/books/2016/mar/11/my-hero-elena-ferrante-margaret-drabble?CMP=twt_gu.

Enright, Lynn. "April De Angelis, the Woman Tasked with Bringing Elena Ferrante's Vision to Life." *The Pool*, March 3, 2017, https://www.the-pool.com/arts-culture/things-to-do/2017/9/april-de-angelis-on-adapting-elena-ferrante-s-neapolitan-novels/april-de-angelis-on-adapting-elena-ferrante-s-neapolitan-novels.

Expert System Semantic Intelligence. "Who Is Elena Ferrante?" February 2017, http://www.expertsystem.com/wp-content/uploads/2017/02/Report-Who-is-Elena-Ferrante.pdf.

Faludi, Susan. "Death of a Revolutionary." *New Yorker Magazine*, April 15, 2013, http://www.newyorker.com/magazine/2013/04/15/death-of-a-revolutionary.

Felski, Rita. *Beyond Feminist Aesthetics: Feminist Literature and Social Change*. Cambridge: Harvard University Press, 1989.

Ferrante, Elena. *The Beach at Night*. Trans. Ann Goldstein. New York: Europa Editions, 2016.

Ferrante, Elena. *The Days of Abandonment*. Trans. Ann Goldstein. New York: Europa Editions, 2005.

Ferrante, Elena. "Elena Ferrante on Sense and Sensibility: I was passionate about Austen's anonymity." *The Guardian*, October 16, 2015.

Ferrante, Elena. *Frantumaglia: A Writer's Journey*. Trans. Ann Goldstein. New York: Europa Editions, 2016.

Ferrante, Elena. *The Lost Daughter*. Trans. Ann Goldstein. New York: Europa Editions, 2008.

Ferrante, Elena. *My Brilliant Friend*. Trans. Ann Goldstein. New York: Europa Editions, 2012.

Ferrante, Elena. "Our Fetid City." *New York Times*, January 15 2008.

Ferrante, Elena. *The Story of a New Name*, Trans. Ann Goldstein New York: Europa Editions, 2013.

Ferrante, Elena. *Story of the Lost Child*. Trans. Ann Goldstein New York: Europa Editions, 2015.

Ferrante, Elena. *Those Who Leave and Those Who Stay*. Trans. Ann Goldstein New York: Europa Editions, 2014.

Ferrante, Elena. *Troubling Love*, Trans. Ann Goldstein. New York: Europa Editions, 2006.

Ferri, Sandro and Sandra, interviewers. "Elena Ferrante, Art of Fiction No. 228." *The Paris Review*, Issue 212, Spring 2015, http://www.theparisreview.org/interviews/6370/art-of-fiction-no-228-elena-ferrante (reprinted in *Frantumaglia*, 270).

Flood, Alison. "Elena Ferrante Pours Scorn on Speculation She Could Be a Man." *The Guardian*, September 2, 2015, https://www.theguardian.com/books/2015/sep/02/elena-ferrante-speculation-she-could-be-man-italian-novelist.

Freeman, Laura. "How on Earth Do You Put 1,600 Pages of Elena Ferrante on Stage?" *The Spectator*, March 4, 2017, http://www.spectator.co.uk/2017/03/how-on-earth-do-you-put-1600-pages-of-elena-ferrante-on-stage/.

Gatti, Claudio. "Elena Ferrante: An Answer?" *The New York Review of Books*, October 2, 2016, http://www.nybooks.com/daily/2016/10/02/elena-ferrante-an-answer/.

Bibliography

Gatti, Claudio. "The Story Behind a Name." *New York Review*, October 2, 2016, http://www.nybooks.com/daily/2016/10/02/story-behind-a-name-elena-.

Gellert, Sonya. "My Brilliant Friend by Elena Ferrante," *Shelf Esteem*, August 10, 2016, https://shelfesteemsite.com/2016/08/10/my-brilliant-friend-by-elena-ferrante/.

Genilloud, Guy, and Claude-Alain Roten. "Determination by stylometry of the probable author of the Ferrante corpus: Domenico Starnone." *OrphAnalytics*, October 11, 2016, http://www.orphanalytics.com/media/press-release-elena-ferrante.

Geok-lin Lim, Shirley. "'Ain't I a Feminist?': Reforming the Circle." *The Feminist Memoir Project: Voices from Women's Liberation*, ed. Rachel duPlessis and Ann Snitow. New York: Three Rivers Press, 1998.

Georgiana. "Book Covers Around the World." *Readers' High Tea*, https://readershightea.wordpress.com/2017/07/20/book-covers-around-the-world-the-neapolitan-novels-by-elena-ferrante/.

Gilman, Charlotte Perkins. "Why I Wrote 'The Yellow Wallpaper.'" *Feminist Literary Theory and Criticism*, ed. Sandra M. Gilbert and Susan Gubar. New York: W.W. Norton, 2007.

Ginsborg, Paul. *Italy and Its Discontents: Family, Civil Society, State:1980–2001*. New York: Palgrave Macmillan, 2003.

Goethe, Johann Wolfgang von. Journal entry, March 3 1787. In *Italian Journey [1786–1788]*, trans. W. H. Auden and Elizabeth Mayer. New York: Penguin, 1962.

Gressel, Madeline. "The Quotidian Ephemera of Women's Lives." *The Brooklyn Rail*, October 5, 2015, http://www.brooklynrail.org/2015/10/books/the-quotidian-ephemera-of-womens-lives.

Hahn, Daniel. "The Man Booker International Prize: A Celebration of Translation." *The Guardian*, May 16, 2016, https://www.theguardian.com/books/booksblog/2016/may/16/man-booker-international-prize-celebration-translation.

Harnett, Emily. "The Subtle Genius of Elena Ferrante's Bad Book Covers." *The Atlantic*, July 3, 2016, https://www.theatlantic.com/entertainment/archive/2016/07/elena-ferrante-covers-bad-no-good/488732/.

Hartigan, Patti. "Success of 'Neapolitan Novels' Stranger Than Fiction." *Boston Globe*, April 11, 2016, https://www.bostonglobe.com/metro/2016/04/10/success-neapolitan-novels-stranger-than-fiction/3GHNc3Doc0jT2XhACcjpWO/story.html.

Harvey, Melinda. "Ann Goldstein on Translating Elena Ferrante and the Inner Workings of *The New Yorker*." *Lithub*, September 1, 2016, http://lithub.com/ann-goldstein-on-translating-elena-ferrante-and-the-inner-workings-of-the-new-yorker/.

Hazzard, Shirley, and Francis Steegmuller. *The Ancient Shore: Dispatches from Naples*. Chicago: University of Chicago Press, 2009.

Hofstadter, Dan. *Falling Palace: A Romance of Naples*. New York: Random House, 2010.

Hooper, John. *The Italians*. New York: Viking, 2015.

"Interview with Francesca Siniscalchi: Foreigners appreciate Naples more than the Italians." *Il Napolista*, March 15, 2016, http://www.ilnapolista.it/2016/03/nyt-elena-ferrante-francesca-siniscalchi/.

Jobey, Liz. "Women of 2015: Elena Ferrante, Writer." *Financial Times*, December 11, 2015, https://www.ft.com/content/1f019b5c-9d18-11e5-b45d-4812f209f861 (reprinted in *Frantumaglia*, 350).

Kakutani, Michiko. "Elena Ferrante Wants Privacy. Her New Book Implies Otherwise." *New York Times*, October 10, 2016, https://www.nytimes.com/2016/10/11/books/review-elena-ferrante-frantumaglia.html?_r=.

Kemp, Sandra, and Paolo Bono, eds. *The Lonely Mirror: Italian Perspectives on Feminist Theory*. New York: Routledge, 1993.

Kirchgaessner, Stephanie. "Elena Ferrante Is Writing Again." *The Guardian*, November 29, 2017, https://www.theguardian.com/books/2017/nov/29/elena-ferrante-writing-again-publisher-says-neopolitan-series-novel.

Bibliography

Kirsch, Adam. "Elena Ferrante and the Power of Appropriation." *New York Times*, October 3, 2016, https://www.nytimes.com/2016/10/04/opinion/elena-ferrante-and-the-power-of-appropriation.html?_r=1.

Kirsch, Adam. *The Global Novel: Writing the World in the 21st Century*. New York: Columbia Global Reports, 2017.

Knapp, Cary. "#FerranteFever Is Raging." *Coastal Illustrated*, December 23, 2015, http://www.coastalillustrated.com/columns/coastal_columns/article_1aba9ec2-a821-11e5-88d8-c3f3049590c5.html.

Kosin, Julie. "Why Isn't a Woman Directing *My Brilliant Friend*?" *Harper's Bazaar*, April 5, 2017, http://www.harpersbazaar.com/culture/art-books-music/a21803/my-brilliant-friend-tv-show-male-director/.

Krule, Miriam. "Dressing a Refined Story with a Touch of Vulgarity, An Interview with Elena Ferrante's Art Director." *Slate*, August 28, 2015, http://www.slate.com/blogs/browbeat/2015/08/28/elena_ferrante_neapolian_novels_cover_design_an_interview_with_the_publisher.html.

Lagioia, Nicola. "Writing Is an Act of Pride: A Conversation with Elena Ferrante." *The New Yorker*, May 19, 2016, http://www.newyorker.com/books/page-turner/writing-is-an-act-of-pride-a-conversation-with-elena-ferrante (reprinted in *Frantumaglia*, 371).

Langstone, Michelle. "*New Yorker* Editor and Translator Ann Goldstein—Interview." *The Listener*, May, 13, 2016, http://www.noted.co.nz/currently/profiles/new-yorker-editor-and-translator-ann-goldstein-interview/.

Laurino, Maria. "Q&A: The Reporter Who May Have Unmasked Ferrante: I have no regrets." *The National Book Review*, November 16, 2016, http://www.thenationalbookreview.com/features/2016/11/16/qa-the-reporter-who-may-have-unmasked-elena-ferrante-i-have-no-regrets.

Laurino, Maria. "Review: Elena Ferrante's New Book: *Frantumaglia*." *Huffington Post*, November 3, 2017, https://www.huffingtonpost.com/maria-laurino/review-elena-ferrantes-ne_b_12775280.html.

Lerner, Gerda. *The Creation of Feminist Consciousness*. New York: Oxford University Press, 1993.

Levasseur, Jennifer. "Exclusive Elena Ferrante Interview: The Full Transcript." *The Sydney Morning Herald*, December 21, 2015, http://www.smh.com.au/entertainment/books/exclusive-elena-ferrante-interview-the-full-transcript-20151221-glt1op#ixzz3vfFeUUaj.

Lotringer, Sylvere, and Christian Marazzi, eds. *Autonomia: Post Political Politics*. Los Angeles: Semiotexte, 2007.

Lucamante, Stefania. *A Multitude of Women: The Challenges of the Contemporary Italian Novel*. Toronto: University of Toronto Press.

Malone, Noreen. "Elena Ferrante's 'Unmasking' Wasn't the End of the World." *New York Magazine*, October 4, 2016, http://nymag.com/thecut/2016/10/elena-ferrantes-unmasking-wasnt-the-end-of-the-world.html.

Marmion, Patrick, "Ambitious Italian Saga Winds Up in a Dead-End." *The Daily Mail*, March 16, 2017, http://www.dailymail.co.uk/tvshowbiz/article-4322464/My-Brilliant-Friend-Italian-saga-winds-dead-end.html.

Mason, Wyatt. "The First Woman to Translate the *Odyssey* into English." *New York Times*, November 2, 2017, https://www.nytimes.com/2017/11/02/magazine/the-first-woman-to-translate-the-odyssey-into-english.html?_r=0.

Messud, Claire. *The Burning Girl*. New York: W.W. Norton, 2017.

Messud, Claire. "Elena Ferrante's Neapolitan Quartet." *The Financial Times*, August 28, 2015, http://www.ft.com/intl/cms/s/0/0b7a4200-4bd3-11e5-b558-8a9722977189.html.

Mitchell, Elizabeth. "The Question for Elena Ferrante." *New York Daily News*, Monday, January 4, 2016, http://www.nydailynews.com/blogs/pageviews/question-elena-ferrante-blog-entry-1.2485045.

Bibliography

Mitchell, Elizabeth. "Who Is the Mysterious Author Spreading #FerranteFever?" *New York Daily News*, December 31, 2015, http://www.nydailynews.com/entertainment/mysterious-author-spreading-ferrantefever-article-1.2480313.

Moore, Fernanda. "Neapolitan Nonsense." *Commentary Magazine*, December 1, 2015, https://www.commentarymagazine.com/articles/neapolitan-nonsense/.

Morrison, Toni. *Sula*. New York: Knopf, 1973.

Moss, David. *The Politics of Left-Wing Violence in Italy*. New York: St. Martin's Press, 1989.

Mullan, John. *Anonymity: A Secret History of English Literature*. Princeton: Princeton University Press, 1980.

Mullenneaux, Lisa. *Naples' Little Women: The Fiction of Elena Ferrante*. New York: Pennington Press, 2016.

Naylor, Gary. "BWW Review: *My Brilliant Friend*." *Broadway World*, March 20, 2017, http://www.broadwayworld.com/westend/article/BWW-Review-MY-BRILLIANT-FRIEND-PARTS-1-2-Rose-Theatre-20170320#.

O'Connell, Alex. "Elena Ferrante Was More Challenging Than Tolstoy." *The Times*, January 13 2017, http://www.thetimes.co.uk/edition/times2/elena-ferrante-was-more-challenging-than-tolstoy-6c7zbq6tf.

O'Grady, Megan. "Elena Ferrante on the Origins of her Neapolitan Novels." *Vogue*, August 19, 2014, http://www.vogue.com/article/elena-ferrante-neapolitan-novels-origin-those-who-leave-and-those-who-stay.

Olsen, Tillie. "One Out of Twelve: Writers Who Are Women in Our Century." *Feminist Literary Theory and Criticism*, ed. Sandra M. Gilbert and Susan Gubar. New York: Norton, 2007.

O'Rourke, Meghan. "Elena Ferrante; The Global Sensation Nobody Knows." *The Guardian*, October 31, 2014, https://www.theguardian.com/books/2014/oct/31/elena-ferrante-literary-sensation-nobody-knows.

Orr, Deborah. "Elena Ferrante's Anonymity Lets Me Concentrate Exclusively on Writing." *The Guardian*, February 19, 2016, http://www.theguardian.com/books/2016/feb/19/elena-ferrante-anonymity-lets-me-concentrate-exclusively-on-writing (reprinted in *Frantumaglia*, 360).

Orsini, Alessandro. *Anatomy of the Red Brigades*. Trans. Sarah J. Nodes. Ithaca: Cornell University Press, 2011.

Parks, Tim. "How Could You Like That Book?" *New York Review of Books*, November 10, 2015, http://www.nybooks.com/daily/2015/11/10/how-could-you-like-that-book/.

Pellas, Francesca. "Michael Reynolds on Ferrante's Class Consciousness." *Literary Hub*, May 10, 2016, http://lithub.com/michael-reynolds-on-ferrantes-class-consciousness-and-rome-vs-nyc/.

Piketty, Thomas. *Capital in the Twenty First Century*. Trans. Arthur Goldhammer. Cambridge: Harvard University Press, 2014.

Prose, Francine. "Sensory Overload in Naples." *New York Times*, June 15, 2003, http://www.nytimes.com/2003/06/15/travel/sensory-overload-in-naples.html.

Rabassa, Gregory. *If This Be Treason: Translation and Its Discontents*. New York: New Directions, 2005.

Rich, Adrienne. *Of Woman Born: Motherhood as Experience and Institution*. New York: W.W. Norton, 1976.

Rich, Adrienne. "When We Dead Awaken." *Feminist Literary Theory and Criticism*, ed. Sandra M. Gilbert and Susan Gubar. New York: W.W. Norton, 2007.

Rogatis, Tiziana de. "'Uncovering' Elena Ferrante, and the Importance of a Woman's Voice." *The Conversation*, October 5, 2016, https://theconversation.com/uncovering-elena-ferrante-and-the-importance-of-a-womans-voice-66456.

Rosenberg, Alyssa. "Elena Ferrante and the Tensions Between Authenticity and Privacy." *Washington Post*, October 4, 2016, https://www.washingtonpost.com/news/act-four/

wp/2016/10/04/elena-ferrante-and-the-tensions-between-authenticity-and-privacy/?utm_term=.e7b8df5250e3.

Saviano, Roberto. *Gomorrah: A Personal Journey into the Violent International Empire of Naples' Organized Crime System*. New York: Farrar, Straus and Giroux, 2007.

Schappell, Elissa. "The Mysterious, Anonymous Author Elena Ferrante on the Conclusion of Her Neapolitan Novels." *Vanity Fair*, August 27, 2015, http://www.vanityfair.com/culture/2015/08/elena-ferrante-interview-the-story-of-the-lost-child (reprinted in *Frantumaglia*).

Schillinger, Liesel. Multilingual Wordsmiths, Part 4: Anne Goldstein on "Ferrante Fever." *LA Review of Books*, May 29, 2016, https://lareviewofbooks.org/article/multilingual-wordsmiths-part-4-ann-goldstein-ferrante-fever/.

Sciascia, Leonardo. *The Moro Affair*. Manchester: Carcanet, 1987.

Shah, Bina. "The Women Who Do." *DAWN*, August 14, 2016, http://www.dawn.com/news/1277487/the-women-who-do?fromNewsdog=1.

Shane, Charlotte. "The Sexist Big Reveal." *The New Republic*, October 3, 2016, https://newrepublic.com/article/137400/sexist-big-reveal.

Shermer, Michael. "Are We All Racists? Private Thoughts and Public Acts." *Scientific American*, August 2017.

Signorelli, Amalia "Women in Italy in the 1970s." *Speaking Out and Silencing: Culture, Society and Politics in Italy in the 1970's*, ed. Anna Cento Bull and Adalgisa Giorgio. London: Modern humanities Research Association, 2006, 43–66.

Silliman, Anna. "Make Your Dad Read Elena Ferrante!" *New York Magazine*, June 17, 2016, http://nymag.com/thecut/2016/06/reading-elena-ferrante-with-my-dad.html.

Skwarna, Naomi. "It's About Making a Person More Herself: Translating Elena Ferrante." March 16, 2017, http://hazlitt.net/feature/its-about-making-person-more-herself-translating-elena-ferrante.

Smith, Zadie. *Swing Time*. New York: Random House, 2016.

Starnone, Domenico. *First Execution*, trans. Anthony Shugaar. New York: Europa Editions, 2009.

Starnone, Domenico. *Ties*. Trans. Jhumpa Lahiri. New York: Europa Editions, 2017.

Taylor, Benjamin. *Naples Declared: A Walk Around the Bay*. New York: Penguin Books, 2013.

Tortorici, Dayna. "Those Like Us: On Elena Ferrante." *n+1*, Issue 22, Spring 2015, https://nplusonemag.com/issue-22/reviews/those-like-us/.

Tuck, Lily. *Woman of Rome: A Life of Elsa Morante*. New York: HarperCollins, 2008.

Traister, Rebecca. *All the Single Ladies: Unmarried Women and the Rise of an Independent Nation*. New York: Simon & Schuster, 2016.

Walker, Alice. *In Search of Our Mothers' Gardens*. New York: Harcourt-Brace, 1983.

Washington Post Editorial Board. "Why We Should Celebrate the Elena Ferrante Firestorm." *Washington Post*, October 6, 2016, https://www.washingtonpost.com/opinions/why-we-should-celebrate-the-elena-ferrante-firestorm/2016/10/06/b26e3fc2-8a79-11e6-875e-2c1bfe943b66_story.html?tid=a_inl&utm_term=.2e754b40cb33.

Wilson, Katherine. "How Elena Ferrante Made the Neglected Naples a Must-Visit Destination." *The Pool*, February 6, 2016, https://www.the-pool.com/arts-culture/books/2016/22/how-elena-ferrante-made-the-neglected-naples-a-must-visit-destination.

Wolf, Christa. *Cassandra: A Novel and Four Essays*. Trans. Jan Van Heurck. New York: Farrar, Straus and Giroux, 1984.

Wolf, Christa. *The Quest for Christa T.* Trans. Christopher Middleton. New York: Farrar, Straus and Giroux, 1970.

Wood, Gaby. "How Karl Ove Knausgaard and Elena Ferrante Won Us Over." *The Telegraph*, February 28, 2016, http://www.telegraph.co.uk/books/what-to-read/how-karl-ove-knausgaard-and-elena-ferrante-won-us-over/.

Wood, James. "Women on the Verge: The Fiction of Elena Ferrante." *The New Yorker*, January 21, 2013, http://www.newyorker.com/magazine/2013/01/21/women-on-the-verge.

Index

abandonment 54–61, 63, 98–100, 103
abortion 165
Acocella, Joan 89, 151
adaptations of Ferrante's novels: BBC Radio adaptation of the Neapolitan novels 21; film adaptation of *Troubling Love* 20; stage adaptation of the Neapolitan Novels 21–22; television adaptation of the Neapolitan Novels 19, 22, 32
affidamento (entrustment) 156, 158
African American feminists 157–159
Alcott, Louisa May, *Little Women* 79
Allende, Salvador 143
anarchism 141–142a
Astarito, Tommaso 77, 171
Austen, Jane 15, 23, 36, 159, 164
authorship: collaborative 30–31, 78, 81–82, 178–179; of Ferrante's novels 6–8, 23–36; of Shakespeare's plays 30
autocoscienza 153–154
Autonomia 141–42

Bady, Aaron 36
Balestrini, Nanni: *We Want Everything* 141–142
Balzac, Honore de 17, 188
Barthes, Roland 24
Batali, Roberto 138
Beckett, Samuel 79, 97
Behan, Tom 145–146, 171, 178–179
Benedetti, Laura: *Tigress in the Snow* 88, 157
Bennett, Catherine 18–19
Biggs, Joanna 13, 16
biological determinism 87, 97, 133
The Blue Fairy 74, 78
Bojar, Richard 39, 44
Bono, Paolo 154
Braidotti, Rosi 156
breakdown of family ties 72
Brontë sisters 23, 26, 36, 164
Bullaro, Grace: *The Works of Elena Ferrante: Reconfiguring the Margins* 2, 5, 24
Butler, Judith 156

Cavanaugh, Jillian R. 47
Cavarero, Adriana 156
Chisholm, Kate 21
Chopin, Kate 84
Clapp, Susannah 22, 138
Clark, Alex 72
class 121–134, 155, 158; bias 128–130, 158; cultural capital 126, 129; downward mobility 130; individualism vs. solidarity 124–125, 129, 131, 133, 142, 146–147; intersection with gender 130–132, 165–166; resentments 103, 128–129; struggle 129, 142, 146, 152–153; upward mobility 53, 61, 121–134
classical literature and mythology 162, 180; Euripides, *Medea* 56, 58, 162; Homer, *Iliad* 180; Virgil, *Aeneid* 78, 98–99, 163
Cline, Emma: *The Girls* 72
Cohn-Bendit, Daniel 152
Collins, Patricia Hill: *Black Feminist Thought* 157–158
Communist Party of Italy (PCI) 8, 111, 141, 144–145, 147–148, 179; *L'Unita* 80
consciousness-raising groups 153–154
contraception 117, 165
corruption 145, 175–179, 183; *Tangentopoli* scandal 175–177
Costanzo, Saverio 32
Cusk, Rachel 75; *A Life's Work: On Becoming a Mother* 83

Dante: *The Divine Comedy* 180
Darwin, Veronique 25
Davis, Lydia (trans. *Madame Bovary*) 48
The Days of Abandonment 2, 16, 25–27, 32, 34, 36–37, 49, 54–61, 110, 160
De Angelis, April 21–22
de Beauvoir, Simone 160; *The Second Sex* 10, 150; *The Woman Destroyed* 60, 160
de Lauretis, Teresa 156
de Pizan, Christine 164
de Rogatis, Tiziana 25, 31

213

Index

Dess, GD 185–186
dialect, Neapolitan 20, 46–47, 127
Dickens, Charles 15, 17
divorce 87–88, 95, 117, 145, 164
Donadio, Rachel 14–15
Dostoyevsky, Fyodor 164; *Notes from the Underground* 184–85
Drabble, Margaret 66
drugs 140; addiction 116, 178; drug trade 177, 180–181
Dutschke, Rudi 152

education 6, 27–28, 46, 50, 55, 61, 69, 73, 77–78, 85, 94–95, 121–124, 133, 145
Eliot, George 15, 26, 36
experimental novel 50, 66, 188–189

Falkoff, Rebecca 46, 161
fascists 94, 135–138, 141, 145, 147, 176
feminist literature and theory 9–10, 150–167; difference 151–152, 154, 160; equality 151; intersectional 150, 189; Italian 10, 153–154, 156–157; second wave 150
feminist movement 9, 103–104, 164–165, 167; Italian 89, 152–153; separatism 153
Ferrante, Elena: *The Beach at Night* 117; *Frantumaglia: A Writer's Journey* 7–8, 10, 23, 27, 29–30, 32–33, 37, 49, 66, 57, 75, 83, 121; narrative structure 66–68, 91, 188–189; Neapolitan Novels 2–3, 5–6, 8–10, 13–17, 19, 22, 30, 34–36, 38, 47, 49–50, 54–55, 66–67, 71, 75, 77–78, 85, 87, 135, 161–163, 165 (see also *My Brilliant Friend*; *The Story of a New Name*; *Story of the Lost Child*; *Those Who Leave and Those Who Stay*); novellas 1–2, 5, 49–50, 53, 67, 75 (see also *The Days of Abandonment*; *The Lost Daughter*; *Troubling Love*); prose style 44–45, 53, 60
Ferrante Fever 13–22
Ferri, Sandra Ozzolo 18, 27, 70, 135, 155
Ferri, Sandro 135, 190
Firestone, Shulamith 156
Foulke, Adrienne (trans. *House of Liars*) 159
Franzen, Jonathan 184, 186
Freudian psychoanalysis 154
friendship: female 2, 8, 10, 13, 16, 19, 53, 66–82; 118–120; male 73, 118–120

Gambarota, Paola 171–172
Garboli, Cesare 37
Gatti, Claudio 5, 6–7, 18, 23, 25–28, 30–31, 33, 36, 73, 161, 169, 189
gender roles 69, 89, 95–96, 107, 111, 116–118, 122–123, 130; gender identity 114–116, 150, 152, 159, 189; "honor code" 95, 113; intersection with class 130–132, 165–166;

men as prisoners of gender 57, 95, 110–111, 113
Gilman, Charlotte Perkins: "The Yellow Wallpaper" 83
Ginsborg, Paul 175–177, 180
Goethe, Johann Wolfgang von 170; *Faust* 77
Goldstein, Ann 2–8, 14, 19, 25, 37–48
Gressel, Madeline 15

Haraway, Donna 156
Harnett, Emily 18
Hazzard, Shirley: *The Ancient Shore: Dispatches from Naples* 170
hereditary traits 59, 87, 133
Hofstadter, Dan: *Falling Palace: A Romance of Naples* 170
homophobia 116
Hooper, John 175–176
housework 105, 117, 132, 150

imagery, recurrent: dolls 61, 63–65, 69–70, 73, 114, 187–188; jewelry 56–57, 69, 87–88, 91, 114, 120, 158, 181, 188
Irigaray, Luce 156
Ischia 62, 76, 79, 97, 99–100, 114, 173
Italy: history 108, 121, 135, 143, 137, 141; prejudice against Southern Italians 127; Southern Italian culture and traditions 87; Southern Italian women 84–85, 87, 95, 166; Southern Italian workers 142, 147

Juola, Patrick 32

Kakutani, Michiko 30
Kemp, Sandra 154
Kirsch, Adam: *The Global Novel: Writing the World in the 21st Century* 14, 28, 37–38
Knapp, Cary 68
Kosin, Julie 32
Krule, Miriam 18

Lagioia, Nicola 148
Lahiri, Jhumpa 37
Laurino, Maria 29
Lerner, Gerda: *The Creation of Feminist Consciousness* 164
Lessing, Doris 84
Levi, Primo 37, 48
Lim, Shirley Geok-lin 155
Lispector, Clarice 48, 159
Lonzi, Carla: *Let's Spit on Hegel* 153–154, 156–157
The Lost Daughter 2, 25, 49, 55, 61–65, 68, 90, 92, 156
Lotta Continua 153
Love, Stephanie: *The Works of Elena Ferrante: Reconfiguring the Margins* 2, 5, 24
Lucamante, Stefania 56, 160, 162

Index

Machiavelli, Nicolo: *The Prince* 175
Il Manifesto 136, 161
Marquez, Gabriel Garcia 39, 48
marriage 94–96; breakdown 54–57, 61, 69; 90–91, 95–96, 117; 102–103, 107, 154; impact of marital breakdown on children 35, 90–91; infidelity 34–35, 54–63, 69, 90, 102–104
Martone, Mario 20
Marx, Eleanor (trans. *Madame Bovary*) 48
Meinhardt, Ulrike 147
mental breakdown 45, 50, 56, 58–59, 65, 98–99, 177
Messud, Claire 19, 68; *The Burning Girl* 72
Milan Women's Bookstore Collective 156
Moore, Fernanda 19
Morante, Elsa 74, 159–160, 163–164; *House of Liars* 25, 159–160
Moro, Aldo 9, 137–138
Morrison, Toni 84; *The Bluest Eye* 52; *God Help the Child* 52; *Sula* 70–71
Moss, David 141
motherhood 54, 58, 61–65, 83–93, 157; mother/daughter relationships 51, 53, 62–64, 85–88, 130, 133–134, 156–159, 185
Mozart, Wolfgang: *Don Giovanni* 105–106
Mullan John: *Anonymity: A Secret History of English Literature* 26
Mullenneaux, Lisa: *Naples' Little Women: The Fiction of Elena Ferrante* 2, 5, 160
Munro, Alice 159
Muraro, Luisa 156
Mussolini, Benito 94; fascism 94–95
My Brilliant Friend 18–19, 32, 40, 66, 69, 71, 77–78, 82, 85, 95, 110, 114, 123, 154–155, 161, 163, 171–173, 187

Nabokov, Vladimir 39
Naples 10; beauty 173–174; difficulties of daily life 173, 183; earthquake (1980) 177–178; history 108, 141, 171–172, 174; immigration 173; Neapolitan dialect 127–128; Neapolitan folk traditions 77; negative images 168, 170; political violence 136; tourism 168–170
Naylor, Gary 22
Noh, Yooyeon 13–14

Olsen, Tillie 83
organized crime 168; Camorra 93, 141, 168, 171–172, 177–181; drug trade 116, 177–178, 181; integrated into Italian society 180–182; Mafia 177; political corruption 179; violence 116, 177–179, 182; waste management 182–183
Orichuia, Nicola 17
O'Rourke, Megan 45
Orsini, Alessandro 136

Paley, Grace 84
Parks, Tim 19
Pasolini, Pier Paolo 37
patriarchy 28, 95, 105, 154
Petracco, Daniela 15
Petzenbaum, Golda Frieda 28
Pevear, Richard 39
Piketty, Thomas: *Capital in the Twenty First Century* 121, 148
Plath, Sylvia 84
politics: left-wing 120, 129, 135–148, 176; leftists' hostility to feminism 152–153; political pessimism 133, 137, 142–143, 148–149, 165; political violence 131, 136–147, 153; worker/student alliances 142–144
poverty 7, 32, 95, 112–113, 171, 174
pregnancy 83, 89, 97–98, 104
Prose, Francine 170
Proust, Marcel: *Remembrance of Things Past* 188
Pushkin: *Eugene Onegin* 39

Rabassa, Gregory 39, 48
Raja Anita 6–7, 23, 26–30, 32–33, 36, 82, 10, 161, 189
Red Brigades 137–138
Reynolds, Michael 14, 16, 19
Rich, Adrienne: *Of Woman Born: Motherhood as Experience and Institution* 83, 156–157
Robinson, Roxana 122
romantic love 97–98; falling out of love 105–106
Rosenberg, Alyssa 28–29
Rousseau, Jean-Jacques 170

Sand, George 26, 36
Saviano, Roberto: *Gomorrah* 177, 182–183
Sciascia Leonardo: *The Moro Affair* 138
sexuality: adolescent 82, 95, 101; female 100–102; infidelity 104–106; intercourse 45, 51–52; 58–59, 100, 102; male 102–106, 132; promiscuity 103, 105–106, 114; revolution 35, 87, 103–104, 132, 139–140
Shah, Binah 13
Shane, Charlotte 23
Shermer, Michael 184
Signorelli, Amalia 94, 153, 166
Silliman, Anna 17
Siniscalchi, Francesca 168
Smith, Zadie: *Swing Time* 71
Snitow, Ann 151
Socialist Party 9, 139, 148, 175; Bettino Craxi 175
sorveglianza (surveillance) 155
Starnone, Domenico 7, 20, 23, 26, 29, 31–32, 36, 53, 82, 109, 133–134, 136, 161, 189; *First Execution* 33–35, 136, 189; *Ties (Lacci)* 26, 33–36, 61, 189

Index

Steegmuller, Francis: *The Ancient Shore: Dispatches from Naples* 170; *The Story of a New Name* 41, 47, 62–63, 69, 75–77, 79–80, 85, 96–98, 108–109, 111–112, 115, 126–127, 131, 138, 152, 162, 180, 187

Still, Melly 22

Story of the Lost Child 35, 45, 51, 67, 70, 72, 76, 84, 89–93, 95–97, 99–100, 108, 129–130, 134–135, 138–139, 145–148, 153, 164, 168, 173–176, 178, 180–181, 187–188

Taylor, Benjamin: *Naples Declared: A Walk Around the Bay* 170

Those Who Leave and Those Who Stay 32, 35, 39–42, 58, 70, 77, 83, 86, 89–91, 100, 102–103, 112, 127–128, 132, 139, 144, 152–155, 162

Tolstoy, Leo: comparisons with Ferrante 17, 23, 164, 188; translation 39

Tortorici, Dayna 26, 36, 50, 54, 156, 163–164

Traister, Rebecca: *All the Single Ladies: Unmarried Women and the Rise of an Independent Nation* 107

transgender identity 114–116, 152

Troubling Love 2, 20, 25, 27, 32–33, 49–55, 61

Tuck, Lily: *Woman of Rome: A Life of Elsa Morante* 74, 160

union organizing 136, 142–143, 147

University of Pisa 79, 85–86, 127

violence: female 54–58, 109–110; female tolerance of male violence 96, 109; male 33, 50, 52–53, 96, 100, 108–110, 113–114, 116–117, 153, 163; organized crime 177–179; political 131, 136–147, 153; sexual abuse/assault 51–52; 100–102 112; sexual harassment 112, 119, 130

Virgil: *Aeneid* 78, 98–99; Dido 98–99

Volokhonsky, Larissa 39

Walker, Alice: "In Search of Our Mothers' Gardens" 157

Warwick Prize for Women in Translation 38

Wertenbaker, Timberlake 21

Wilson, Emily (trans. *The Odyssey*) 38

Wilson, Katherine 170

Wolf, Christa 26, 28, 160; *The Quest for Christa T.* 161

Wollstonecraft, Mary 164

Women in Translation (WiT) 38

Woods, James 5, 14, 49

Woolf, Virginia 159

Years of Lead (*Anni di piombo*) 134, 136, 146

www.ingramcontent.com/pod-product-compliance
Lightning Source LLC
Chambersburg PA
CBHW032054300426
44116CB00007B/735